D0412083

THE CENTURY
GIRLS

Also by Tessa Dunlop:

The Bletchley Girls
To Romania with Love

THE CENTURY GIRLS

*The Final Word from the Women
Who've Lived the Last Hundred
Years of British History*

TESSA DUNLOP

**SIMON &
SCHUSTER**

London · New York · Sydney · Toronto · New Delhi

A CBS COMPANY

First published in Great Britain by Simon & Schuster UK Ltd, 2018
A CBS COMPANY

Copyright © Tessa Dunlop, 2018

The right of Tessa Dunlop to be identified as the author
of this work has been asserted in accordance with
the Copyright, Designs and Patents Act, 1988.

1 3 5 7 9 10 8 6 4 2

Simon & Schuster UK Ltd
1st Floor
222 Gray's Inn Road
London WC1X 8HB

www.simonandschuster.co.uk
www.simonandschuster.com.au
www.simonandschuster.co.in

Simon & Schuster Australia, Sydney
Simon & Schuster India, New Delhi

The author and publishers have made all reasonable efforts
to contact copyright-holders for permission, and apologise
for any omissions or errors in the form of credits given.
Corrections may be made to future printings.

A CIP catalogue record for this book
is available from the British Library

Hardback ISBN: 978-1-4711-6132-2
eBook ISBN: 978-1-4711-6133-9

Typeset in Sabon by M Rules
Printed and bound by CPI Group (UK) Ltd, Croydon, CR0 4YY

Simon & Schuster UK Ltd are committed to sourcing paper
that is made from wood grown in sustainable forests and support the Forest
Stewardship Council, the leading international forest certification organisation.
Our books displaying the FSC logo are printed on FSC certified paper.

In memory of Bernard

DÚN LAOGHAIRE-RATHDOWN LIBRARIES	
DLR27000010466	
BERTRAMS	29/03/2018
GD	02323692

Contents

Introduction

'You're as young as you feel, surely?'

'It's a pity, but yes, dat's right!' At 102, Olive inverts my cliché
and laughs loudly. She is surrounded by the paraphernalia of old age:
walking frames, pill pots, pads and plasters, dusty corners and dis-
infectant. Assistance is required to get dressed and go to bed. Carers
drop in three times a day, they comb and plait her hair, cut her nails,
wash her body and prepare her food. Captive in a reclining chair,
physically Olive feels old. She can't just get up and go – there is no
spontaneity any more. A room full of astonishing dresses, sequins,
fur and frocks groans overhead; the clothes tell a story of one hundred years. That story is ongoing but Olive can no longer mount the
stairs to reach her glittering wardrobe – she has to wait and hope.

When company eventually arrives Olive is transformed; she feasts
upon it, slaking her thirst and sitting upright for more – down come
the dresses and out pour the stories. She berates me for not visiting
sooner: 'You playin' away, you cheatin' on me, eh?' And there are
anecdotes about the doctor who still flirts with her, and St George's
Church, where she's the star of the show. Olive dips between time
zones and continents; childhood and adolescence flash past until
we arrive sooner or later in 1950s London. 'It was a very unusual
relationship!' There is nothing Olive loves more than talking about
her late husband, Trinidadian Ray Gordon, whom she met on her
first night in the Mother Country's metropolis. She's right, the
story is complicated, as was the era. A black woman from British

Guiana, there's nothing straightforward about Olive's life in post-war England. She shakes her head, this is not the time for questions; it is imperative I understand the intensity with which Ray once loved her – 'I was his illustrious wife!' – and that in the end, 'Yes, I can't tell it otherwise, I've had a wonderful life.' In these moments, Olive is no longer old, she is travelling down a highway of cherry-picked memories, once again a woman in her prime, a player, a beauty, a survivor. She has edited (and re-edited) her Great British century; the highlights are her gift to subsequent generations.

As the scribe, I take what I can get. Olive has no interest in delivering a neat thesis on empire, migration, colour, politics or change over the last century. She wants to tell *her* story of her life, around which I am permitted to extrapolate historical parallels and analysis. I can ask questions, but if Olive isn't interested she shrugs and doesn't answer. One of the first women I met when researching this book, she taught me much about how memory works. I adapted the shape of the unfolding narrative accordingly. This story is the history of six women who have lived one hundred years, specifically the years that followed the political enfranchisement of British women aged thirty and over in 1918. Like so many historical watersheds, that date has provided the *raison d'être* for a far richer, more nuanced history.

The story spans more than ten decades (the youngest Century Girl was born in 1918), but in the retelling of their lives those decades are rarely accorded equal importance. During our numerous meetings and interviews, Prime Minister Tony Blair and his 'new dawn', which claimed the women's ninth decade, was not touched upon by any one of them. The recent past is tainted with today's contemporary agenda, and (perhaps more importantly) it is not exclusively *their* past. When I mentioned Margaret Thatcher (she was a woman after all), I invariably met reluctance, even resistance. Generally, the further back in time, the more vivid the memories and the more willing the storyteller. They are called formative years for a reason. Napoléon Bonaparte famously declared, 'To understand the man you have to know what was happening in the world when he was twenty.' Given the political, social and legal restrictions placed upon women at the beginning of the twentieth century, that supposition works even better when applied to girls born during the First World War; these were young women who came of age when the political tumult of W. H. Auden's 'low dishonest decade' approached its grisly climax.

There are exceptions. Olive's desire to focus her story predominantly in the 1950s is unusual for a woman born in 1915, but understandable. Those first challenging years in London decided the rest of her life. Nor will everyone admit to having a defining moment or epoch. Joyce is an academic; to gain access to the revered world she inhabits I gave a lecture at her former Oxford college. In return, the Principal of Somerville wrote to her most senior alumna and asked if Joyce would grant me a hearing. Dr J. M. Reynolds has been engaged in the pursuit of learning most of her life; an honorary fellow at Newnham College, Cambridge, Joyce is still working, with a reputation to maintain – it has always been thus. She resists the suggestion that she belongs to one particular era but does concede that perhaps 'how one arrives at a destination is the most interesting bit'. Following Napoléon's benchmark, at twenty she was already at Oxford University and would defy the odds to emerge, mid-World War Two, with a first-class Classics degree. An achievement which set her up for life. However, she is clear that 'today, what I do now, I don't consider it a diminishment, it's just as important as it has always been. Only I do get very tired.' Whatever her protestations, Joyce's manners, her speech, even her style belong to another era. To sit and listen to her trained, resonant voice is an evocative delight, made all the more extraordinary when she expounds a broad sweep of liberal views.

Joyce was born in 1918, a month after the First World War's November armistice. She is the product of a distant, very different world and yet in conversation many of her opinions are contemporary. 'I suppose I have always worked with students and in that respect I was part of the change that was taking place. I find young people interesting.' A fascinating blend of old and new, Joyce has been an astute guide; a witness to decades of incremental social progress, she didn't need to be part of a new world to understand it. And yet she chides me when I take a generalisation too far, or get overexcited about modernisation. 'We cannot rely on progress. Most certainly not!' Joyce has studied the rise and fall of empires; she is also a woman who has lived through the gradual flowering of free tertiary education and its subsequent decline. Dr Reynolds has been at university a very long time.

Perhaps the best of us never stop learning. An enthusiastic correspondent, in our first written exchange centenarian Helena Jones explained, 'I am going to a monthly political meeting tonight and it's poetry club tomorrow night!' Four weeks later, bent double (surely in constant pain?), she walks out of her little home in Brecon to welcome my arrival in a swirl of snow. 'Well! We haven't had proper snow in this part of Wales for four years. It's global warming, you see.' Helena was recommended by a loyal member of Powys Brecon Women's Institute. In 2015, the year I started my research for this book, the Welsh WI enjoyed its own centenary celebrations. (The first UK meeting had been held in Anglesey one hundred years earlier.) A century on and two sentences in a newsletter asking for women born in 1918 or before left me fielding calls and emails for over a week. Seven women got in contact, each proudly informing me of their very own Welsh centenarian. The numbers belied a larger trend. There are approximately 14,000 people over a hundred alive today in Britain; the figures are unprecedented. The Department of Work and Pensions, which oversees the administration of the Queen's birthday cards, now employs a seven-strong 'centenarian team' just to keep track of the nation's oldest subjects. Meanwhile, I quickly realised that living for one hundred years wasn't enough to qualify as a Century Girl. In Wrexham, a miner's wife was still going at 104 years old, but her daughter admitted, 'I suppose Mum's a bit forgetful now and again'; a Scottish centenarian nurse who married a Cardiff GP was introduced to me by a proud neighbour, but she confessed, 'I'm quite a private person, so it might not be for me'; and I received a hopeful email about a very old department store sales assistant, who, on further research, wouldn't manage to talk for

longer than an hour. (Being one hundred takes it out of you.) And
then there was Helena Jones.

Vital, exceptional, dramatic, in very old age Helena has become
something of a celebrity in her Breconshire locality. Fortunately, she
revels in the attention. 'I've got my picture in the *B&R** again this
week! Making Welsh cakes on the street to raise funds for Trallong
Eisteddfod, with all my friends ... I haven't missed a year since
1984. It's good fun. Every police officer that passes begs for a Welsh
cake!' In 1916, Helena was born into a farming family; one of eight,
dependent on meagre acreage and a pony and trap, she grew up
in a world minus modern contraception and incessant motor cars.
Everything has changed save the silhouette of Brecon's Beacons and
the recipe for Welsh cakes. Even Helena is not the same person as
she was back then. How could she be? 'But that's a good thing,' she
reassures me before doling out advice for girls today. 'It all depends
who you are ... let that decide what you are going to do because life
is too short to be unhappy. I've been very lucky, I've always loved my
work.' Although drawn from her own experience, this advice has a
telling contemporary resonance; meaningful choice for (most) girls
is a recent phenomenon.

Edna smiles. She doesn't mind me admitting that she is the poorest
woman in this book. That elixir of modern life, choice – the elusive
gamble we value and chase above all else – simply didn't exist for
Edna and legions of other young girls born a century ago. She is very
sad about that but refuses to let the past dictate the way she lives
the present. 'You see, I've been far happier in the second part of my
life. Before that it was hard.' For hours, we sit and discuss why Edna
was dealt such a difficult hand – a slip of a girl, she was forced into
domestic service at the tender age of fourteen. A product of rural
England, Edna is very different from Helena, her contemporary in
rural Wales. No two women growing up in Great Britain one hundred years ago share the same narrative, but perhaps it is in the peaks
and troughs, where similarities collide and differences stand out,

---

* *Brecon & Radnor Express.*

that the next generation is really able to learn about a Britain that no longer exists. I admit to Edna that early on she was a must-have character for the book – not just for her impeccable hearing and wise words during our first telephone conversations, and later those soft beguiling green eyes that still feel and understand, but because of the poverty and restriction that's accompanied so much of her life. 'And look at me now!' she laughs. Edna knows her challenging life has novelty value in modern Britain – thankfully she's willing to share it.

Halfway through 2016, I had found four Century Girls. Olive an immigrant from British Guiana, Joyce an Oxbridge academic, Helena a crofter's daughter and Edna an English servant. As my voice recorder filled up with their stories, I had to acknowledge my hand in the selection of each one. The breadth of Great Britain's narrative over the last hundred years insisted that the women in this book spanned different social classes, different nations, differ-ent ethnicities. I first saw Olive on a BBC1 documentary *The Age of Loneliness*. She was filmed at a charitable tea party with other elderly people, in her sitting room bemoaning the absence of friends, and rifling through sepia photographs of a family life that has since disappeared. I cried out at the television – I wanted access to the woman behind the pictures, a woman who had the gumption to move her life from one corner of the globe to another. Instead, the documentary cut away to a different corner of lonely Britain. It took two months to track down Olive; she was hard to reach for a lonely person. I was immediately honest: 'I want your story.' She replied, 'Well I want to tell it, it is time.' There is an exotic otherness to Olive's early life that contrasts sharply with the nostalgic drudgery of Edna's upbringing in Lincolnshire. So too a riveting juxtaposition that exists between the vast imperial project that defined Olive thou-sands of miles away in Guyana* and the Welsh corner of the British Mother Country where Helena has been pocketed almost all her

---

* Upon Independence in 1966 British Guiana became Guyana. In this book when referred to as British Guiana the spelling of Guiana with an i will be used, otherwise it will be Guyana.

life. The hurly-burly of gender politics has seen women's lives change unrecognisably in the last hundred years and that unsteady trajectory dictates the thrust of much of this book, but the 'liberation' of women is just one among an assault of changes that has swept British life. Womanhood means something totally different in today's world, but so too does Britishness and all that it encompasses. Hierarchies and identities which once defined people's daily lives no longer exist. Nothing is the same. Edna agrees. 'Nothing! Nowadays people don't even know what being poor means.'

Edna is a terrific woman, mindful, wise and modest. Ditto Helena, Joyce and Olive, for very different reasons. But how many women can a reader genuinely care about over a 300-page story? The truth is I don't know. I care about more centenarians than the six etched into the fabric of this book but I have met these women face to face, photographed them, recorded them and played with their lives on the page. Of course I care. A good narrative demands empathy; too many women would water down the intimacy of each story, too few would leave the nation's story unjustifiably shorn, so I limited the cast of Century Girls to six. I might have eked out that number to seven or eight but there was no need. As soon as I'd met the final two, Phyllis and Ann, one seated in our archipelago's most northerly capital, the other in salubrious south-west London, I knew the diverse canvas of their long lives more than did justice to Britain's modern century. Six was sufficient.

Phyllis has lived in Scotland from the age of twenty-three. At one hundred, she remains alert and mobile; the spread for lunch is entirely her own making and I never leave without a tin of home-baked shortbread thrust under one arm. In many respects, Phyllis is an archetypal old-fashioned Edinburgh widow. Conspiratorially (fully aware of how times have changed), she will share her doubts about working mothers. 'I think they should spend more time with their children. When the kiddies are wee, I think it's important they're with their mother.' In old age, Phyllis plays a convincing traditionalist, but her views are far from one-dimensional. In the same breath, she will tell you, 'I never liked babies myself, I was a tomboy, you see.' Phyllis was born in British India, where her father's capacity for work propped up the end of empire and an ever-expanding brood of children. No wonder Phyllis didn't think much of babies. She liked her dad and shooting for the pot, joining the mela and swimming in the river. Her face creases in delight; the shadow of a young girl is there in her bright eyes and the same child is smiling out audaciously from numerous photographs. 'Father was a keen photographer.' Phyllis is a chameleon – that's how she survived the journey between different continents and epochs. But it is British India, her childhood home, that dominates Phyllis's story. Her son Geoff is insistent: 'To understand Mum, you have to understand the British Raj.' Neat longhand in numerous notebooks, her own meticulous recollections reiterate this early focus. Memoirs, photograph albums and Phyllis's vital mind, on a sofa in Edinburgh together we time travel, and I am reminded this is less a story about extreme old age, but rather a story told by extremely old women.

And, finally, there is Ann. Brainy, well connected, thoroughly independent and highly amusing, thank goodness I found Ann in the hot summer of 2016. 'You're coming tomorrow? Okay, well my forgettery is terrible, so I'd better write that down.' We speak often, most recently on the telephone last night; at her own request, she has been proofing the *Century Girls* manuscript. Apparently, I've much work to do – somewhat terrifyingly, Ann has already 'made over six sides of corrections on my life alone!' A wordsmith and fully 'compos mentis', by the time you're reading this, the text will have passed its harshest critic. She explained the process has taken rather longer than she would normally expect, as her 105-year-old sister, Elizabeth, died last week. Finally, aged 103, Ann is the matriarch of the sprawling, accomplished Sidgwick family. She is also the indisputable matriarch of this book and therefore the natural starting point for what comes next – a story about six remarkable women: Olive, Joyce, Helena, Edna, Phyllis and Ann.

I hope you enjoy getting to know them as much as I did.

THE CENTURY GIRLS

IN ORDER OF APPEARANCE

Ann Baer (née Sidgwick), b. 4 April 1914
A London bohemian, an artistic entrepreneur, a wordsmith

Joyce Maire Reynolds, b. 18 December 1918
A scholarship girl, an Oxford classicist, a Cambridge Fellow

Edna Cripps (née Johnson), b. 13 August 1915
A Lincolnshire lass, a servant girl, an English patriot

Helena Jones, b. 27 August 1916
*A Welsh woman, a Breconshire farmer, a schoolteacher,
a National Eisteddfod champion*

Olive Mable Gordon (née Higgins), b. 1 May 1915
A child of empire, a Guyanese dressmaker, a London migrant,
an 'illustrious wife!'

Phyllis Ramsay (née Gargan), b. 15 July 1917
An Indian-born nurse, a wartime factory girl, a Scottish housewife

CHAPTER ONE

A RICHER DUST CONCEALED

ANN

Ann Baer (née Sidgwick) is matter-of-fact about the privileged world she once inhabited. There was Mary, a fecund Anglican mother, Frank, a tall creative father, a maid called Missy and a clutch of siblings romping around a spacious nursery in the English shires. Born in the spring of 1914, baby Ann arrived just before the First World War, that giant killing spree that inured humanity to modern horror. Her first steps were taken in the shadow of death. The arc of this unimaginably long life stretches right through to the present day where now, 103 years later, Ann lives alone in Richmond upon Thames; a spectacular individual who accidentally embodies so many stereotypes of her age. Stoic. Resilient. Remarkable. 'Am I? What choice do I have?' She doesn't even covet the company of television. 'I've never had a television, so how could I possibly miss it?' She first talked on the telephone when it was screwed to the wall in the downstairs cloakroom, somewhere between the galoshes and the washbasin.

Very old age is an abstract concept, almost impossible for younger bystanders to fully comprehend. Platitudes about war and duty and endurance don't begin to make sense of how far back Ann reaches. It requires her own inimitable style to do that. Ann is quirky and artistic; she likes oddities, coincidences and connections that together paint pictures which are entirely otherworldly. These are the teleportals to Ann's story. Take her anecdote about the name Jeremy – nowadays a commonplace English moniker for a middle-class British (more likely English) boy. But in Ann's time, it wasn't. Back then Peter had only just become fashionable, courtesy of J. M. Barrie's *Peter Pan* in 1904 (names have always been susceptible to stardust). Jeremy fared even worse than Peter – Ann is certain most people did not call their children after Beatrix Potter's fictional frog. Therefore, when her younger brother was christened Jeremy in 1917, it was considered a highly unusual choice. So much so that two years later, her father discovered his writer friend Hugh Walpole had borrowed the name for his eponymous book. *Jeremy* was a huge hit; a *Jeremy* trilogy followed. England was inspired and the popular boy's name Jeremy was born.[1]

'You see,' explains Ann, 'it's fascinating. There have been all sorts of little coincidences like this throughout my life.' (Her familial anecdotes stretch back as far as Charlotte Brontë.) But surprise on her part is misplaced. After all Ann grew up in a very different version of England; it was an imperial epicentre where class structure was more rigid, social circles – especially influential ones – much smaller and the population 20 million lighter. Ann's family inhabited a prestigious literary stratum in this tailored hierarchy.

> I suppose I was born into a sort of Establishment, yes. My parents got engaged walking on Richmond Green, but what Father never knew is that Mother had a rat in her muff at the time of asking. She loved pets. Perhaps he wouldn't have proposed had he known. Then I wouldn't be talking to you today.

Does she miss her other life? 'To quote Bernard Shaw, "I miss the man I used to be."' It's an apt reply, for above all else, Ann's generation was born into a man's world.

That the famous historian A. J. P. Taylor starts his odyssey through English history between 1914–45 from the perspective of 'a sensible law-abiding Englishman' is not surprising. He was a product of his time and writing about an era when men were fully in control. Before the Great War, Taylor's Englishman 'could live where he liked and as he liked'.[2] Not so an Englishwoman; if married she was invariably her spouse's dependant; any children belonged to her husband, as did the exclusive right to cry foul play in marriage. Women were poorer, less well protected and barred from vast swathes of public life. Nor was there much they could do about the ignominy of their situation. They had no voice. Women were not enfranchised.* Since 1832, votes for women had been on the agenda, an uncomfortable and growing controversy that politically minded Victorian men carefully picked their way around, fearful of relinquishing their own protected status. Soon, women could vote in imperial New Zealand and Australia but not in the Mother Country. The groundswell of indignation gathered momentum. Millicent Fawcett was the punctilious champion behind the push to grant an elite educated sisterhood the vote. But progress was slow. By the turn of the century, the flamboyant Pankhursts had bigger ideas; the heft of working-class women was needed and rules would have to be broken. 'Civil war' was declared. By the time Ann was born in 1914, women were rioting, striking, marching and starving themselves to death to obtain the ultimate remedy – the right to vote.

Ann was just a baby. Her mother, 'a good-looking woman with chocolate-coloured hair', continued to churn out children (four by 1917, two more followed in quick succession). There was little time for public protest, which anyway ceased shortly after Ann's nativity in honour of a greater violence – war. 'One of our neighbours, a woman that we didn't much care for, we were told by my mother, had been an active suffragette.' Ann shrugs. 'I called my doll Panky after her. You know, by then it was all in the past.' She adds, 'I feel I don't give you the answers you want.' But why would girls of her generation care? Enfranchisement was not their fight and the subject a distant memory by the time Ann reached adulthood. The volte-face had come in the war, when women's labour proved essential. They

---

* They could vote in municipal elections.

emerged with a clear national value in 1918. Meanwhile, the elector-
ate was sufficiently broadened to make the (partial) enfranchisement
of the fairer sex a less terrifying prospect. Women over thirty could
vote in the 1918 general election (that discounted Ann's mother, a
pregnant mother of four).

There was little cleavage between the family's well-established
bohemian style and the suffragettes' bawdy antics. Nonetheless,
pioneering Frank, a meticulous man, would make sure all four
daughters were equipped to tackle a modern world where women
had just pushed down a door few knew how to walk through. The
Sidgwick pedigree for education began early – all six children were
subjected to the Greek alphabet on the nursery wall. 'My grandfather
used to translate English nursery rhymes into Greek and Mother
learnt them automatically and recited them to us.' Physical agility
matched mental stimulation.

> I remember a swing in the nursery. The ceiling had wooden beams
> across it and my father screwed in thick hooks, and we could hook
> in two ropes and then we could hook the seat on the bottom or
> we could hook a trapeze bar or leather-covered rings, so we were
> always doing gymnastics. We were surprised to find that when
> we went to school, in their little gymnasium, the other children
> couldn't turn somersaults easily and climb ropes and so on.

Boys and girls tumbled together in the Sidgwick household. 'Well I
was the second eldest child, behind my sister Elizabeth. There were
four girls so we outnumbered my brothers, Jeremy and Christopher.
I didn't feel it was a disadvantage being a girl. No.' A statuesque
woman with the posture of a Victorian at the age of 103, she held
her own against predominantly younger siblings, as did the sextet of
Sidgwick children among their peers in the Buckinghamshire village
of Great Missenden.

Exactly one hundred years after Ann was born, the *Guardian*
declared that Great Missenden 'has been prime stockbroker belt for
over a century'. For the *Telegraph*, it remains in the top five locations

to bring up an English family. Small wonder Roald Dahl chose it as his home and literary inspiration in the 1950s. But Frank Sidgwick got there well before him, identifying the irresistible charms of this English village just as they were becoming attractive to an insecure post-war world. The timeless qualities are the same ones that still impress today's broadsheets. 'Ancient beech woods, deep valleys, rolling Chiltern Hills, higgledy-piggledy streets.'[3] Even then it had easy rail links to London's financial quarter. But, crucially, Ann's father was not a stockbroker. Frank was an esteemed publisher and talented, irreverent wordsmith (*The Times* wrote in a glowing obituary in 1939).[4] The Sidgwicks were a touch classier than the average Buckinghamshire family.

Like many stories from this period, Frank's rise in the world of publishing was bittersweet. His firm, Sidgwick & Jackson, made serious money with the publication of Rupert Brooke's *1914 and Other Poems*. It is typical of Frank's vision to have scooped up the talented Brooke before he fatally went off to war. 'The handsomest young man in England' had his prophetic words read out in St Paul's Cathedral in April 1915.

> If I should die think only this of me,
> That there is some corner of a foreign field
> That is for ever England.

Within three weeks, Rupert Brooke was dead. The same war killed Frank's publishing partner and his brother Hugh. Brooke's gallant poetry masked gruesome loss. Frank was still standing, but much changed. Perhaps he is the root of Ann's robust realism; certainly no one influenced her more. 'The words of "Land of Hope and Glory", they were written by my father's first cousin – Arthur Christopher Benson, his father was the Archbishop of Canterbury.' She recalls a patriotic festival at which the hymn was on the musical programme.

> Land of hope and glory, mother of the free,
> How shall we extol thee, who are born of thee?

Years later, her father confided, 'I've never sung more loudly or more cynically.' Even when it came from the depths of their extended family, the Sidgwicks didn't buy into conventional British tub-thumping, especially after 1918. Each town would bear its own memorial to the dead. Pain ran deep and Ann is sure everything was different: 'The idea of hope and of an easy future was dissipated.' She doesn't remember talk of votes for women but war talk was everywhere. 'I was surrounded by it. The adult population was stunned.' Ann had an imaginary friend called Veevee. She recalls, 'Veevee's father had black, khaki clothes and he met a German, and the German took him to the other end of the world.' The story does not end happily. 'The German took a spear with a light on the end of it – and so Veevee's father died.'[5]

In early childhood, Ann was cushioned in a sunlit nursery, swinging upwards to the beamed ceiling, but already this little girl knew that the world was not straightforward. Nor did her mother's devotion to an Anglican Lord and Ann's Sunday obligation to the catechism provide any reassurance. 'I am not religious. No, I never have been. There are several things in my life I avoid and church is one of them.' It was not unusual to question God by the twentieth century and a futile world war had done little to allay fears – why had the Lord let this happen? Conventional religion had begun its downward spiral. Nonetheless, Ann's unapologetic rejection of the Christian message was indicative of a free spirit. She won't be drawn on her personality – 'I can't answer in black and white terms' – but the recollection of her first day at school is unambiguous. All the Sidgwicks began their education in Whitefields, a fee-paying elementary school bang next door to their house in Great Missenden. Her father removed a few boards from the adjoining fence to provide his children with ease of access in the mornings. But the proximity to home provided little succour.

I can remember very clearly the first day, going, sitting on the brick steps on the porch of our house and putting on my shoes, and looking at the rain falling gently in the shadows of the trees of our garden and thinking to myself, 'It's not just today, it's tomorrow, and the next day, and the next day, and the next day. I shall never be free again.'

JOYCE

Born in April 1914, Ann is the oldest woman in this story. Joyce Reynolds is the youngest. Baby Joyce arrived near the border where London meets Essex just one month after the armistice, in December 1918. 'I was born at home, with a midwife and a doctor in the room. My mother couldn't bear the midwife. Halfway through the pains she said, "Enjoying yourself, dearie?"' Joyce is still angry on her mother Nellie's behalf. 'It was totally unsympathetic! Absolutely shocking.' The recollection is comforting for its domestic detail and filial loyalty. No Germans with spears loiter among Joyce's early memories; family connections did not link the Reynoldses to a prematurely dead officer class. Instead, cheeringly, during the war schoolteacher Nellie Farmer had fallen in love and got married to a civil servant called William Reynolds. Nellie came from earthy East End stock – the family album is full of faded pictures of young men in worn leather boots and women with bat-wings of hair scooped clean of their foreheads, aprons protecting their skirts. At the turn of the century Joyce's mother was part of a large working London family, replete with soldiers and servants and carpenters who enjoyed a singsong and a jar of beer.

Over one hundred years later her daughter is sitting erect but comfortable in front of a cluttered writing table, flanked by a wall of books. Joyce's diction is smart and her conversation educated and precise. With a fixed, inscrutable gaze and her grey hair swept back, on first meeting she is an intimidating prospect. Joyce doesn't suffer fools (or foolish questions). She is the product of a rigorous intellectual upbringing that actively sought out the new opportunities available in early twentieth-century Britain. Within one generation, her mother would travel from the steps of a Walthamstow tenement to a charming residential house in a London suburb (the Essex border was a stop along the way). Joyce, an esteemed Cambridge academic, completed that process of self-betterment.

'Highams Park was the station before Chingford on the train from Liverpool Street. We lived on Preston Avenue, number 41, and just a minute away there were fields with cows in them.' Joyce concedes that perhaps back then there were even 'real people who had been born and brought up there, but it was already becoming townified'. Instead of cows, the immediate vicinity now offers a pink Glitz & Glam nail parlour, Sea Breeze fish and chips, and a convenience store; a smattering of modern services for the same red-brick, end-of-terrace Edwardian house that still stands with its well-appointed windows and pocket-handkerchief garden. A hundred years ago, Joyce's parents had gone to considerable efforts to buy the house. Like the Sidgwicks and thousands of other couples, they wanted a home within reach of central London. 'I developed a rather good forehand drive against the brick wall of the house; all other games I was no good at.' This was an ideal place to bring up a family but a little slice of convenient real estate came at a cost. Joyce laughs, 'Yes, I do remember Father hanging up his bowler hat at the end of every day.' William Reynolds endured a daily commute back and forth on the train into Westminster. Civil servants also had to work a Saturday morning; the week was long but, one senses, well worth it. William, from a modest family of Methodists, had capitalised on an increasing commitment to nationwide education in the late nineteenth century. In general, the results were patchy and hard to obtain, but diligent William won a scholarship to the local grammar school, later supplementing his education with additional evening classes. The end result was a stimulating job in Westminster. 'He loved his work.' Joyce is sure of this.

The purchase of the family house on Preston Avenue confirmed the family's arrival into the rapidly growing middle classes. The trend towards 'the professions' had begun under the Victorians. This much-heralded section of society came into its own during the war – mass destruction needed management. Civil servant numbers more than doubled to 130,000 in four years.[6] As the government expanded to cope with the impact and aftermath of a total war, power increasingly lay behind the scenes. William Reynolds was well placed to capitalise on a changed social and economic landscape. 'He worked in a part of the Ministry of Labour called the Industrial Court. He was the Secretary. This was a court to which disputes were brought between owners and workers.'

As weary George V looked out over the unhappy crowds from the safety of his royal balcony, he surmised that the war had been an unsettling time for monarchy. Typically for this modest king, his was an understatement. Across Europe, social upheaval, revolt and the spectre of communism cast long shadows. Britain's own brief post-war bubble burst in 1920; unemployment, strikes, socialism, the labour movement and unions pressed forward scary new ideas in an unsettled land. It seems appropriate that William Reynolds, part of a new generation of socially mobile, educated men, was on hand to mediate between the discontented worker and his economic master. Britain's industrial heartlands contracted under stubborn unemployment; William, based in the opulent South East, would attend hearings all over the country, secure in the knowledge that the sanctuary of a new home awaited his return.

Joyce recalls the evening meal with Father: 'Mother prepared it. Yes, I think we did have fish on a Friday. If he had been at an industrial hearing, he would bring home sweet stuffs from that region. Mostly they were delicious but I hated Pontefract cakes.' Her father's departure and arrival punctuated an early childhood of simple pleasures. 'The milkman delivered in a cart drawn by a horse and if I had been good I was allowed to give a piece of sugar to the horse. I can remember very strongly the horse licking my hand. I still feel his tongue.' For company, there were snatched chats over the fence with the neighbour's daughter, Margaret, a lump older than Joyce, with masses of fluffy hair. These were memorable meetings but other children proved harder to reach. 'There were two little girls at the far end of the garden but it wasn't so easy to chat over that fence.' Otherwise home alone with Mother, Joyce had to wait four and a half years for the arrival of her only brother, David. Unimpressed with the midwife, this time Nellie opted for a private nursing home, Twilight Sleep. The name evokes a smile. 'My father took me to visit. He went to see his wife and I was left in a great room full of babies. I stood by this little infant in a cot and he opened his eyes. When I was taken to see Mother I remember saying, "His eyes are blue!"' Joyce's delight with her new companion was palpable, and a photograph captures this joy – big sister in a wicker chair proudly clutching a terrified-looking baby David. 'We became great friends.'

~

Interwar prime minister Stanley Baldwin, with his reassuring English manner, spoke for many when he commented, 'There is nothing in the first twenty years after the war that can make good to this country the loss of so many men.'[7] The pall of pointless death hung over Britain for two decades. 'Have you heard news of my boy Jack?' wrote Rudyard Kipling mournfully. Over three quarters of a million young men didn't come home after 1918. Others, maimed and sick, stood around in branded blue hospital garb, tarnished for life. Small wonder then that the birth of a baby boy was often savoured as a miraculous event. Here was a new male bud, full of promise and potential. Many girls, including women featured in this book, recall the preferential treatment their brothers received. But not so Joyce, nor Ann. The absolute certainty that they were treated no differently from their brothers is very unusual. Perhaps it is no coincidence that these two women, both exceptional in later life, were treated exceptionally as children, or more specifically as girls. Ann gestures, almost blasé. 'Oh, Father was *all* for women's education! Women's education was a sort of Sidgwick thing. It was important. Father's sisters went to Oxford High School for Girls.'*

Joyce is equally adamant. 'My mother minded very much that her

---

* Founded in 1876, Oxford High School for Girls was one of the pioneering independent girls' schools established in Britain in the latter half of the nineteenth century.

daughter should be well educated. She resented the fact that in her own family her father was prepared to educate her brothers more than he was prepared to educate his daughters.' Nellie Reynolds was ideally placed to ensure her own daughter was not sidelined in the same way. 'Mother was a primary school teacher and she was a very, very good one. She taught the first year in reception – normally she had a class of sixty with no assistants – and if they couldn't all read and write at the end of a year she said, "I was ashamed of myself."' Once married, the sole receptacles for Nellie's extraordinarily energetic teaching were her two children. She oversaw a creative programme. While others were still chastising 'the Hun', Joyce, not yet eight years old, was conjugating German verbs under the supervision of perhaps the only German in Highams Park.

My mother, who felt very strongly in favour of internationalism and that there shouldn't be another world war, invited this lady to come and teach us German. I can half remember her face. It was rather exciting and subsequently the only German I could ever talk was what she'd taught me.

Visionary, a pioneer even, surely Nellie was an early feminist? Joyce shakes her head. 'There was no such term then.' Joyce doesn't tolerate retrospective, loose generalisations but she does concede that her mother provided a formidable early education. The seed of learning was planted early, and amidst piles of papers and jottings, Joyce's academic engagement continues today. 'You can come only if you don't stay too long, I have a lot of work to do.' In her ninety-ninth year, time is short.

EDNA

Although from very different backgrounds, Joyce and Ann were both born into loving, progressive, relatively affluent families. Psychologists now tell us that these early years are crucial, developmentally more important than any other time – in which case both girls were set fair to handle whatever life threw at them. Not everyone was so fortunate. Up a wheelchair ramp, inside a purpose-built semi in a Wiltshire close, 102-year-old Edna Cripps puts down her Cup a Soup and shakes her head. She always knew things weren't fair, her certainty the gift of someone born at the bottom of the pile. From Jane Austen to Virginia Woolf, the public voice and image representing women for nearly a century was overwhelmingly middle class, but most girls born during the Great War were poor and baby Edna, arriving in August 1915, was no exception.

For hundreds of years her family's fate had been linked to the Welby dynasty in Denton, a small Lincolnshire village.

> I can remember that by the time I was born, there was my grand-dad, the estate carpenter, Uncle William, the estate shepherd, there was Uncle Tom, who worked at the dairies, and Uncle Harry, as we called him, he used to drive the manor van – that was horses in those days. My mum worked up in the big house.

Edna's ability to reel off her family's long service for the Welbys belies a certain pride. After all, Sir Charles Welby, 5th Baronet, was quite a man – a Conservative MP, prime mover and shaker in Lincolnshire local government and personal friend of Neville Chamberlain. Edna talks enthusiastically about Denton's overlord – the marriages, the mishaps and the fire in the manor. Her knowledge is encyclopaedic and impersonal.

> Oh no! We never mixed, they were titled folk. But I can't say we never saw them because they always went to church. Sir Charles read the lesson and they had a special pew at the front. We liked to see what the children were wearing. We never talked to them, you just didn't.

Little Edna, hunched over her kneeler, imbibed the word of the Lord and the Anglican-approved social order. 'You didn't wave, they came in that way and we came in another. The church clock was always five minutes fast so they were on time. They had a good long walk, mind you, down the drive, around the ponds.' She retraces their steps with the accuracy of a silent observer: Welby's daughters in their finery, deigning to grace the local church with their presence before retreating behind the manor gates. Edna lived in a different world in the same village. She enjoyed singing and saying her prayers; a shy girl who understood early on the importance of maintaining standards, she never talked back, especially not to her elders. In many ways, Edna was perfectly equipped for a modest rural life, surrounded by extended family with a loving mother and father. 'It would have been okay, I think, yes.' If only she could change one thing. 'I wish he hadn't died, if my father hadn't died, well, that would've made all the difference.'

One of Edna's earliest memories is going to church with her father, a precious moment sitting together on the Sabbath. It is also one of her only memories of her father. Aged just twenty-nine, Mr Johnson died of double pneumonia in the spring of 1920. Double pneumonia? 'I know, people don't die of that now.' The details are cloudy. In a glass cabinet is a picture of a sombre man cross-legged, outside in a bath chair. 'He must already have been sick then, cos he was sitting down.' Arms folded, teeth clenched around a pipe, waistcoat neatly fastened over a collarless white shirt, Mr Johnson's long, handsome face is expressionless. The picture is of a man too young to die. Edna pores forensically over the image, hunting for clues. 'That was our cottage, it belonged to the estate, it had been Grandpa's before us.' The house's ironstone wall is covered with a climbing rose not yet in bloom, but at Mr Johnson's feet there are sprays of delicate flowers. 'It must've been the spring shortly before Dad died, he died on 18 April 1920. My brother was born in the September, but Dad was dead by then. I remember him coming in and leaning on the mantelpiece with his hand in his hair.' She pushes her own hand through a silver thatch. '"I don't feel well," he said.' Six weeks later Mr Johnson was dead, and nearly a hundred years later this one moment captured in time still represents the turning point in Edna's long life. 'I was meant to begin school in that September, instead I went to stay with my grandparents in Great Gonerby.'

Mr Johnson had, in keeping with family tradition, done a stint of gardening on the Welby estate, but a job in the local engineering business, Ruston and Hornsby, tempted him to neighbouring Grantham. Riding the wave of expansion heralded by the production of aero-engines during the war, newly married Mr Johnson clocked in and out of the factory gates daily. A married man of independent means, he paid a monthly rent for the estate cottage his father had once received in lieu of additional wages. 'You see if my father hadn't died, then maybe I might have gone to Grantham High School like Margaret Thatcher.' Edna has constructed a mythical other life that might have been, 'but people in them days died when they weren't old, that was the problem'. With a dead father (another loss for a village already mourning a slew of young men), the Johnson family's prospects plummeted. 'Poor, we were very poor.' A widow's pension was 21 shillings. It wasn't nearly enough to bring up three young children and pay the rent and rates. Mrs Johnson resorted to taking in washing for a shilling ('I've known my mum to be standing up ironing at two o'clock in the morning') and returned to the Welbys' enormous mock Tudor manor house for piecemeal work.

> My mother was a parlour maid – they look after the dining room table – and Mother would lay the table and wait on the table. I listened from my bed and heard her leave very early in the morning and make her way. It was a long walk through the churchyard and up past the fishponds.

It pains Edna to recall her mother's weary tread and stooped frame, but she's insistent it wasn't all bad. 'Sir Charles was very good to people like my mum, the widows. At Christmas, people like us got half a ton of coal cos mum was on the list.' Edna said her prayers every night and thanked God for providing. 'It could have been much worse, there were people much worse off than us.' Like Ann, Edna learnt the catechism. She promised to do her duty towards God, her neighbours and, above all else, 'to do my duty in the state of life which it has pleased God to call me'. A bright girl, it didn't take Edna long to work out what God had intended for her; the signs were even there in the Lord's own house. The Johnsons would not have dared sit near the front of Denton's St Andrew's Church, which boasted in its northern apex (and still does) a stone monument of a Welby. Fatherless, penniless and isolated in the countryside, it was simply a matter of time before Edna began her working life as a servant.

HELENA

Perhaps it's a coincidence, but the six women featured in this book, still alive and alert at the time of writing, were the eldest siblings in their respective families and have outlived nearly all their brothers and sisters. (With the exception of Ann, who was the second eldest of six and whose older sister, Elizabeth, died in 2017, in her 106th year.) Welsh-born Helena Jones was the eldest of eight. 'Yes, Mum didn't need a maid, she had me. I had seven younger siblings. I looked after them. Can you believe it!' Actually, when you meet Helena you can believe it.

Oh, you've caught me hoovering!
Have a French fancy, go on!
Now, let me make you a cup of tea.

Her crooked, kindly frame and open face are so set that it's impossible to imagine her any other way. When you hear Helena's story, you realise there was no other way. 'Ahh, life revolved around a Sunday morning. We'd go to chapel and I think we used to leave before the sermon, so I'd come home and my mother would've bathed the baby. There always seemed to be a baby.' Aged 101, Helena's hair is smudged with brown and she still lives in the shadow of the sandstone mountains where she grew up. In a miniature house on the edge of Brecon, a small Welsh market town, she recounts the Sunday routine that defined her youth.

Mother would put the baby in the pram and then I'd have to take the baby and the other children. It was tiring. I remember where we used to go, it would be at least two miles, pushing this big heavy pram so that my mother could prepare lunch and get on with dinner.

She laughs – she loved her brothers and sisters (just one remains), but looking after seven siblings was hard graft. 'I can remember when I realised there was another baby coming, I used to think, "Oh no! Not again!" There was a real drudgery, wasn't there? It wasn't fun being the eldest, you know.'

But being the first born had its perks. John Jones, Helena's father, was a committed performer; from Welsh farming stock, it was in his blood to sing, worship and work. A revival of the Welsh eisteddfod's bardic tradition a century earlier ensured there were ample local opportunities for John to showcase his talents. Local eisteddfod festivals peppered the country. Serendipity and genes gifted him an eldest child who shared his passion. Bonded in their work of performance, early on father guided daughter.

'My father would come in at nine o'clock, having fed the cattle for the night and the horses, and he'd be coming in then to rest and, as soon as he came in, he'd say to my mother, "Well, call her down then." I'd gone to bed and I had to get up from bed.' In her nightie, four-year-old Helena would pick her way across the stone slabs and stand on a piece of carpet that was waiting in the middle of the room specifically for her. 'Reciting for my father, I would have to do the poem two or three times until he was happy, you know, and then I'd go to bed and then I'd compete.'

Helena stops suddenly, just when she is about to broach the subject of her first eisteddfod performance. She has a broader point to make.

One of the best feelings that I can have, and it still applies even in this last eisteddfod: if you're up on that stage and you have everyone looking at you, listening, and you can hear a pin drop and you've got them in the palm of your hands, it gives you a wonderful feeling, a feeling of power in a way.

She touches her 101-year-old finger on a recently won glass trophy. 'It's nice, isn't it?' She cups it – 'heavy, too' – before returning to the past.

> The first time was in Cwm Camlais Chapel. We lived about half a mile from the chapel, I suppose, and my father was the treasurer, I remember. They lifted me up to the big seat where the deacon sits and put me to stand on the seat so I could be seen. I recited and I won. I don't remember much about it, but I can remember even though it was nearly one hundred years ago someone lifted me up.

Inside a modest, white Welsh chapel in the middle of a green field, Helena had her first taste of what she would decades later describe as 'a wonderful feeling, a feeling of power'. She returned home a winner, perched at the front of her father's bicycle. 'None of my brothers and sisters really enjoyed eisteddfods like I did.' The passion for performance more or less stopped with Helena, who competed in at least eight local eisteddfods a year; only with the benefit of hindsight does she concede that perhaps she was a hard act for her siblings to follow. 'Glenys says I was the favourite. No. But I enjoyed learning recitation with Father and they didn't.' It's impossible to separate the intimate distinctions that formed and motivated the performer in young Helena, but without doubt her father was the alchemist. Edna is right, what a difference a dad makes.

~

A well-matched couple, there were clear differences between Helena's mother and father. Small, dark, Celtic Ada was from a big South Wales mining family and her father and brothers worked the pits; in contrast, lean, long John was a Welsh-speaking liberal from a farming background. 'Mother was from the Valleys; she was always a Labour voter and Dad, Liberal. I remember them arguing about it.' John only joined the miners under duress. In 1914, he was working on the family homestead and that's where he would have liked to stay. There was widespread apathy towards the war in rural Wales; the chapels held sway and they believed 'soldiering to be sinful'. But Welshman David Lloyd George (munitions minster from 1915 and prime minister from 1916) did much to persuade his countrymen that the war was a crusade in support of small nations. Soon, John found himself with little choice: either he joined the army or became a miner and helped deliver the black lifeblood of Britain's war effort. A peaceful man who'd just married Ada, he opted to stay in Wales and dig for coal. Or, as Helena puts it, 'work in some way in the pits. Isn't it strange, I never remember him talking about working underground. Maybe he worked above ground.' Helena still finds the idea that her sylvan father was once a miner odd; a quirk of war that meant his first child was born in the pit village of Seven Sisters during the summer of 1916. The hooters summoning the men back to work were the standout sound of Helena's earliest years.

By the time war ended, a second baby girl had been born and a third was on the way; John was eyeing up options which would take him and his young family back to the Welsh hills. Helena's life, in all its full-bodied rural glory, really began once the family moved to Libanus, a small village in the Brecon Beacons, where her father had risked everything he owned, and his future too, on a forty-acre smallholding. 'I can remember furniture being loaded onto a horse-drawn gambo. What a challenge for a young couple!' Helena nods her head approvingly. John Jones's gamble was well timed. Of the two Welsh staples – coal and agriculture – it was the latter which benefited from a boom in prices and profits after 1918. Making a success of their Welsh croft was hard work, but the Jones family didn't go short.

We always had plenty of food and a pair of best shoes, black lace-up ones for chapel. I remember at the weekend my mother would go shopping and come back with a bag of bananas for a shilling and give us each one, and there was a quarter pound of Toffee Rex for Dad.

In stark contrast to agriculture, by 1921 miners had gone from the top of their country's wage table to the bottom. Only in Wales had militant pit workers been on strike during the war and industrial action persisted long after, climaxing in the General Strike of 1926. Pit owners demanded longer hours and lower wages of their workers. 'Nowt doing' came the robust reply. The chasm between the two sides epitomised a wider class struggle – coal, which fed into every branch of British industrial life, was the symbol for discontent. All the large unions approved a general strike that began on 3 May 1926. Camaraderie ran deep. 'When there was the very big strike, my uncles, two of them, came up and stayed with us on the farm. You see, in those days if you weren't working there wasn't any support. They used to help my father with whatever he was doing.' When it began, the strike had novel appeal.

> I remember going to stay with my gran in Seven Sisters, which had a big colliery. I was walking up through the village and outside the church there was a long queue of children, all holding basins. I said, 'What are they doing, Nan?' 'Oh,' she said, 'that is the soup kitchen; cos their fathers are out of work, they are providing food for the children.'

Helena thought the smell so delicious she wanted to join the queue. Meanwhile, back on the farm she loved having her uncles: 'They used to spoil me, take me for walks and play cards and games with me.'

Inevitably in Wales, where so much of the workforce depended on the pits, the strike's impact was almost total, but even small children in London's suburbs never forgot 1926. Eight-year-old Joyce had just left the confines of her mother's kitchen table in Highams Park to brave Walthamstow County School when the strike stalled the trains. 'I had to walk the distance, and it was quite a distance, each day. In the mornings my father took me, and in the afternoon perhaps it was the maid.' But it was not the walk through cow pasture and ribbon development that stood out, rather the one occasion when Joyce's mother had organised a children's party. 'A friend in my form had a brother with a car, and private cars were very rare at that point! The boy carried in his car all my little friends and me. It was a bit dangerous and would not be allowed now. There were a lot of us!' Not a naturally excitable woman, the novelty of that first hugger-mugger automobile ride has never left Joyce. Gone were the days when paralysing the railways could bring Britain to a standstill; the strike was undermined by mobilising growing numbers of vehicles, driven by well-meaning volunteers, lumbering staples and passengers across the country. A middle-class sigh of relief went up when the strike was called off; even Joyce's moderate father, with his industrial relations expertise, believed it had gone on too long. But the miners held out. In Wales, Helena remembers the weeks rolled into months. 'My father said to my mother one day, "Well, if this strike doesn't end soon your family will have to go back, because we can't afford to keep them."' John Jones was mindful of just how many children he had to feed by 1926 ('at least half a dozen of us'). The prospect of shortages frayed family loyalties. After six months, hunger eventually drove all the miners back underground for lower wages and longer hours, Helena's uncles included.

CHAPTER TWO

EDUCATION FOR ALL

EDNA

'There you are, dear.' Edna hands me a photograph from the *Grantham Journal*; under the heading 'Denton School Revisited', numerous children smile from wooden benches. Overleaf, Edna has carefully noted the names of her 1927 contemporaries. Johns and Alfs, a Molly and Nellies, and one Edna. The name guide wasn't necessary; in a simple handmade cotton tunic Edna is unmistakeable – face upturned into a grin, legs obediently folded at the ankle, shoulders hunched in anticipation, the girl in the picture is a happy one.

> Oh, school was lovely. We had a lovely headmaster. Mr and Mrs Dove were very elderly and rather old-fashioned. I can see Mrs Dove now; she taught the infants. She wore a long black pinafore and she would answer the school door scratching her head with her pen.

In 1918, 'Education for All' was an obvious democratic slogan but its novelty should not be underestimated. Only with the Elementary Education Act in 1880 did school mean school for all children until the age of ten (the 1918 Act extended the leaving age to fourteen). For Edna, those precious years of education took place exclusively within the confines of her local Lincolnshire village.

Denton Elementary School had a headmaster, two mistresses and 120 pupils. A gallery of wooden steps accommodated the youngest children, whose laps made do as desks. Each child had a slate, a chalk and a rag, all eyes projected forward where the teacher focused on basics – reading, writing and arithmetic. Break times were a highlight, as was the warmth in winter from a huge coal fire, its guard strewn with sodden garments that belonged to the children from outlying farms. Edna worked to the gentle hiss of drying clothes. 'Oh no, I wasn't mischievous! I was actually very shy.' She soaked up all that was presented to her, but some aspects of teaching remained a mystery. 'I was never any good at maths – I discovered I was dyslexic, you know, at the age of ninety. That's why I failed my eleven-plus.' Even when pressed, Edna is not exactly sure what she learnt and instead argues that subsequently the 'school of life' taught her much more; this indifferent evaluation of the education on offer contradicts her fondness for school itself. Perhaps a clue lies with the ebullient faces in that one class photograph and her description of playtimes chock-full of singing games. 'Here we come gathering nuts in May' and 'The farmer wants a wife' drifted into the vast expanse of sky beyond the playground. School was fun, and crucially a break from domestic chores.

> I was ill a lot, mind. We all were. Sometimes the school was closed when there was an epidemic. I shared a bed with my sister, so she always got everything. One year, I think it was 1925 – yes, that's right, I was ten. Well, I had yellow jaundice in the spring, I had mumps in the July and measles in the August. There were no vaccinations in those days.

Edna is now 102 years old; her immense longevity proof that she has a staggering constitution. 'Perhaps I built up resistance!' she laughs. Her thin body shakes, she coughs and takes a sip of water. It isn't hard to imagine her as a sickly child, lying in bed waiting for Doctor

MacDonald. 'Dr Mac, we called him. He always came with a hat and briefcase. And leather gloves, of course leather gloves! One glove on his hand and the other glove inside his gloved hand. I can see it now.' She is distracted by memories, of how she hallucinated when fever gripped in the summer of '25.

I saw my great-grandmother, I know I did; she was Victorian, I could tell from the clothes. She wore a long, white summer dress and a Victorian bonnet. Widow Johnson, that is who I saw. I have Romany blood, you know, my mum's mum was from gypsy stock. I never allow people to run down the gypsies.

Edna has sat up in her chair, defiant – there must be no doubt, she saw her great-grandmother and she was a gypsy.

We return to Dr Mac, one of the three pillars of Denton village life, his status shared only by the rector of St Andrew's Church and Mr Dove, the head teacher. Edna's childhood was shaped by a masculine trio of moral rectitude, no wonder she remembers the leather gloves at her bedside. She nods – a visit from the doctor was quite an occasion. 'Oh yes, he had a bag of tricks. A stethoscope and pills. They might've been aspirin, I don't know.' For the reassuring knowledge that Dr Mac would visit her poorly child, Mrs Johnson paid into a club, a form of local insurance particularly necessary in rural areas. Domestic service wasn't covered by Lloyd George's 1911 Insurance Act, the patriarchy was expected to make up the short-fall. Perhaps Mrs Johnson didn't have to pay very much, Edna's not sure, but she is certain they were sick a lot. 'Yes, I suppose it could be dangerous. Occasionally someone died.' She goes back over the summer of '25. 'I know it was that year cos that is the year that Mum left us with a neighbour to go to Uncle Tom's funeral. I was very weak. The year after that, almost everyone got chickenpox and whooping cough.' Death lurked in the village. Edna shrugs – she has always lived with death. 'I tell you something else, we had to take a Beecham's Pill every Friday night. They came in a little box. No, I've no idea what was in them but it must've been a laxative cos they made you go to the loo.' She claps her hands and recalls the slogan, 'Beecham's Pills are a very good thing!'

Edna's right (she usually is), Beecham's Pills did contain a laxative; unlike other cure-alls, this nineteenth-century combination of ginger, soap and aloe actually impacted on the digestive system.

> Hark the herald angels sing,
> Beecham's Pills are just the thing.
> Moves ye gently meek and mild,
> Two for an adult, one for a child.

Garden vegetables, one tin of laxatives and the odd drop of cod liver oil were the only medicines that stood between the Johnson children and a swarm of possible infections. It would be three more years, in 1928, before Alexander Fleming discovered the life-saving qualities of mould on stale bread, otherwise identified as penicillin. Edna survived her childhood without it.

HELENA

'I couldn't wait to go to school.' Like Edna, Welsh Helena went to her local elementary school and, as with everything else, Helena did school intensely. Aged ninety-one, she even wrote about it in a short book. In *My First School, by a Libanus Lass*, the reader is gifted a kaleidoscopic sweep of anticipation, joy, gentle bumps and an unfurling love affair.[1] Helena is convinced school changed her life. Once again, her father John was the puppetmaster, securing a smallholding one mile from a main road with easy access to Libanus village in time for Helena's first term. Holding firmly on to her father's hand, togged out in a fleecy button-up liberty bodice, taped petticoat, bloomers, her 'best' brown velvet frock, white pinafore and soft brown boots, she skipped through two meadows, down a high-hedged lane, past Libanus Mill, up the hill and across two stiles, where, beyond a little row of houses, Helena finally came face to face with a big, stone-built building. Surely the biggest building in Wales! Certainly bigger than the chapel where she performed at eisteddfods. There, in the care of a school mistress, John left his daughter clutching a small packet of ham sandwiches.[2]

It is easy to pick out similarities between Edna's and Helena's experiences. Theirs were country schools with a mix of village and farm children, and both were governed by married couples. Mr and Mrs Price ran Libanus (regrettably the marriage bar which restricted the employment of wives left Mrs Price, a superior teacher, with no official role). The women recall obedient, happy atmospheres, abacus counters and inkwells. There was skipping and football with a pig's bladder, and discipline came from a cane on the wall. If epidemics shut Edna's school, at Helena's, rigorous attention was given to medical hygiene – ringworm was a particular scourge for farm children. The 1902 Education Act insisted on annual medical examinations and the results were startling. In 1913, 3 million pupils needed urgent dental attention. Ten years later, Helena wasn't one of them, but fear of the dentist lingered. 'He was short and dark, with a stern unsmiling face. His hands were hard and cold, and they tasted of Lysol.' The school nurse was another dreadful prospect. After a military-style line-up, it was bitter aloes for thumb-suckers and nail-biters and a shaming visit to Mother for those with lice infestations. Helena sat next to Nell: 'She would scratch her head and lice would fall and crawl on her desk or her shoulders.' Wary of the pomade and toothcomb, Helena smacked them dead with a school book.[3]

Rural elementary schools were about covering the basics; survival for a girl meant more than sums, if it meant sums at all. At Libanus, there were big wooden needles and balls of coloured wool, 'country skills' that included bulrush-weaving and art lessons with pastels. Meanwhile, the boys maintained the prize-winning schoolhouse garden. Three of Helena's sisters, like Edna, left Libanus school at fourteen and went into domestic service. 'Well, what choice was there? In those days, there wasn't a Woolworths in Brecon.' Helena, however, was an exception. The clues were there early; a child who was already learning poetry pre-school to impress at local eisteddfods caught the teacher's eye. She failed a maths times table test one morning and Mr Price (otherwise uninterested) actually bothered to come in from the 'big' room to dress her down. 'You can read and learn poems, why can't you learn your tables?' Never again did Mr Price have cause for concern. Five years later, Helena was the headmaster's first entry for the examination to the county school in Brecon. 'I had worked hard at writing compositions, reading and doing comprehension, writing out dictation.' She even gave 'subject, predicate and object' her best shot. No stone was unturned. The other children felt sorry for Helena, sitting on her own, unable to talk, taking the test. It led to a second examination in Brecon's Mount Street County School. Helena, in possession of a new pencil and rubber, was terrified. She need not have been. She would enter the county school in the autumn of 1927, the youngest in her class.

Helena is living proof that nearly a hundred years ago, in the state system some girls could chart a different course. She was lucky to be born in Wales, where the impact of social class was less dominant than in England and fewer secondary school pupils were obliged to pay fees. But in Wales, girls at the county schools were still exceptions, not the rule. Helena attributes her success to parental support (although it would be another fifteen years before a second Jones sibling entered the county school). But perhaps greater than her home environment was Helena's early understanding of why she needed to learn. 'I always knew I wanted to be a teacher.' There were few other professional female role models in rural Wales, so it was fortunate that Helena had an urge to teach. Without it, her destiny would've been much less clear. She shakes her head, nope, it's not easy to imagine what she would have done. What else did women do, except become servants, have babies or deliver them? 'When Mother was about to have a baby, Alice Williams, the district nurse, would turn up on her motorbike.' Helena had had enough of babies at home, she wanted to be a teacher and characteristically wasted no time mastering the art. 'You know, we had at the school this sort of cellar, where the boiler was for the fires. There were steps going down and I used to take three or four friends and I'd say, "C'mon!

Let's play school." Outside the classroom, Helena recreated (perhaps improved) the instruction of Mr and Mrs Price. A bright face, an efficient manner and a considerable brain, she subjected her contemporaries to pre-prepared lessons on slips of paper carefully written out the night before. 'I don't know what was on them, perhaps spelling or reading. As soon as I was sixteen I taught at the Sunday School. Apparently I was ... ' Helena doesn't finish her sentence, she doesn't need to. 'All I wanted to do was to be a teacher. That's all I ever wanted, you see.'

~

All the other Jones sisters went into domestic service, but in the early years it would be inaccurate to portray Helena as the family's sole educated warrior, the original Miss Jean Brodie breaking free from her sibling pack. 'Back then I did everything with Vanu, who was the sister closest to me in age; there were just two years between us.* We were always together and she was very bright, much better at sums than me.' Peppered through Brecon's surrounding uplands, farming families lived far apart; bucking the declining birth rate nationally, here large sibling groups were common. Lineage, blood, a new generation to work the land and help at home – having lots of children was an insurance against life's unpredictability. They also provided ready-made companionship in remote areas. Sometimes among Helena's anecdotes it is hard to discern one Jones sibling from another (there were eight, after all), but not Vanu. The second eldest child, this sister really mattered. She was beautiful, of that Helena is sure. 'I was very plain-looking but she had lovely dark, curly hair, beautiful dark-brown eyes and she was very pretty, you know.' Boarding in Brecon with an old woman during the week, Helena couldn't wait for her sister to join her at the county school. 'I knew she would pass the scholarship. It was very competitive, but I knew she would pass.'

---

* Her first name was actually Myfanwy, but the family called her Vanu for short.

But Vanu didn't pass the exam. She didn't even sit it. Helena rubs the arm of her chair and a tear travels down her cheek. 'Oh dear, it took me ever such a long time to get over. We were terribly close, you see.' There is a vague story about Vanu getting her head knocked against the school pegs; she walked all the way home rubbing her temple, complaining of a terrible headache. Helena came back from Brecon that weekend to find Vanu in bed. 'She had been ill now for quite a bit, I don't know exactly what we thought was wrong.' Helena occupied herself with keeping the younger siblings quiet, shushing them outside Vanu's door, making sure her mother was supported, as ever the vigilant daughter. All the while there was a nagging drag inside her: Vanu was properly, inexplicably unwell. Different doctors, official and brusque, carrying bags and outdoor coats, brushed their feet upon entry and washed their hands in water collected from the well. More hushed tones. 'Then one morning this doctor came, it was different somehow, and I was trying to keep the children quiet downstairs, you know. I knew that something was wrong, and my mother came and asked me to come upstairs and kiss my sister.' Helena followed her mother's heavy tread. 'I could see at once that she had died, you see.' Vanu lay pale and silent and so still, Helena's precious dead sister. 'I remember that my mother had to lift me up and I kissed her. I was crying.' Helena is crying again, ninety years on, a pattern of grief well worn, pulling her back to that same haunting loss. 'I leaned over and there was a tear I had left on her cheek. Ohh, I didn't know what to do. I didn't have a hanky or anything.' Her mother reassured her, hugged her and then, holding her by the shoulders, she looked straight at her eldest daughter and said, 'I've always relied on you, will you go downstairs and tell the other children what has happened?' Helena froze. 'I thought, no way could I go down and tell all the others, but I had never said "no" to my mum. Ever.'

Duty came first, it always did. Helena walked downstairs. There, met by an assault of laughter and child's play, she panicked. 'I thought, I just can't tell them.' She picked up a ball and led them out of the house. Still unsure of her next move, she chivvied, 'Come on!

Let's go out to the field!' Detached, she watched them as they hoofed about in the meadow, still puzzling over how to break the news. 'You see, I didn't want them to go running to the house, crying to Mum.' Just twelve years old, Helena's instinct was to protect her mother. 'It would've been horrible, wouldn't it, if they all . . . ?' The thought trails off. Helena shifts in her chair, she has told this story before, she knows what comes next. 'Well anyway, I just couldn't think, and I noticed the sun was going down in the corner of the field, it was fairly low and rays were out all around and one ray was coming right to the top of the field.' With the artistry of a well-trained performer, she paints a near biblical scene, etched out on the majesty of Brecon's landscape.

> Suddenly, you see, I knew what I was going to say. I called, 'Come here, all of you! I've something to tell you. You know Vanu hasn't been well?' I said, 'So today she's going to be an angel!' Connie asked, 'Isn't she going to play with us any more?' 'No,' I said, 'but she is very happy cos she's on 'er way now, she's going to meet Grandpa.'

Helena crouched down and pulled the children in around her. 'Look! Have a look at all those paths of light going up there! Which is the trail that you think she's taking?' Her three remaining sisters looked up and discussed the dazzling light. Even the boys, a lump younger, joined in. 'Oh, we know, it's the long one! Look! Look! The one coming down to the top of the field.' '"Yes, yes," I said, "that's what I think too. I am sure you're right. She's on her way to see Grandpa!"'

Euphoric with their discovery, Helena's brothers and sisters turned and ran towards the house. 'Mam! Mam! Come out! We've just seen the path where Vanu's gone to be an angel!' Helena watched them go, a lonely figure silhouetted against the evening light. 'And that was it, you know. No tears or anything. So, erm,' she pauses and looks up, 'God was good, he just showed me the way to tell them. Yes, God was good.'

JOYCE

At the beginning of the twentieth century, Britain had two well-established education systems: public schools, which cost money (their name alone an ironic reminder that only one 'public' really mattered), and schools that were paid for by local authorities. Attendance at the former helped mark students out as future members of the ruling class (or, if a woman, an accessory to it), while the latter confirmed an individual's place among the ruled. However, with the rapid growth of the middle classes, institutions existed which blurred the distinction between state and private. They included the newly founded High Schools for Girls. Unmarried women in particular had to earn something and, by the late nineteenth century, intellectual credibility required academic qualifications. The suffrage movement fed into this wave of enthusiasm; if women could prove they were men's intellectual equals, then surely they must be granted the vote. The Endowed Schools Act of 1869 helped convert exuberance into serious educational institutions; by 1894, there were eighty such schools.

On the border of Epping Forest, hawthorn, wild rose and cattle had been removed, the motto 'Neglect not the gift that is in thee' adopted, and soon numerous girls from the surrounding area were daily attending Walthamstow's new county school in the borough where Joyce Reynolds' mother, Nellie, had grown up. By 1925, there was a distinct green uniform and actress Sybil Thorndike opened its swanky Greek theatre, complete with columns.[4] Walthamstow County High School for Girls had ambition. That same year, it was decided by William and Nellie Reynolds that the time had come for Joyce to attend school. Walthamstow, with its own elementary division and just a short train ride away, was the obvious choice for their seven-year-old daughter.

My mother won a scholarship to a mixed school and she always swore, since she was a very pretty girl, that she spent too much of her time flirting with boys and she would never send either of her children to a mixed school. She was quite firm about that.

Joyce's schooling from the outset was minus boys and, as Nellie had hoped, her daughter was a model student. But despite its single-sex criteria, Walthamstow County High School did not live up to expectations. 'There was good teaching but the girls, by and large, thought the only thing that mattered was to play games – the games mistress was very prominent and she was a nasty woman.' Although possessed of a good constitution and a sturdy frame, Joyce was not an athletic child. Perhaps her mind has always been on higher things. 'I hated games, but if the whole of the rest of your form thinks games are wonderful and that to be able to do them well is all that matters, you feel a bit lost.' In an obligatory green tunic, a reluctant Joyce endured hockey, netball and athletics. The sporty ethos and Spartan appearance of leading male public schools had influenced the culture in new girls' schools. It was quite common for pupils 'to flatten their chests in gymslips and thrash neighbouring teams at hockey'.[5] In her county school in Brecon, Helena remembers 'my breasts getting slightly enlarged and I thought, "I don't like that!" So I bought some wide elastic and I stitched it up, and I used to wear it to stop my breasts getting big, cos I wouldn't be able to run and I was quite athletic, you see.' Not so Joyce, who 'felt a bit other, a bit miserable, because your peers thought you were so dreadful'.

Many girls had to balance the sporting pressures at school with the need to be domestic and winsome at home. But again, Joyce was different. 'No! Not at any stage did I help my mother and the maid with the housework. I was learning, both my brother and I had to be doing something constructive.' In their modest Highams Park house, at first Nellie had help from a daily who lived locally, but the arrival of baby David and husband William's progression up the civil service ladder soon ensured there was both the need and the money for a live-in maid. Joyce remembers liking the respective servant girls, considering them friends even, but she was not permitted to join in their chopping and mopping. Nellie ran the home, the maid was her assistant, meanwhile Joyce was granted 'an elevated position to be able to learn'. In 1923 the Board of Education had published a report on the need to differentiate between boys and girls at secondary level. Concerned that 'old delicate graces had been lost and the individuality of woman had been sacrificed upon the austere altar of sex equality', the board recommended that girls were given less homework, to counterbalance the extensive housework most were expected to do.[6] Nellie Reynolds placed no such domestic pressure upon her daughter. Yet again out of sync with her peers, Joyce regretted her lack of culinary expertise. 'I didn't learn to cook and that was one of the things I resented. You see, all my friends at Walthamstow, they learnt how to cook at home and I didn't.' The perks of having a highly unusual avant-garde mother were not so easily discerned aged ten.

With learning the key aspect of her childhood, Joyce was an avid reader. She smiles. 'Well, again, my mother didn't believe in my reading the sort of standard things that girls read. Those were *not* good for children, so she thought.' Breezy weekly *The Girl's Own Paper* was illicit material in the Reynolds household. 'I borrowed my friends' copies of this. I read them under the bedclothes, and that is partly why I am short-sighted.' Joyce pushes her glasses back up her nose towards her distinct blue eyes and tries to explain something that perhaps even she never fully understood. 'Mother thought this reading material did not encourage girls to be learned, to be interested in learning. That it encouraged you to play around, based on playing with boys or aiming at boys.' Nellie need not have worried; despite her forbidden consumption of *Girl's Own* 'propaganda', sheltered in a single-sex environment Joyce was not lured from the pursuit of learning. Far from it. Within three years, she had passed the entrance exam to the most academic girls' school in the country, St Paul's for Girls in London's Hammersmith.

Joyce's place at St Paul's was the fruit of her own academic graft (at the entrance exam, her mispronunciation of a poet's name the only hiccup she can recall), as well as the strategic planning of her parents. Attending an exclusive private day school in the west of London proved possible only because William Reynolds became a relatively successful civil servant. His improved position permitted a domestic upgrade from Highams Park (too far east to ever be considered desirable) to Southfields, a charming leafy glade neatly positioned between opulent Wimbledon and Putney. From there, both father and daughter could easily travel to their respective London destinations.

Personal matters also came into consideration. Joyce's mother had four living brothers and sisters. In contrast, by limiting herself to just two children, Nellie ensured the Reynolds family could afford the very best for Joyce and David. Contemporary demographers noted with concern that between the wars, the birth rate fell; this was particularly the case higher up the social ladder (with the exception of prolific aristocrats).[7] People were living longer but there were fewer children under five than there had been in 1871. Joyce agrees it 'seems likely' that her parents deliberately limited their family size but she can't be sure – such conversations were never held in front of the children.

It was in 1918, the year Joyce was born, that Marie Stopes's gushing book *Married Love* was published. For the first time, laboured metaphors were used to bravely extol the virtues of sex for married women.

> One might compare two human beings to two bodies charged with electricity of different potentials. Isolated from each other the electric forces within them are invisible, but if they come into the right juxtaposition the force is transmuted and a spark, a flow of burning light arises between them. Such is love . . .

Married Love was a bestseller and supplemented by Stopes that same year with birth control advice in *Wise Parenthood*.[8] It's unlikely Nellie would have indulged in such flouncy literature, but the fact that publicly the idea of sex for sex's sake was being discussed and barrier method contraception, although scarce, was available to married couples, points to a sea change among Britain's middle classes. Regular sexual activity no longer needed to result in extensive breeding. Family sizes shrank, while consumerism and personal wealth rose. The old adage 'the baby Austin ousted the baby' certainly had a ring of truth,[9] although Joyce is quick to point out that in her family's case it was a Morris Minor. Her recall of the number plate – 'PU3 202. It's one of the few things I really remember' – is an indication of how significant the family car was. Fewer children also meant private education was more widely affordable. For their daughter, Joyce, her parents had singled out St Paul's with characteristic care.

Twinned with and built opposite one of the four incarnations of the boys' school (founded four hundred years earlier), St Paul's School for Girls has always enjoyed a fearsome reputation for academic excellence. Established during the second wave of pioneering public schools for girls, it had a declared aim to be 'of the highest educational rank'. In keeping with its intended status, there was a prestigious opening in 1904 attended by the Prince and Princess of Wales. However, while clearly not a run-of-the-mill high school, St Paul's didn't attempt to attract the daughters of aristocrats or royalty; its *raison d'être* from the outset was about educating bright young women – background and religion were less important.[10] For intellectual Joyce, freshly pressed from the aspiring middle classes, St Paul's was the perfect fit. 'It was a delight' she confirms without a moment's hesitation. Even the architecture, 'sweetness and light' under the deft touch of Gerald Horsley, with its Queen Anne revival façade, strawberry-pink brick and delicate Arts and Craft embellishments, suits the idea of this clever girl with her birdlike face and appropriate, bobbed hair. But for Joyce it was the academic environment which made her feel so at home. 'I remember the pleasure of being in a small form, where every girl could make her mark, where all girls were intelligent and reasonably interested in the work, so that my interest wasn't regarded as out of line.'[11]

Walk down the eighty-foot 'marble', as St Paul's black and white chequered entrance hall is affectionately known, and embossed in gold on a prestigious honours board of former scholars are the names of two girls. Joyce Reynolds is credited with winning a Classics exhibition (read academic award) to Somerville College, Oxford University, and directly beneath her, in the same academic year is

Ruth Jacob, who won a place to study mathematics at Cambridge. It is no coincidence that these two girls – Ruth, dark-haired and Jewish; Joyce, pale with a slight Essex accent and non-believing parents – became firm friends. They were sparring partners in all subjects. Meet Joyce in extreme old age, and you see a woman encased in decades of academic achievement and accolade; with long silver hair and large round glasses, she physically embodies her position as a leading light in classical studies. Ruth was a friend who clearly challenged her, and therein lies the crux to understanding Joyce: she has always been driven by a zeal to broaden and nourish her mind. If she found St Paul's a 'delight', without doubt this distinguished school reciprocated the sentiment. Within a year, Joyce had won a prestigious John Colet Foundation scholarship and retained scholarly status to the end of her schooling in 1937.

Outside the classroom, extras included elocution lessons to iron out Joyce's Essex accent, which 'was not approved of' despite the school's focus on ability not class. The reams of poetry she enunciated her way through led to a deep appreciation of English literature and by 1933, under the nom de plume of Mousie, she won a prize for seven poems, 'serious and comic', submitted to the school magazine. Seventy-five years later her attractive low voice still has the enduring diction of a pre-war BBC announcer. No hint of Essex remains. Meanwhile in St Paul's modish tiled baths, Joyce had the rough edges removed from her swimming technique. 'The school wasn't interested in distances, only style.' She emerged with an elegant breaststroke, but at least there was no overbearing emphasis on 'games'.

Joyce refers to these anecdotes concerning extracurricular activities as 'gossip' or 'nonsense'. Study was always her primary motivation. Preparation for the all-important Oxford and Cambridge examinations was extensive (in those days students could apply to both universities) and her decision to study Classics not taken lightly.

I couldn't make up my mind between English, History and Classics and, after a lot of thought and some discussion with my teachers, I came to the conclusion that if you took Classics you would have literature, you would have history and you would have languages all rolled into one.

NO! I never read from translations. Good heavens, no!

A poet, a linguist, a classicist, a scholar, in an era when girls were not generally expected to have more than accomplishments, throughout her childhood Joyce not only took great pleasure in learning, but harnessed that learning for her own ends. 'I always read the newspapers and we could see women were beginning to take high positions in the workplace. Okay, perhaps not many, very few in fact, but one just thought, 'Wonderful, I am going to be like them!' In 1919, a sequel to women's enfranchisement was the Sex Disqualification (Removal) Act, which stated that neither gender nor marriage should disqualify an individual (a woman, in other words) from any public function; numerous legal barriers were removed from the professions. Apparently, the door had opened wide for the fairer sex. But in reality, things remained ominously static and male. There were no female directors of large companies, in the civil service few women were promoted to high office, many London hospitals would only train men – teaching and clerical work were the best most women could hope for.[12]

However, Joyce was undeterred and in 1937 she won exhibitions to both Oxford and Cambridge. Regarding her future, Joyce identified not with the majority, making do in dull jobs, but rather the exceptions. After all, in one version of brave new Britain, amidst the post-war furore of flappers and bohemians emerged a series of firsts: a first female Member of Parliament, a first female veterinary surgeon, a first woman barrister, a first British female delegate to the League of Nations. 'It was that women could do things, that one was conscious of. There were enough to give you ambition. No, I would not call it hope. It was ambition.' Indubitably old-fashioned and naïve in so many ways, here was a young student who had discovered the rush and push of an emotional driver few girls had experienced. Joyce Reynolds was ambitious. 'One had a goal. Yes, that was the thing!'

ANN

'I allocate twittering entirely to birds!' That was Ann's quick-fire response when her homemade Christmas card was much admired on social media. Aged 103, she is a witty woman. Ann is also very artistic. The card, delicate blue flowers amidst a sea of green foliage, picked out in ink and paint, was worthy of praise. 'I knew about colour from infancy as we each had a paint box. I knew exactly vermilion was an orangey red, raw sienna inclined to yellow. I knew all the names, and I was rather surprised when other children didn't.' Ann is unabashed about her rarefied upbringing. Even the teacher at Whitefields infant school (the private one accessed through a fence from her childhood home in Great Missenden) failed to live up to the seven-year-old's unusual standards. 'This teacher criticised a pupil's painting, saying, "Errgh, you shouldn't have painted that purple!" I thought, "She is a stupid woman if she thinks crimson lake is a bad colour."' Ann liked art but she didn't like school. What came after Whitefields was a move to Hayes Court; in Ann's words, this was a fee-paying girls' school 'on the fringes of the Bloomsbury set', located in a large Georgian country house. Surrounded by banks of rhododendrons and fine emerald lawns, fashionably near London yet airy enough to be Kent, Hayes Court was a compelling mix of pre-debutantes, wealthy bohemians and Home Counties girls. Infinitely classier than St Paul's and less earnest about conventional learning, it was deemed a suitable fit for the daughters of an eminent publisher. (Naturally the Sidgwicks knew the founder and headmistress, Katherine Cox.) Ann's parents employed the architect Horace Marshall to build an attractive brick country house in neighbouring Keston.

Mother didn't want her daughters boarding.
What do I mean by the Bloomsbury set? Oh, you know, Virginia Woolf would give lectures there and that sort of thing.

Ann shrugs. It wasn't that the school didn't make an impression, it clearly did, but it *was* just school after all.

'The drawing room, where morning assembly was held, had two wide bow windows, curtained with indigo batik curtains, and on the walls were facsimiles of Renoir pastels taken from the Marées Society portfolios.'[13] Visuals made an impact on Ann, classroom particulars less so.

> Maths was totally mysterious. I used to look at the blackboard with all these quadratic equations in little letters and numbers and brackets, and think those would make a very nice embroidery design, and then realised this was totally the wrong attitude.

School struggled for attention in a full young life. Ann recalls a flamboyant (predominantly adult) fancy dress party in a very large house. There the twelve-year-old girl came face to face with 'two sisters, and they had dressed themselves up as a Dresden shepherd and shepherdess. It was all absolutely perfect.' She can still remember the intricate detail of their costumes – varnished American cloth mimicked porcelain and cake doilies became cuffs and collars. The sisters went on to establish the Motley Theatre Design Group, which by the 1930s was winning Tonys in the West End. 'I wasn't surprised. They were very, very clever and versatile.'

While recounting these stories from an extraordinary childhood, Ann sits with beautiful poise in her London home. She is bathed in a pool of sunlight that blazes off her white linen shirt and white hair. Even (or perhaps particularly) at her great age, she is a vision to behold. As is her house. Fruit in a Cézanne print and a Kokoschka adorn the walls and when she sweeps the dust covers off her dining chairs so we may sit and eat, two exquisite embroidered masterpieces are revealed – lilies for one seat, irises for another. 'As each flower came into perfection, I would paint it in watercolours on a piece of paper and slide a drawing under the canvas and then I could pick up the coloured wools and follow the pattern.' A pastime in old age, completed with a precision acquired decades before.

Most 1920s schoolgirls would've been proud of Ann's considerable accomplishments, knowledge and contacts. At home, she enjoyed

Old English and was fascinated by *Beowulf*, and Jane Austen has been a companion for life. Yet when telling her story, Ann stresses her early academic failings – 'I was no good at languages, loathed maths' – and repeats that she left school with no exams. Her concern is surprising given she came from a generation which treated educated girls with extreme caution. With three quarters of a million dead, the shortfall of young men after 1918 exacerbated a fear of blue stocking career women. Invariably single, there was a nasty backlash against these 'spinsters' who were believed to be beyond masculine control. (Outside the narrow corridors of academia, Joyce's path was neither encouraged nor revered.) But the Sidgwicks were not the type of family to be cowed by pejorative commentary; they were among society's liberal leaders.

> My father assumed that his daughters would go to university and my elder sister, Elizabeth, behaved perfectly and became a Latin and Greek scholar. She went to Newnham Girls College in Cambridge because, after all, it had been founded by Great Uncle Henry Sidgwick!

A small biography of Ann's life can be found in a reputable journal, *The Book Collector*, which gives context to her impressive claims. Introducing the Sidgwicks as a 'well-connected family of distinguished scholars and school masters', among them was 'Great Uncle Henry', a philosopher who did indeed help found Newnham, one of two colleges that catered for women long before a hostile Cambridge University fully embraced them as members. Henry and his wife, Nora (sister of Edwardian Prime Minister Balfour), epitomised 'the family passion for education, especially female'.[14] Elizabeth, Ann's elder sister, carried that family legacy forward. 'It was frustrating. She was brainier than me, and she was doing everything that my family thought suitable.'

Ann, meanwhile, did not. The story of the two sisters is significant. Interwar, among Britain's Establishment, networks of families and friends sustained children but they did not necessarily dictate their course. It is perhaps no coincidence that Joyce Reynolds, from a class below the Sidgwicks and with no legacy of family entitlement, worked towards the academic world with unbridled passion (her two exhibition offers included one to Newnham). Ann, meanwhile, actively avoided engagement with the learning that surrounded her (starting with those Greek alphabets on the nursery wall). Exposed to other exciting options, cushioned by her family's position, and with a sister who excelled academically, nonconformist Ann was free to chart a different course.

CHAPTER THREE

EMPIRE GIRLS

'I didn't feel particularly English or British, those sorts of things weren't emphasised in those days. You see we just learnt by rote.' Edna shakes her head, she is dutifully roving through her mental archives. 'Of course we learnt about the empire! Queen Victoria was queen of so much of the world thanks to people who went out and searched. We had a great empire.' Edna smiles. Nostalgia in its right form is reassuring. The details are patchy but no matter, the essence of an idea is still there; an uncle who left for Canada before she was born, a large pull-down map on the classroom wall, a school holiday for Empire Day, that sort of thing. If the specifics of what Denton's village school taught its pupils about imperial Britain between the wars are lacking, there are the standard texts that remained a staple across the country for over half a century. Preserved in brown paper, these school books regurgitated a glorified idea of Great Britain and her colonies to children long after elite culture had moved on. The giant atlas was another ubiquitous classroom feature. Joyce nods – at Walthamstow County High School, Empire Day also required a performance.

In First Form, each child was given one bit of the empire and you walked onto the stage with a pointer in your hand and you pointed at your bit on the map and announced, and my bit was Hong Kong, and I can still see myself going up onto the stage waving the pointer and saying loudly, 'HONG KONG!'

Although unaware at the time, the impact of this small ritual on Joyce's identity endured. 'Later during the war, when Britain was losing the Middle East and Singapore and Malaysia one bit after another, my response was very controlled, I didn't show emotion, but when we lost Hong Kong I wept.' As the British sociologist A. H. Halsey recalled, 'The world map was red for the empire and dull brown for the rest, with Australia and Canada vastly exaggerated in size ... Empire Day and 11 November ritualised an established national supremacy.'[1] Some children thought it was the Greenwich Meridian that placed London at the centre of the world, but for Edna it was Big Ben, which she could hear strike as if by magic.

> Christmas, Whitsun and Easter we always used to go to Great Gonerby to stay with Grandma. It was one New Year and we all went next door to Mr and Mrs Wakely, cos they had a radio and we wanted to hear Big Ben strike nine o'clock and that was really *something*. We all gathered around the wireless cos it was coming from London. Yes, it was exciting!

Published in 1937, George Orwell's *The Road to Wigan Pier* observed 'twenty million people are underfed but literally everyone in England has access to a radio'.[2] That Edna, otherwise blighted by poverty, found her way to a wireless as early as 1926 is a case in point. A decade later, more than 9 million radio sets had been sold. Simple patriotic history lessons and access to the advent of finely tuned BBC broadcasts swathed in Edward Elgar's bold tunes and Big Ben's bongs reinforced a vague, pleasing idea of imperial Britain. Edna remains fond of 'the empire'; she has never travelled out of England but that is beside the point. She was, from an early age, connected to it by the aural bellybutton of the universe – Big Ben.

Arguably, the world's largest empire, which by the end of 1918 had again grown, gobbling up an additional 13 million subjects, could have expected to represent more than a faintly pleasing idea to the Mother Country's subjects. With colonies and dominions spread over nearly a quarter of the planet, allotted shopping weeks, official Empire Days, with Empire Day broadcasts, a giant Wembley Exhibition, plus a rash of glitzy Empire Cinemas showing back-to-back swashbuckling movies, Britain's imperial brand hoped for traction with its home audience.

But Ann is dismissive. 'Well, I think at my first little school we celebrated every 24th of May, singing "God Save the King" and waving Union Jacks. We did have a radio by 1926 but no, we didn't really listen to it. My parents didn't regard it as much ... ' She trails off. 'It was sort of common. It didn't feature in the house.' Whether it was the radio set that was common or the contents of the broadcasts is not clear, but certainly the BBC's first ring-master, Director General John Reith, believed the corporation's programming, which began in November 1922, should reach the whole nation. Special emphasis was placed on ritual, empire and royal events. The bohemian Sidgwicks did not tune into these patriotic ideas and sounds; instead they would talk and read in the evenings.

Irrespective of its national remit, Reith's imperial gloss couldn't eradicate awkward trends. The protracted, expensive Boer Wars at the turn of the century dented the morale of the governing classes. The empire was no longer cheap to run, nor could it claim the moral high ground. The era of jingoism and 'Rule Britannia' vigour had lost its way, with the First World War compounding doubts over Britain's imperial status. Despite her junior school efforts and subconscious commitment to a British Hong Kong, Joyce is quite sure of the reception empire got in her household. 'My mother wasn't left wing, she was just very anti-war and very anti-empire, yes, yes.' Nellie Reynolds was firmly committed to the growing tradition of liberal internationalism, which attacked imperialism as a major cause of the Great War. Once again Joyce's reading material came under scrutiny. 'The mistress of the elementary class at Walthamstow was a dear, and she read from authors whom my mother thought were imperialist and bad, and I wasn't allowed to read them at home.' The imperial literati – G. A. Henty, Helen Bannerman, Edgar Wallace,

Rudyard Kipling – were banned from 41 Preston Avenue, although
Joyce thought 'they were terrific! Lovely stories!'

After the 1923 Imperial Conference, when the white settler colonies (Australia, Canada, New Zealand, South Africa) demanded
greater autonomy as dominions, even the Westminster–Whitehall
power axis had to admit that there was little hope of a close-knit
imperial future. A new way forward had to be found. David Low's
Colonel Blimp, first featured in the *London Evening Standard*, was
more than just a pompous cartoon character, he was a reminder
that empire was a brittle entity too easy to mock and despise, a
giant conglomerate that had to be handled with care. Emollient
Conservative prime minister Stanley Baldwin did what he could
with soothing words on the wireless. After all, what better pana-
cea in the face of strikes and economic depression than a glorious,
familial empire? But family tended to begin at home. Welsh Helena
was a keen student, and that included geography. 'I used to read a
lot, I did geography for my School Certificate. What's that you said,
dear? Empire?'

Helena stops and ponders the question. Empire, what did it mean
to her? 'Well, I was very proud of being Welsh. Welsh came first
always, always for me. I felt Welsh. As a young child, there was only
one country and that was Wales, the rest was over the water.' When
she identifies 'the rest', they are Scotland and England, not Britain,
which hardly gets a look in, never mind the empire. However, she
does concede, 'I always remembered the King and Queen in my
prayers. And we got a half-day holiday for Empire Day, the purple
lilacs that were brought into school smelt lovely.'

For many in the early twentieth century, a distant empire was an
imaginary world populated with exotic flowers, Colonel Blimps and
Little Black Sambos; a sprawling mass miles away from the humdrum reality of life in 1920s Britain. Emigration fell dramatically
after the war and by the 1930s more people returned to Britain than
left. Ignoring empire, or simply enjoying the fripperies and high days
and holidays which accompanied it was standard fare in the complacent Mother Country. But in the peripheries, where 400 million

colonial subjects spanned the globe, connected by an inconsistent cobweb of telegram wires, steam liners and English-speaking officials, there was less choice. Britain was omnipresent.

OLIVE

Olive's speech is rapid, her accent distinct* and the story she is telling fluent – she has told it before. Often. 'I just thought about de Governor. Yes, I met him cos we went to parties at de Governor's house as children and den I was a Girl Guide and would go to parade at St George's Church when is de King's birthday and it always raining. *Hahaha!*' She laughs – Olive laughs a lot, a warm, engaged, occasionally raucous laugh that invites you to laugh with her. *Hahaha.* 'De Governor had a lovely big government house and at de parties we used to have chocolate – cocoa tea! We in Guyana used cocoa and you use tea!' The way Olive tells her early story is uncomplicated and affirming, 'I had a wonderful childhood!' And that childhood – from its genetic complexity to the cultural overtones that defined it – was the product of very deliberate imperial policies.

Guyana's existence as a British colony was a classic piece of nineteenth-century imperial consolidation. By the time this ear of land on the northern tip of South America was annexed from the Dutch, Britain already had an extensive collection of Caribbean islands. British rule, which formally began in 1814, united the separate territories under the banner of British Guiana and continued to develop the hundreds of sugar estates carved out along the coast of this plantation economy.

'Me, I am a MIX!' Olive shouts this word, sitting in her north London home. She is 'a great big MIX-up!' She knows that at 102 years old, bright as a button, with her smooth black skin and delicate features, she is surprising. Her identity's surely worth shouting about? 'My father was a mixture, his parents were mixed and, um, his father was from Scotland and his moder from India. He was

---

* See Appendix 1.

born in Guyana. My moder, she was a mixture too. She was half aboriginal and black too.' Olive's extraordinary ethnic heritage gives bite to the phrase 'living history'. Absolutely present in a reclining chair, she is the very embodiment of the four vital points in Britain's imperial equation.

Take her father, Mr Higgins. 'A businessman,' says Olive proudly, 'with rice and a mill.' The two sides of his family tree – Scottish and Indian – underline the empire's most important export: manpower. It is well known that Scots – educated, hardworking and with fewer homegrown opportunities than the English – were the Mother Country's great empire-builders. Across the West Indies, Scotsmen alongside their fellow Europeans ran colonial plantations; it was a lucrative business that depended on the arrival of black slaves from the African continent. In 1834, the end of Britain's trade in human lives brought Guyana's most profitable industry to an abrupt halt.* Imperial economics demanded a cheap alternative workforce and one was found. Between 1838 and 1917 (when the practice was banned), 240,000 indentured East Indians duly arrived in Guyana. Displaced, dispossessed and obliged to work for five years in return for their 'freedom', Olive's Indian ancestors were part of a much larger trend. From the 1820s onwards, nearly 1.6 million Indians left to work elsewhere in the empire. Britain's imperial arm had once more picked up the globe and given it a shake; the mass movement of whites and blacks and then Asians founded and consolidated Britain's overseas brand. The world was never the same again. To quote Olive, it was 'a great big MIX-up!'

Indentured Indians don't interest Olive – too far in the past. Rather she focuses on her father's success. In him plantation owner and Indian servant became entwined, leaving this pale-skinned, fine-looking man well placed to move from the stigma of plantation work to the cultivation of rice. Mr Higgins was an 'overseer', a man of status, a man who shot wild animals with his brother, and took

---

* The law banning slavery in the British Empire was passed in 1833 and implemented in 1834.

a shot in the leg. 'After dat his foot was straight, so he looked after his rice fields on a horse.' Broad savannas, mangrove swamps, the dark snaking Essequibo River, these are the hallmarks of Olive's very early childhood. But the union between Mr Higgins and her mother Rosalind didn't last. Olive doesn't dwell on the split, preferring the original love story. Her mother Rosalind was a natural beauty, with an ancestral heritage that touched two more points in the imperial paradigm – the trade in slaves and the dislodged native. Rosalind's lineage went beyond the story of European arrival and exploitation: not only was she half black courtesy of her slave ancestors but also half Amerindian, tying Olive to the first inhabitants of Guyana. It was this dark, alluring woman who turned Mr Higgins's head, leading to a union that bucked and blended the distinct racial strata led by the ruling whites in British Guiana. 'Tis so. And why not an Indian man with a black woman? Huh? So an Indian man would not fall in love cos she is black?!' Olive shakes her head knowing well love and attraction don't work like that. 'Dat doesn't stop a man loving a woman, and when dey are young, you know what dey do!' More laughter, and the arrival of baby Olive on 1 May 1915.

~

'Here, let me tell you ... ' Olive's carer has arrived and is included in the conversation. But the tangled family saga is complicated so Olive, aware she might lose her audience, breaks the impasse with a song. 'I'm going to sing you something I learnt at school':

> Born in the land of the mighty Roraima,
> Land of great rivers and far stretching sea;
> So like the mountain, the sea and the river
> Great wide and deep in our lives would be.

She bangs out the rhythm on the arm of her chair, delivering a mighty crescendo for the chorus.

> Onward, upward, may we ever go,
> Day by day in strength and beauty grow
> Till at length we each of us may show
> What Guyana's sons and daughters can beeeee!

'Dat's me!' she shouts with gusto, pointing at her chest, '"Guyana's daughter"! Hurrah!' Briefly the room is filled with euphoria. 'The Song of Guyana's Children' has all the qualities of a great national tune, it is catchy, evocative and unifying. It is no coincidence that it was written by Reverend W. Hawley Bryant, an early twentieth-century English missionary working in Guyana. He wrote music with a divine purpose.

The elevated aspirations of Victorian Britons ensured that by the middle of the nineteenth century they were no longer content to rule the world but also sought to redeem it.[3] With slavery outlawed, the Christian missionaries spearheaded a 'civilising' campaign that sought to tackle the spiritual welfare of the heathen peoples. Olive's song, sung without a shred of irony in the now obsolete 'Mother Country', is testimony to the lasting impact of their efforts. Raised almost solely by her black mother in Georgetown, Guyana's capital, it was this exported version of Christianity that provided the backbone of Olive's childhood.

> I went to St Philip's School. I was confirmed in St Philip's Church when I was eleven years old and it was Church of England. Oh yes, dey talk a lot about England. We spoke about Wilberforce, he is de man who brought back de Bible. And we knew about Canterbury Cathedral and de knights who murdered dat man.

Alongside a litany of English history snippets, Olive describes a sunny bright life within a wooden house with open windows and lace curtains waving in the sea breeze; nearby was the wooden church, St Philip's. Her mother was God-fearing and Olive a diligent student. 'Church was more devout over der.' The God she learnt about as a child was the God who has guided her throughout the rest of her life, the same God that led her by the hand to Great Britain. Another rendition, this time a poem:

> A is for Adam, the first man made
> B is for Bethlehem, where Jesus was born
> C is for Cain, who killed his brother Abel . . .

Faultlessly she performs through all twenty-six letters of the alphabet. '. . . Z is for Zion, the home of the blessed!' It could be a miracle (she is 102). Olive's God is unfaltering and he is word for word, hymn for hymn the God that Britain brought to Guyana nearly 200 years earlier. As deliberately as the Dutch had planted sugar before them, the British planted their Christian Lord with his army of Anglican and Presbyterian foot soldiers. Paid for from the public purse, above all else their mission was to convert Guyana's population (in particular the Africans) to the word of the Lord. There were giant edifices on hand to bind loyalties. 'We had St George's Church, look it up on your machine.' Olive nods assertively at my phone. 'It's a cathedral, and de biggest wooden church in de world! Everybody want to get married in St George's Church.' It was in this building (a magnificent timber structure completed in 1899, tickling heaven at 143m tall) that Olive and her school friends celebrated Empire Days and the King's birthdays, stories which bring our narrator neatly back to tales of the (British) Governor who protected Guyana. Above him was King George of Britain and above him, 'God of course! *Hahahaha.*' Lots more laughter.

Olive is a wise woman. Sitting in her living room in 2017 she knows that the Guyana of her youth was a mild despotism ruled from far away, an economic outpost of a British Empire well past its prime. A slump in the price of sugar and rice after the First World War left the economy depressed and the people angry; there were riots and strikes. British rule looked increasingly like the thin end of the wedge. But memory isn't reality, it is the version of our story that we believe fits us best. For Olive that means remembering and reconnecting with the simple lines that defined her youth. 'De Moder

Country, we always knew about de Moder Country. We were from Guyana *and* we were British!' She claps her hands, keen to stress her dual nationality. The missionaries did a thorough job. Alongside the word of the Lord, they exposed Guyana's mixed population to British culture, education and political structures. Their groundwork was enduring; Olive grew up a well-schooled, proud subject of His Majesty's exclusive world club, the Great British Empire. Unlike her contemporaries back in Britain whose imperial understanding invoked vague notions of national superiority (Edna), or personal squeamishness (the families of Joyce and Ann), Olive was absolutely sure of the strong, invisible umbilical cord that linked her life in British Guiana to the life-giving Mother Country.

PHYLLIS

> Linked to the chain of Empire one by one,
> Flushed with long leave, or tanned with many a sun.

Kipling's famous poem 'The Exiles' Line' captures the regular ebb and flow of Imperial Britain's workforce as they criss-crossed half the globe, pausing briefly to reconnect with the metropole, only to leave. Again.

> And how so many score of times ye flit
> With wife and babe and caravan of kit.[4]

In British India by the late nineteenth century, regular trips to the Mother Country were the hallmark of a ruling family. Like the West Indies, the subcontinent was governed, it was never 'settled'; returning home was an important mechanism by which the upper echelons of the British Raj asserted their superiority and right to rule. However, this transnational to-ing and fro-ing was not available to every British Indian. Throughout her childhood, Phyllis Gargan had understood she was British, that Britain was her homeland and that this invisible British identity somehow made

her special, and yet aged fifteen she had never been to the Mother
Country. Now, aboard a steam liner bound for Tilbury, Essex, in
March 1933, all that was about to change. Nothing could diminish
the thrill of this epic voyage. 'A lot of people never came to England.
The lower classes didn't have the money. We only came because it
was paid for by Father's work. It was very prestigious. Yes! Quite
an event.'

The grey, wet March air and the dismal tinge of a global depression could not diminish London's splendour. 'My father took me
around to show me the historical sites and museums. We used to get
a bus and Dad would say, "That is Trafalgar Square!" and "That is
Marble Arch and that is the Cenotaph!" And he'd tell me a bit about
the history. He was very good.' Phyllis adored her father; a handsome
Dubliner who left Ireland in 1911 to try his luck in the British army,
William Gargan had oodles of Gaelic charm. Equally devoted to
his eldest daughter, the pair had forged their relationship all over
India and Burma – baiting mongoose, fishing in the Hooghly River
and shooting peacocks for the 'pot'. But in 1933, with the flexibility
demanded of an empire-builder, William was now his daughter's
guide around the empire's most prestigious city. Beneath a tweed
cap, through the fog, he pointed out Great Britain's star-studded
architecture. 'I just accepted Britain, that's my nature. I knew a lot
about England before I arrived. No, I wasn't disappointed.'

Phyllis's parents had always made a conscious effort to reinforce
their family's British heritage. Whether in the dusty heat of Calcutta
or the humidity of Rangoon, on Christmas Day – that ultimate
English celebration – 'a gramophone appeared with a big horn and
Mother got our finest carpet for the sitting room'. Traditions were
upheld and standards maintained. An early family picture shows
off a proud husband and wife with their first four children (Phyllis
and two younger sisters in starched white European frocks and a
polished little brother, Terence). The photograph is startling for its
formality. 'A tailor used to come to the house, and Mother was very
good at making clothes too.' Rakish William sports a black suit
with bow tie, his wife Irene is sitting upright on a dining chair of

dark wood, a dainty stockinged leg extended beyond the child on her knee. Elsewhere William cuts a dash on the veranda reading a broadsheet in woollen stockings, leather brogues and a polo shirt. The impression given is that of an English Edwardian family but the reality was very different. All of them bar their father were born and raised in India. Irene, Phyllis's mother, was a third-generation white Indian, and even Dubliner William belonged to a country which by 1921 was no longer even British. But Britishness was a deliberately flexible, inclusive concept and one primarily built abroad. Like nothing else, the common mission of empire focused hearts and minds on a shared idea of a British identity and 'homeland'.

> It was a Cambridge education. I took Cambridge exams. I went to ten schools in India and Burma before I finished but I knew more about Britain than the people who lived there. Years later I said to a friend of mine who came from Luton, 'Do you know what Luton is famous for?' She said, 'No.' I replied, 'It is famous for making hats, I learnt that in India!' And I learnt what they made in Glasgow – shipbuilding and in Newcastle too . . .

William was a wireless operator for the Indian Post and Telegraph Service. There was no money to send their growing brood to school in England but the Gargans had done the next best thing, they sent them to government boarding schools and convents sprinkled across the remote uplands of India. Deemed an escape from the dirty heat of the city, in 1924 seven-year-old Phyllis, with her younger sister Babs, set off for Dow Hill School near Darjeeling in the Himalayan foothills. The journey from Calcutta was long; an overnight train ride plus a 'toy train' through the mountain forests, with coolies on hand for the final ascent. 'A motorway runs up there now,' sighs Phyllis in wonder; back then it felt like the world's end. Crisp cool nights, days walking in the woods, digesting yellow raspberries, counting monkeys and bears, feasting her eyes on the snowy caps of the Nepalese range. 'We had no electricity or gas, but there were hurricane lamps in the main hall and we slept in dormitories. The rainy season brought the leeches out but we got used to them in time.' It was at Dow Hill (then an entirely European school) that the sisters began to formally learn about the Mother Country. Hats in Luton, shipbuilding in Glasgow, 'and in November we had an annual bonfire night, logs of wood and a guy made by someone in Class Seven. It was a very rounded education.' Brought up on the other side of the world, Olive speaks equally highly of her education at St Philip's Church of England School in Guyana's Georgetown. The British brand, and by definition British influence, had long, convincing tentacles.

For schoolgirl Phyllis, perhaps the most compelling evidence that the Mother Country was something special came in more tangible form.

I remember a girl in boarding school, her name was Sheila Gorey, and her family were tea planters. She had an aunt in England and at Easter she sent the most beautiful Easter egg. It was all made of icing. You don't see them any more. It was beautifully decorated in two parts and you opened it and there were chocolates inside.

Wistfully Phyllis says again, 'You don't see them any more, it really was a beautiful work of art,' before reinforcing the point: 'It was from her aunt in England. I used to think, "I wish I had an aunt in England who would send me something like that."' In fact Phyllis did have an aunt in England, but not one with the money to express-deliver iced eggs halfway around the world. Aunt Mary was surviving on a widow's pension of 21 shillings a week. Still, a contact in England (London no less), was worth cultivating. It was Aunt Mary who helped facilitate the Gargans' trip to the capital in 1933.

She didn't have the space to accommodate the whole family so they rented somewhere in north London's Finsbury Park. Restricted by a poor exchange rate, the musty Victorian terraced house was a far cry from the Gargans' spacious existence on the subcontinent. Phyllis is phlegmatic – it's hard to know if her solidly calm disposition was inherited or learnt, but either way it has stood her in good stead. 'Yes, London was very different but you accept that as a child.

Even after Calcutta I had lived in Madras, then miles away in remote St Thomas Mount, there was Burma also.' Growing up, Phyllis had moved with her father's job every two years, always to another bungalow within a military cantonment, with numerous siblings and servants in tow. 'We never mixed with Indians, except our servants of course, and I remember playing with their children. The *ayah* was like a nanny, and then there was a cook and the cook had an assistant, and the *dobbe*, who washed our clothes and another fella ... ' She stops. 'There was no toilet, you see, so we had a commode and he emptied it. He did the sluicing.' Phyllis agrees there were a lot of staff: 'They were very cheap, everybody had them.'

There were no servants in London; the 'glamorous' Mother Country in 1933 was a levelling experience. 'My brother and sisters came rushing home one day saying a man had been chasing them.' The man in question knocked on the door of the Gargans' temporary home and met their mother; a flinty Irene, dark, angry and with an unusual accent.

'Were you the man who was chasing my children?'

'Yes,' came the firm reply. 'I am an education officer and I want to know why they were playing in the park when they should've been at school?' Irene explained what by now must've been apparent, that they were from British India. The man was unrelenting. 'I still think your children should go to school, they will be much safer in school than wandering about in parks.' After all, these were British white children, weren't they? Irene acquiesced, and the younger Gargans went to the local school but sixteen-year-old Phyllis was exempt. For her, a Singer sewing shop was recommended. 'I went twice a week and I got instruction, not that it did me much good.' Freewheeling Phyllis bent her head to the demands of London life and sought out perks where possible. There were tickets to a 'real theatre', a tour around Madame Tussauds and a visit to Lyons Corner House in Piccadilly with an older cousin, Kathleen. Together they heard Ivy Benson and Her Girls Band and gorged on a giant knickerbocker glory – it was Phyllis's first and she remembers still the cost at 2s 6d. In comparison, 'Woolworths, with nothing over 6d, was a magic place!'[5]

Memories of a small London house and high prices matched the reduced circumstances that returning British Indians often endured in the Mother Country. Orwell, in his novel *Coming Up for Air*, writes of repatriates residing in 'little dark house[s]' in 'those buried back streets' who would look 'twice at a sixpence', their grander days gone.[6] For Phyllis, the London trip was just a temporary 'status' holiday, but a photograph taken on her sixteenth birthday captures the effort made by the family. 'Look! Mother is wearing a fox around her neck and it was July!' Phyllis, meanwhile, smiles in a stodgy two-piece suit and white ankle socks; the oppressive English sunlight gives the picture an uneasy edge. Despite their best efforts, the Gargans don't belong in London, but they're not Indian either.

Just a teenager at the time, Phyllis is non-committal over recollections of Gandhi and the rising nationalist movement.

It was mainly clashes between the Muslims and Hindus that caused the problems. There would be scuffles in the streets, people fighting with sticks, then the police would break them up. We never had any problems. My father was very friendly, he spoke Hindustani.

In fact, the reality between the two world wars was much more than internecine scuffles. Emboldened by Ireland's example, Indian nationalism surged post-1918; the National Congress gave it form, and skinny, scantily clad Mohandas Gandhi gave it unlikely leadership. The game was up for British rule in India. The Gargan family responded to this looming crisis like the majority of their imperial contemporaries – they continued to blithely live the only lives they'd ever known. By November 1933, husband, wife and their four daughters were heading south back through the Suez Canal. Only Terence was left behind at boarding school – as a boy, an 'English' education was imperative.

Phyllis won't be drawn on her emotional response to London nor her departure. She accepted living in a state of permanent impermanence, and this tolerance girdled her young life. In comparison with Kipling's 'poverty-stricken officer class', whose rigid faith in the imperial project left them stranded when change swept in, Phyllis's peripatetic childhood gave her an enduring flexibility. 'You just got on with it. I didn't know any different. I was tough.' In her hundredth year, Phyllis has an Edinburgh accent (she's lived in Scotland for nearly eight decades), but listen carefully and there are faint, clipped Indian undertones. 'I suppose yes, I suppose I was multicultural.' She grins, and says the newfangled word again. 'Multicultural.'

CHAPTER FOUR

A GREEN AND
PLEASANT LAND

The endearing 'British' touches knitted into the Gargans' way of life
in India and then Burma – that little bit of rolled out carpet and the
gramophone at Christmas, meticulous Edwardian dress and dark
European furnishings – were gestures that, in accumulation across
the empire, translated into something much bigger. Stanley Baldwin,
testing out his vision and voice as the leader of the Conservative
Party, acknowledged the work of these empire-builders in 1924.
They were men who had uprooted themselves in service of the greater
good, 'for that love of home, one of the strongest features of our
race', but he did not credit Britain for this 'love of home'. Instead,
on St George's Day, he focused his praise exclusively on the English.
It was *England*'s empire that one day he hoped would be held in
equivalent esteem to the Romans', anticipating how in the future
'the men of the world of that day may say, "We still have among us
the gifts of the great English race."'[1]

Prime minister three times during the interwar period, with the
adopted style of a provincial English country gent, sucking gently on
his pipe, his faded hair neatly parted, avuncular Baldwin sought to
embody a new familial national image. Shaken by the bloody messes
of first the Boer War and then the Great War, he identified a country in need of healing, whose national character sought affirmation

and reassurance. And he was quite clear that that country, distilled into its purest form, was England. Addressing a home audience, he admitted his 'feeling of satisfaction and profound thankfulness that I may use the word "England" without some fellow at the back of the room shouting out "Britain"'. It was this retreat away from a bold imperial Britishness to an idea of the essence of Englishness that lay at the heart of his interwar appeal. He articulated his own vision of the nation's cradle,

> the tinkle of the hammer on the anvil in the country smithy, the corncrake on a dewy morning, the sound of the scythe against the whetstone, and the sight of a plough team coming over the brow of a hill, the sight that has been seen in England since England was a land.[2]

This timeless evocation had roots in the late nineteenth century. By 1851, more than half the English lived in towns. England was the world's first major urban nation and London the world's biggest city; from the crowded streets and polluting stacked chimneys, a new 'ruralism' gasped for air – a love of the 'real' original England was self-consciously declared. Even empire's greatest champion, Rudyard Kipling, turned to England's rural past to placate his imperial anxieties.* In 1902, he bought a seventeenth-century Sussex manor house and settled down in a country he saw occupied by a happily 'primitive peasantry' and old-fashioned landed gentlemen. His England was made up of 'trees and green fields and mud'.[3] The early twentieth century saw a market boom in books and articles that nurtured bucolic visions of the English countryside. Riding the crest of this nostalgic wave, H. V. Morton quickly became Britain's most famous travel writer; *In Search of England* celebrated the English village and enjoyed numerous reprints.[4] The middle classes were energised by this fresh focus on their own country. Between the wars, walking for pleasure acquired mass appeal. Slow, puffing trains from Charing

---

* Rudyard Kipling was Prime Minister Baldwin's cousin.

Cross to Battle and Kings Langley catered for hikers and ornithologists with shooting sticks and waxed hats. Uptake was particularly keen among suburban dwellers with time, money and a hankering for the great outdoors.

ANN

'Did I like to walk? Yes, of course we walked!' Ann is adamant.

> We called it hiking and it was something that you could do for no money other than the cost of a sturdy pair of leather boots, and it was something that you did with friends, especially good if you were poor students or unemployed. We went walking in Sussex, absolutely yes!

She keenly stresses that Stanley Baldwin was a Conservative, 'and no one in our family voted Conservative'. His popular politics and nostalgic nationalism had no traction among the Sidgwicks. However, rural England appealed to both left and right. By the time Ann was eleven she'd been relocated twice, from Battersea in London to Buckinghamshire's Great Missenden, and then one step further into idealised English village territory – Keston, in Kent. 'My friend Elizabeth and I used to go out into the country and walk. Perhaps we'd spend a night in a village pub and walk further, and so on, and have an evening meal. Both in Kent and further afield.' Practical Ann, with brown bobbed hair, open honest features and milky skin; it's easy to imagine her in the folds of Morton's book, feasting on herring pie and plum broth, visiting inns with fat tabby cats and ancient open fires, sleeping beneath thatch so low the window has a man's 'stubby beard'.[5] And young girls with limited funds, Ann and Elizabeth soon looked beyond the standard country pub and joined the growing youth hostelling movement.

Founded in 1930, by 1939 the Youth Hostelling Association had over 83,000 members and 297 hostels, with a stated objective 'to help all, but especially young people to a greater knowledge, use and love of the countryside'.[6] Their success reflected the growing popularity of walking and cycling, but just occasionally members broke the rules.

> Sometimes I would borrow my brother's two-seater Austin 6 with a dickey seat. The car was very old and stiff and you could only change gear by putting both hands on the stick so Elizabeth would lean across and steer while I was doing this. When we stayed in youth hostels we would hide the car behind a haystack then walk the last mile to the youth hostel, because you were supposed to either walk or bicycle and we were cheating!

Teenage girls in tweed trousers and sensible shoes hurtling between hostels in an old car has an endearing appeal. Ann laughs, it *was* fun and the more daring the better. 'We didn't restrict ourselves to England. Once we drove it all the way to Glasgow because there was an exhibition I wanted to see!' Great Britain had opened up courtesy of multiple grey veins that crisscrossed the landscape; the open road was transforming the countryside and the lives of those who toured across it.

JOYCE, HELENA

Joyce can't remember exactly when her parents invested in that first unforgettable car, the family Morris Minor, but she thinks it was the early 1920s, sometime after the birth of her baby brother. By then, car manufacturers had realised that the future lay in the 'Lure of the Small Car' and deliberately targeted a middle market. Soon an armada of Baby Austins and Morris Minors fanned out across Britain's ever-expanding road network where surface quality was inconsistent and road rollers in constant use.[7] Welsh Helena's family didn't have a car ('we had a pony, mind you') nor had all Brecon's local tracks been blessed with tarmacadam, but that didn't stop private vehicles from careering along. By 1927, one in seven Welsh families owned a vehicle, anyone over seventeen could drive and where speed limits existed they were difficult to regulate;* walking in a country lane was no longer safe.

'I was quite delighted with the responsibility of shopping for 'Miss'. She sent me to Mrs Hiron's little shop in the village that sold sweeties in jars, I was to pick up three pencils.' Elementary schoolgirl Helena rushed to execute her grown-up task, dashing across the snowy road minus a coat to collect the teacher's pencils. 'Good girl,' said Mrs Hiron, rolling her purchase in a slip of paper.

> I've no idea what happened next. I started back across the road. I don't know that I ever did remember. Mr Miller, an old man in his eighties, was driving his car and apparently he braked when he saw me and skidded across the road, pinning me against the school railing!

When Helena regained consciousness it felt like the whole of Libanus village was staring down at her. Then came the hospital ward and six lonely weeks with a crushed foot, elevated and in traction. Numerous villagers sent books and treats and letters. 'Everyone was so caring.' She is sanguine about the accident and seems to have forgiven Mr Miller: 'He never did say sorry and there wasn't any compensation in those days!'[8] Helena had a lucky escape. In 1934, road accidents and fatalities broke new records – that year vehicles caused 7,343 deaths and 231,603 injuries, half the victims being pedestrians. (In 2016, there were just 1,780 fatalities on Britain's roads.)[9] The statistics shocked Britain and a test was introduced (only for newcomers – Mr Miller would've been exempt), and a speed limit of 30mph set in built-up areas.

~

---

* The first speed limit was introduced in 1861, however it was over a hundred years later, in the 1960s, before Road Traffic Regulation Acts were introduced that controlled the setting of speed limits.

Joyce's father, William Reynolds, was a careful driver, his manner behind the wheel in keeping with his gentle temperament. His little family felt safe and excited as they bundled into the Morris Minor and drove away from their London home in search of England. 'We often went on tours at the weekend. I suppose travelling fifty miles or so.' Unlike some of her fellow pupils at St Paul's, Joyce wasn't yet permitted to learn to drive but, used to strict parental control, her pleasure went undimmed. Canterbury, Winchester, Brighton, there was no end of delights to uncover – the Reynoldses loved motoring and within easy distance of their southern home they could feast on that much celebrated 'Old England'. By 1933, Yorkshire novelist and playwright J. B. Priestley added his name to the roll call of men articulating their vision of this England; for him it was 'the country of cathedrals and ministers, of manor houses and inns, of Parson and Squire'.[10] Joyce nods at Priestley's name, but insists 'we were touring before he started writing about it. My mother began her teaching in a little village near Rugby where she fell in love with the English countryside.' Nor were the Reynolds family hidebound by their car. 'When I was a child we would go for a fortnight or maybe three weeks on several walking holidays in the Lake District.' Joyce was not alone; in a Windermere traffic jam at Lancaster, H. V. Morton ruefully concluded that the Lakes' most famous poet, Wordsworth, 'was a great, but unconscious publicity agent' (an appeal supplemented by Beatrix Potter's more contemporary efforts). Between the wars, rising disposable incomes, more cars and the vogue of rural escape put pressure on England's most famous mountains. When he finally arrived, Morton identified two different groups of Lakeland tourists: those who stayed at water level, sailed in boats and sought suicide in their cars on narrow roads and an altogether heartier set: 'who, rising early, put on khaki shorts, grasp stout sticks, and leave the ground level before the first group have had their morning tea'.[11] Joyce *never* wore short trousers but does concede her family took their holidays seriously.

We stayed in a B&B but the proprietor gave us more than breakfast. We took sandwiches and spent the whole day on the mountains. I don't think we conversed much. I mean, if one saw something in the way of a plant that you had never seen before you would talk. Ask the parents, that sort of thing.

No, I don't think I knew their Latin names at that stage!

Joyce, with her insatiable thirst for knowledge, was keen to learn about all that surrounded her. 'Yes, yes, I would want to be able to identify the difference between a kestrel and a buzzard. Absolutely.' It was this time out, spent exploring, breathing lungfuls of bracing air, miles from the sounds and sights of relentless London, that established Joyce's great love of walking, a pastime she's held dear her entire life. By 1937, she was a twenty-year-old student at Oxford University; when in need of a study break,

we would walk in the country for fun, fun, fun! We would go out in the afternoons into the surrounding countryside and I often went alone on my bicycle. Just before our final exams, we stayed away for the night in some fairly nearby cheap place, the Cotswolds perhaps, and walked. We would look at nature and chat. Do you never do that?

EDNA

Although living in the countryside was frequently discussed in news-papers and on the wireless after 1918, there was no mass exodus of people rushing to live in rustic England. The interest expressed was primarily one of sentiment; the countryside represented a repository for middle-class hopes, pursuits and holiday ambitions. And per-haps inevitably the focus of these rural aspirations were squires and landowners with money and status, who lived in appealing manor houses – the sort who were frequently featured in country-living magazines and articles. Whether a tourist or a resident, enjoying

England's remote corners required money. Even with a modicum of cash, the community myth of the English countryside didn't always convince. In 1926, writer H. E. Bates wondered if he would 'die of solitary loneliness' in Northamptonshire's Rushdene:

> God knows how people keep alive here. It would be easier for bananas to grow in their gardens than for them to live on what happens to them. Everything is so silly and dull – one has to flirt with every conceivable girl and gibe at the pious and interest myself in the local Labour Party and trespass myself into other people's woods in order to get anything out of the business. I can't write, I can't read, or think.[12]

Edna listens to Bates's angry, condescending words (she's a good listener), and then nods. 'Well, yes, it could be dull. I mean, no, nothing ever really happened. I suppose you would say it was very slow and closed off.' Of the six women featured in this book, Edna, who grew up in Lincolnshire's Denton, is alone able to claim she lived in genuine rural *England*. Her childhood was indeed framed by green glades and burbling streams and wood smoke, and she can follow her family tree back 400 years and still find Johnson peasants working in Denton. But her life was neither romantic nor idyllic. Baldwin's imagined green paradise didn't exist, not for Edna nor anyone else in her family. She neither hiked nor rambled, but she did walk. She walked to fetch water from the Willybriggs stream; she walked to gather kindling, without which there was no fire; she walked to collect milk, carefully carrying the little glass bottle. She had not the energy nor inclination left to walk for pleasure. From an early age, Edna's life was defined by endurance.

> Washing, well – washing was totally different from what it is today. It was a case of lighting the copper fire and boiling the water. But first you had to fetch the water and then you washed the clothes by hand with soap, you scrubbed them. Then the white clothes were put into the copper, having been soaked and cleaned,

and they were boiled. My first job was to do the handkerchiefs. You did the same with the coloureds, but they weren't boiled.

What she describes from the depths of an armchair in her small, centrally heated home sounds so spectacularly dated it has quaint charm.

Monday was washday and then they all had to be pegged up on the line, but if it was raining they were pegged indoors on proper thick cord in front of the fire. I've known in winter the washing's been out and you take the pegs off and the washing still hangs on the line, like ghosts, that's Jack Frost.

Edna was used to frost, in the winter it lined the inside of her bedroom window; she'd wake breathing out plumes of grey mist and rush to scratch her name on the glass pane. We laugh together at the idea of this eager little girl, and then Edna remembers and she stops. As a child, Edna knew she was not merely helping her hard-pressed mother, she was also in training for a job that would occupy the next forty years of her life. The verdant expanse outside the window did not feel large and liberating; the patchwork of fields and hedgerows were an integral part of the rural order in which Edna, as a skivvy, was destined to be at the bottom. Merrie England was nowhere to be seen.

I didn't want to go into service, you must understand this. It was a waste. I would've liked to've worked like my friend at Chambers, as a dressmaker. She was a sleeve hand, but you had to pay for the apprenticeship and my mother couldn't have afforded that.

In neighbouring Grantham, Chambers & Co became the town's first department store in 1911, an emporium of relative luxury (it sold ladies' clothes). Edna's childhood dream was to work in the backrooms as a seamstress. 'Or I would've liked to have been a shop assistant, ooh yes, that would've been nice.' But with no money at home, one less mouth to feed was eagerly anticipated; by the time she was fourteen, Edna's fate had already been decided. She became a domestic servant. Her long hair ('I could sit on it at school') was cut short in preparation. The same man who'd crossed water on baby Edna's peachy forehead, preached weekly at her from the pulpit of St Andrew's Church and guided her adolescent self through Anglican communion became her first employer. 'I worked for the rector and his wife as soon as I left school. His appointment had been approved by Sir Charles Welby.' The pinnacle of Christian authority in Denton Village had just become Edna's lord and master. Initially, she walked across the rectory field from the little estate cottage she called home, but the length of her working day meant she soon lived in. Rising before the sun was up and readying herself with an apron and cap, she went downstairs to clear the grate of ash and light the fire in the big range. 'Oh no! You didn't take their tea into the bedroom! You don't do that!' Edna recounts the order of her morning with terrifying precision. First the water had to boil, only then could it be poured onto the tea leaves through a strainer, and a small jug of milk was placed on the tray. ('The milk was always kept separate!') Edna then set off up the back stairs, tray in hand, along a passage and up a second set of stairs, where she placed the tea on an appointed table and knocked upon her master's bedroom door. The time was exactly quarter past seven. Quickly and discreetly she turned on her heel and re-entered the kitchen, where she began preparations for the couple's breakfast.

'I realise now that a lot of the work I did wasn't really suitable for a fourteen-year-old.' Edna stares wistfully at a watercolour of St Andrew's Church; all these years on her forlorn face encapsulates the disappointment that so many girls felt when entering a life of servitude on the cusp of adulthood. After the First World War, the press panicked about a 'servant problem', but the predicted shortage of girls never materialised. An economic slump in the early 1920s followed by the Depression of '29 kept one in four women in service between the wars; most were under twenty-five and invariably they came from the countryside, where alternative work was limited. For a period in the 1920s, Joyce Reynolds's mother sourced her maids from Evercreech, a remote village in Somerset. 'It was very rural then,' concedes Joyce. 'Nowadays it is virtually unrecognisable, an upstage place for second homes. We once went and stayed there, and all the daughters I met went into service.' Like Evercreech, Edna's village, Denton, had few employment opportunities for young girls. With the nearest town, Grantham, a nine-mile round trip away, the fourteen-year-old teenager had to take work where she (or rather her mother) could find it.

Looking back on the rapidly disappearing era of domestic service, sociologists in the 1970s and '80s concluded that female servants between the wars tussled with polarised emotions; apparently deference and defiance were the standard hallmarks of a girl's response to her employer. 'Mainly I was very shy – back then I wouldn't have been able to talk like I am talking to you now.' If timidity kept Edna quiet, convention and necessity helped mould her into a biddable worker. 'No, you didn't curtsey, that had gone out of fashion, but I suppose I would call the rector "sir". You might give a little inclination of your head if the situation demanded it.'

It was a long working day. After breakfast and prayers and general cleaning, Edna prepared lunch.

Perhaps if there was a piece of lamb, I'd roast it and make a mint sauce. There was mint in the rectory garden, I would chop it up with a bit of sugar and vinegar. The gravy would come from what was left in the pan, I would add a dod of flour and mix it up. Sometimes we'd eat pigeon. They kept domestic pigeons and the gardener would first have to wring one's neck.

Food preparation was a magnum opus. Teenage Edna regularly grappled with a fresh carcass – plucking, skinning, gutting. 'Oh yes, I skinned rabbits wherever I worked if it was necessary. And I can tell you the only thing that I can't cook from a pig is its squeal!' Lunch was served and cleared and washed up, and only then might she have an hour in the afternoon for a spot of knitting or reading – 'but I had to wash and change into a black and white uniform and get tea ready. So no, it wasn't much of a break.' Just two half-days off a week yielded minimal respite. Nor did Edna enjoy the camaraderie of a colleague. Like the majority of domestic servants, she worked alone; middle-class couples relied heavily on their solitary 'help', and the rector and his wife were no exception. Mechanised devices were on their way but in the meantime, as H. G. Wells suspected, Edna had to go 'up and down, up and down and be tired out'.[13] In the 1930s, it was cheaper and more reliable to put a girl in the spare room than to be one of the few households that risked investing in gimmicky contraptions like washing machines.

The rector and his wife, they were called Mr and Mrs Buss, well they didn't own a washing machine but they did own me! I was owned, I really didn't have a life. It was a waste. Even on a Sunday, which was meant to be my half-day, I never got away before four o'clock because Mrs Buss made me wait until after she'd written her letters so I could post 'em. Oh, she was a besom.

Open defiance was out of the question, but Edna was not happy. 'I didn't like the rector's wife. She was a so-and-so.' Isolated in private houses, the labour movement and trade unions overlooked domestic servants, and frequently despised them. Unfairly derided as lackeys of the rich, between the wars over 1.5 million domestic servants managed the arbitrary whims and moods of their individual employers while drudging their way through longer hours and less pay than any other sector. In her first posting, Edna was easy prey for the rector's wife.

On a rare Saturday off, I had been with my mother and sister to Smith & Dicksons, a shop in Grantham where you could pay so much a week – you know, 'on the never-never'! Anyway, Easter was a big deal and I had bought a lovely straw hat, cos summer was coming, and a new coat and a dress.

This was a shopping trip laden with expectation. Edna, having completed her first stint as a working woman, relished the opportunity to spend some money on herself. She'd always had an eye for clothes and now, for the first time, she could choose her own. With the arrival of factory-produced fashion, everyone could indulge in beautification: domestic servants included. George Orwell regarded this mass consumerism as a vital palliative that 'averted revolution'. 'In your new clothes you can stand on the street corner, indulging in a private daydream of yourself as Clark Gable or Greta Garbo which compensates for a great deal.'[14] Edna was never the revolutionary sort, but still, clothes (and the two picture houses in Grantham) meant a lot to her. On this occasion, the precious garments were squirrelled back to her mother's house in their paper wrappings before she returned to the rectory in time for Sunday morning duties. 'Well, on Sunday afternoon I got home for tea, where I changed into my new clothes before I went to church for my evening off. It was six o'clock church, and my brother Charles was in the choir.'

Edna, upright in her appointed pew, shiny as a new penny in a bright straw bonnet and best coat, caught eyes, the rector's wife's eyes among them – the local girl was coming of age. But servants needed to know their place, did they not? 'Well, on the Monday, do you know what Mrs Buss told my mum? She complained I had spent the Sunday morning admiring myself in the mirror with my new clothes. My mum said, "She'd've had a job, cos those clothes were at our house!" Old bitch!' Edna smiles wickedly, enjoying the opportunity to right the grubby little wrong administered by the omnipotent Mrs Buss. The tale is full of the claustrophobic corners that she negotiated as a domestic servant and resident of Denton. Nowhere could she go unobserved; even off-duty, her behaviour and demeanour were jealously guarded (then misconstrued) by her employer and keeper.

But what other option was there? Edna shrugs. 'Things were like that then. That's how it was.' Beneath the surface, defiance still wrestles with deference. It was a very simple life, but a complicated one too. 'Yes, look at me there, don't I look angry ... ' Edna holds a black and white picture of her much younger self. 'I suppose I was about eighteen here. Yes, I probably was fed up!' The girl in the photograph glowers back at old Edna, arms folded, frame strong, brows dark and sure.

'How dare you?' her expression seems to say, 'How dare you serve me this lot and call it a life.' And yet it was that same girl who played by the rules; young Edna was a willing supplicant on bended knee in the rector's church; she didn't seek out London for a service job in the city or to try her luck in a new industrial world, she instead stayed the course she knew. There was no television, and only rare access to the radio, but the *Grantham Journal*, 'that had everything in it, all the news and we read that every weekend and cut interesting bits out so I knew that Stanley Baldwin was a very popular prime minister.'

The rector, the local school, *Grantham Journal*, her mother – these were Edna's points of contact with the outside world; and circling beyond them were the Welbys in their big house, the prime minister and the Royal Family. 'I thought, given the circumstances, George VI did a very good job and his daughter has been a very good queen.' Edna was never told whom to vote for, 'although I knew some servants that were taken to the polling station, and it was just presumed they would vote the same as their employer'. But conservatism was in her blood; an essential part of the rural hierarchy, Edna voted to keep things how they were and 'how they should be'. 'I always voted Conservative, always, all my life until 2015.' No matter what it cost her personally, she reinforced the strong provincial sense of social order and place that prevailed in Britain between the wars. Her inner contradiction – that fight between deference and defiance – is quite as old as she is and still it persists. 'I was owned, you see, it wasn't my own life' – this is Edna's frequent and understandable refrain, but rarely does she fall into self-pity, there's always a reason to be cheerful about her past. 'People were friendlier then, it was a friendlier country. Everybody knew everybody. You knew what was in your neighbours' drawers!' In all its many contradictory forms, the village community was the crux of Edna's life. Without Denton, who was Edna?

ANN

Ann's mother, Mrs Sidgwick, was chaotic when it came to running the household – sometimes impossibly so. 'My mother was terribly messy. And she was bad at employing staff; she didn't like having servants in, but we had at least two.' This statement on the inconvenient necessity of staff underlines the vagaries of Mrs Sidgwick's domestic regime as well as the family's class. 'All my contemporaries had live-in maids, cooks, chauffeurs and so on.' Ann doesn't remember friends commenting on the individual treatment of servants but there was a paragraph in her mother's memoirs that stood out.

> She was a young girl and had been told to clear up her things because the maid wanted to lay the table and Mother, who was fed up, said, 'Why should I bother? She is only a servant!' Well, for this she was terribly rebuked for the rest of the day by her parents, and I thought when I read it, 'To react so violently, it does seem to indicate a feeling of guilt.'

This pricking conscience – a distant jangle of an idea that as the world woke up to the democratic behemoth, servitude in the home would (must) evolve – touched some households more than others. The discomfiture between 'upstairs' and 'downstairs' seemed to particularly trouble a coterie of wealthy bohemians in the 1920s and 1930s. Relations between a mistress of the house and her servants often became emotionally deep and dependent (as opposed to deferential and defiant) – with Virginia Woolf and her staff a case in point. Ditto the Sidgwicks: a working relationship that was tinged with guilt for Ann's grandparents evolved; by the time Ann's mother was in charge, the servant–mistress paradigm was a vital source of emotional and practical stability. 'Missy' was a centrifugal force in the Sidgwick household.

> When my parents were first married they lived in a flat in Battersea, where they had two live-in servants. When my sister was about to be born in 1912, Mother employed a monthly nurse, Sister Mitchell, to help her with the baby. This was common middle-class practice. Well, that worked out fine but at the end of the month my mother said she didn't think she could cope with a

baby, despite having a very helpful husband and two servants and a mother nearby, so Sister Mitchell recommended her own sister, Ellen, who was looking for a new family.

One of ten children from rural Aylesbury, Missy Ellen duly arrived in London with a suitcase and a wide-brimmed hat covering a large roll of brown hair.

Missy wasn't so good at storytelling and reading aloud and she was not involved in our religious education. We knew that she was, as it were, under my mother and she and my father were always very polite to each other. 'Yes, Miss Mitchell. Good evening, Miss Mitchell.'

But for children, matters of social rank carried little stock – as far as the Sidgwick brood were concerned, Missy was their second mother. In an era when upper-class women were actively discouraged from over-cosseting their children, Missy more than compensated. 'Oh, she was more loving than my mother, yes! I think that Mother, having had six children in ten years, had had enough of maternity. In fact, my younger sister said she felt guilty that she loved Missy more than our mother.' Mr and Mrs Sidgwick would go on an excursion or out to dinner, but Missy was always there. 'She was a fixture, we sat on her knee, she made our life permanent and she loved babies.' Throughout their lifetime, Missy remained resolutely single.

No, I don't remember there ever being a man, she belonged to our family. If Missy had decided when we were all children that she would move elsewhere, I think my mother would've been absolutely lost. They had an intuitive relationship and Mother became more and more dependent on Missy as an organiser.

For the few days at Christmas when Missy returned to her family home in Aylesbury, nothing was left to chance. 'She would make sure everything was organised, with sufficient bread and milk and cold meats in the larder.' The novelty of being in charge in their own home encouraged japes amidst the preparations. Mr Sidgwick tackled the onerous task of gutting the turkey with his student daughter's medical dissecting tools, and the bedecked Christmas tree ominously dripped wax onto the carpet.

Full of curiosity, the children occasionally quizzed Missy over her pay. They clambered on her knee and pressed for an answer. 'Ooh yes, I get paid lots and lots' came the reply. 'How old are you?' they queried. 'One-hundred-and-fifty-six! That was the age she always gave.' Ann sighs, 'We never did discover how old she was.' Missy's age was not relevant. She was one among legions of women who lived in the shadow of someone else's marriage, seamlessly servicing someone else's family, as if it were her own.

> She did all the housework, all the cooking, she oversaw the other parlour maid, she dressed the babies and took them on walks. Mother totally depended on Missy and at the end of the Second World War, after we had left home and father had died, they set up a household together and lived more or less on equal terms.

Ann admits that it was not the ending her mother had envisaged, but the two women loved animals and gardening and the same six Sidgwick children, so they made it work. Missy was family, after all.*

~

Edna sits up in her seat and clasps her hands. She has patiently listened as I recounted the story of Ann, her fellow centenarian: she's learnt all about the Sidgwicks and their Missy and now she is rejoicing. 'Yes! Yes!' she says, 'Yes, if you found a family like that as a servant, you were made for life.'

---

* Missy's sister, the monthly nurse, Sister Mitchell, attended Mrs Sidgwick at all five of her subsequent births.

CHAPTER FIVE

GROWING PAINS

HELENA

In the 1920s and 1930s, self-conscious Englishness emanating from the seat of power in Westminster did not cross borders. England could keep provincial Prime Minister Baldwin and his cohort of writers, with their quaint rural connotations; the resurgent nationalism of the late nineteenth century ensured Scotland and Wales discovered their own potent symbols. Sir Walter Scott had already draped his country in one-time Highland tartan and the romantic Scottish idyll had subsequently been converted into political capital: cue a modest home rule movement, a Scottish Office in government and a guaranteed national share of public expenditure in the UK. Wales lacked Scotland's weight and institutional independence, but the Welsh fightback from Anglocentric hegemony saw a concerted push against the centuries-old subjugation of their national language.

When Helena was a child, she recalls that in some chapels recital competitions still took place in Welsh, with local villages like Crai and Sennybridge and Trecastle doing their best to preserve the language. Slowly Welsh would position itself at the vanguard of a twentieth-century reassertion of national pride helped by the emergence of a new group – what national historian John Davies refers to as 'middle-class Welsh speakers confident in their Welshness'. By

1937, their influence was considerable, and even the BBC relented, at last granting the Welsh nation a separate wavelength.[1] But for many families it was too little, too late.

Helena sighs. 'When I was young, you weren't encouraged to speak Welsh; in fact if children spoke Welsh in school they were put in the corner or kept in at playtime – oh, I can remember that very well.' Even at local eisteddfods, Helena invariably performed in English.

> I once had a dear little doll, dears,
> The prettiest doll in the world;
> Her cheeks were so red and so white, dears,
> And her hair was so charmingly curled.

In her beautiful lilting voice she begins to recite her first publicly performed poem. The four-year-old standing before the deacon's seat in a cleft of the Black Mountains recited not Welsh prose but an English classic (Charles Kingsley no less). She laughs apologetically, 'Oh, but I did sometimes perform in Welsh; Father would help me.' John Jones's first language was Welsh, and he taught his daughter to reproduce titbits of his mother tongue for performance purposes, but John was a pragmatist. England's unchallenged dominance across Britain for hundreds of years had bullied and harried the Welsh language. By the time Helena was born, English was the established language of commerce and education and, in Helena's case, the language at home. 'I do wish my father had spoken to me more in Welsh, but it was different in those days and my mother didn't speak Welsh, you see, she came from the Valleys.'

This linguistic absence was the only blemish on her otherwise unimpeachable national credentials. A wordsmith and performer, Helena knew the names of the local mountains and wild flowers, could tell the stories of the ancient House of Gwynedd and colourful Henry Morgan, the pirate king; she understood the importance of David Lloyd George (even though her mother refused to waste her first vote on his Liberals) and best of all she adored the land she lived in. Helena had no need for England's disproportionate power and distant pomposity. Had their sanitised rural fantasia reached her ears it would've been laughable codswallop. Unlike England, in Wales (as in Scotland) agriculture held up its numbers against other industries. As a farmer's daughter, Helena lived an outdoor life. It wasn't possible to romanticise something that was so real, nor was there a novelty in the everyday.

> Some days I worked very hard. When father was cutting the hay in the morning, I would be up at six o'clock with him and I'd have a rake, and he'd start there and back with his horse and I would have to run from one side of the line to the other to turn the back swath, which was the grass he'd cut.

Next came turning the hay, then hauling it into heaps. Uncles and brothers and neighbouring farmers with brawny arms forked it onto gambos ('We never called them hay wains, not in Wales'), and there again was Helena, on the wagon, jumping up and down and inhaling the pungent ripe aroma of fresh hay. 'Be careful!' her father would shout, 'Be careful and don't fall off now!'

Life-affirming and life-giving, the rise of the sun, the fall of darkness and the turn of the seasons dictated the rhythm against which the Jones family lived out each day. Strong, muscular and competitive, this farm work was ideal training for Helena the athlete. Anxieties about national fitness after the Boer War and the First World War had translated into a public preoccupation with sports and strength. Edwardian ideas of minimal physical exertion for women were banished, so too modest bloomers and corsets. The pioneering *Health and Strength* magazine declared that war work had resulted in the emergence of a 'new and virile race' of women who took to athletics 'like ducks to water'.[2] Helena needed no encouragement. With her chest strapped into elastic and her practical short hair tucked back, she was a regular winner at Brecon's annual county sports. 'The 100 yards, 200 yards, jumping. Oh yes, I won a lot. I didn't wear shoes, because if it was lately mown grass you could run better in bare feet.' Sports day was a much-anticipated annual event, with the additional bonus of prize money.

If farming and competing took up the holidays, there was no physical let-up in term time.

Once we moved farms, I had a long journey into the county school. I would walk three miles to catch the bus into Brecon. In the summer, I would cycle all the way on the old Roman road and sometimes in the evening I would cycle home, have my dinner and cycle all the way back into Brecon to play tennis. It was about seven or eight miles. Father was furious but I wanted to play tennis, you see; it was always my ambition.

A mesmerising warren of small lanes, flanked by high hedges bursting with rosebay willow herb, creamy dog rose, alder and ash, Helena furiously pedalled the distance; bent double over handlebars, she flew across stones and puddles and grassy verges to achieve her dream. 'We had three houses at school; I was in the Green House and I always wanted to be picked to play tennis for the Green House. I was chosen in the end! I'm not sure how good I was, I was a bit of a titch in those days!' Distance was no obstacle until the winter came, bitter cold and snow-filled, blanketing Brecon's uplands. 'Then I had to stay in an aunt's house. I was a lodger. She wasn't a real aunt, more a maiden aunt.'

During the coldest months, Helena endured long evenings miles away from her family's little farm in the nook of the hill. 'I suppose I was a bit lonely then. You see, Vanu was meant to have joined me . . . But well . . . ' Vanu was dead, so Helena lodged alone. The house was unfriendly and the sheets unclean, Helena itched incessantly. 'There were fleas, my mother was horrified!' It was there in the inky black, lying flat, her sheet tucked under her chin, that Helena experienced sharp unpleasant pains in her abdomen. 'I couldn't think what it was. I thought, *Am I ill?*' Candle light revealed blood. Helena stops and shakes her head. 'I was very ignorant, you see, my mother didn't tell me anything. She never told me about menstruation and when it happened, I thought, *What on earth?* I didn't have anything to use.' Bleeding and in pain, Helena ransacked her panicked mind. What was happening to her?

> Then I remembered. I remembered when I used to make the beds at home, that was my job at the weekend and I had to empty the chamber pots. You had a slop bucket, each pot kept under the bed was emptied into this bucket and you had to go down to the garden to get rid of it. Anyway, under mother's bed I remembered seeing something white, a towel or something, and there was blood on it and at the time I thought, *What on earth? Has she hurt herself?*

The memory of this small detail reassured Helena in the middle of the night that perhaps her bleed was not life-threatening but rather a crimson marker on the way to womanhood, made all the more painful by the silence that surrounded it. 'Can you believe I was allowed to be that ignorant! My mother never said anything.' Helena, a country girl, brought up to the sound and sight of birthing ewes, calving cows and a constantly pregnant mother, was bewilderingly clueless about her own body. 'Well, had I stayed on at Libanus School I suppose it might have been different. In the county school, we moved from class to class, we didn't talk much ... ' She trails off, still coming to terms with the naïvety of her former self, how one so fit and able-bodied could have understood so little about her own physique.

The eldest child, Helena was dependent upon her mother for a better understanding of her body. That information was not forthcoming. 'No, even when she had a baby, the midwife would come and the door was firmly shut.' A marital photograph of Mr and Mrs Jones reveals a strong-featured, proud Welsh woman; modestly dressed in a homemade suit with a wide belt, long skirt and low brimmed hat, she is covered from head to toe. Ada was someone who bore pain silently; a product of her time and place, this Edwardian woman found it easier to say nothing about the female body than risk the embarrassment of indecent talk. Beneath her voluminous clothes, Ada's own female parts were a private mystery from which life miraculously sprang. 'She never said anything, nothing at all.' Like her mother before her, Helena would have to work it out for herself.

OLIVE

'My moder never told me anything!' Both born in 1915, on different sides of the world, Guyanese Olive was as ignorant as her Welsh contemporary.

> I was at church on my way to school and in de church yard I stubbed my toe on de roots of de trees and when I reach school I find de blood runnin' down on me and I went to my teacher and I told her, 'Miss, I stubbed my toe and it's burst my fallopian tube!'

Rather than explain what was happening to the distressed young girl in front of her, the teacher wrote a private note to Olive's mother and sent her pupil home, where she was bathed and given a pad of cotton. The next day in school, Olive shared her experience among friends; advice was forthcoming.

'I was told eat cassava bread and dis will never happen again.' Obediently indulging on quantities of bread, the following month Olive discovered she was bleeding once more. This time her mother explained, '"Every month you are going to get dis ting and every month you must show it to me!" But no, she never tell me nothing more. Dat's all, I must show it to her.' None the wiser, Olive did as she was told.

Entrenched Victorian etiquette, which dismissed bodily functions with embarrassed disdain, especially female ones, hobbled generations of young women, who didn't understand their own anatomy. Terrified of the faintest whiff of promiscuity, society opted for total ignorance. Period. Silence within the family home compounded the problem. Joyce recalls:

When I was about to go to St Paul's School, various bits of information arrived in the post and one talked about 'monthly periods'.
I said to my mother, 'What's a monthly period?' and she replied,
'I've told you all I want you to know at present,' which was nothing! I talked to friends and guessed roughly what would happen.

Ann was briefly grateful that she had an elder sister. 'Elizabeth and
I shared a bedroom and she was two years older than me, so I knew
what would happen. I have heard of women who had no idea and
thought they were dying. It was cruel and unnecessary to leave them
in such ignorance.' On the whole, the obstructive veil of silence on
feminine matters endured, extending well beyond the 1930s into
the latter half of the twentieth century. Polemicist Caitlin Moran,
who enjoys smashing the taboos of masturbation, abortion and
menstruation in today's Britain, admits that as late as the 1980s 'my
own mother never told us about them [periods]'. She only discovered
'what the whole menstruation deal was' when she 'came across a Lil-
Lets leaflet stuffed in the hedge outside our house'.[3] No such clue was
available in rural Wales or colonial Georgetown fifty years earlier.

   Firepower and aviation innovation in the First World War, computer wizardry and nuclear advancement in the Second, conflict has
long been credited with delivering seismic technological advance;
less well known is war's impact on the development of female sanitary products. It took bleeding men to legitimise women's use of
disposable bandages made from wood pulp. In 1921, an early Kotex
advertisement explained how it was soldiers who inspired American
nurses in France to use them as menstrual napkins.[4] But even in brash
America, a discreet money box on the counter in exchange for these
towels was necessary in order to save women's blushes. It wasn't
until the Second World War that significant numbers of consumers
moved from towels to tampons. *Vogue* chided its readers, urging
the use of Tampax instead of 'the old, clumsy, uncomfortable methods'.[5] Behind the glossy enticement once again was a masculine war
machine – like never before the nation needed women to work, and
it was hoped that more 'modern methods of sanitary care' would

stop them taking time off.[6] Even in this most private matter it was men who effected meaningful change and only when it suited their agenda.

EDNA

However, in the 1930s tampons were the future, and disposable sanitary towels a luxury most couldn't afford. Like so many other girls, Edna had no clue what was happening when she got her first period. 'It started when I was at the rectory, but at the time I was going daily, it was before I was living in. Mum had got everything ready cos in those days you didn't have what there is today.' Edna describes a piece of folded cotton held in place with elastic that was tied around her waist. 'These pads, they weren't to be thrown away, they were washed. You had to put them in to soak. You would then scrub them and boil them.' Considerable industry was involved in cleaning her own handmade sanitary towels and, when working as a live-in servant, it was an additional complication. 'You think about it, now all you've got to do is discard it but there was no way you could do that then. No. I had to make my own pads and I had to wash them discreetly.' Edna pauses, the effect is to emphasise her final point. 'People think they are hard done by today but believe you me, they have a very easy life.'

Adjusting to the practicalities of womanhood and coping with unexpected hormones, especially when working alone in someone else's house, was a challenge. Edna's stint with the rector and his wife only lasted eighteen months. 'I don't quite know why I left. They were an elderly couple, and I rather think I had been quite enough for them. They got rid of me, I expect they probably told my mother.' Edna laughs. Domestic service was sufficiently unpopular to ensure that demand outstripped supply – she had no difficulty in finding another job. 'When I was about seventeen I went to Normanton to work for the Wards.' Eleven miles from home, Edna had the invidious task of being the sole maid for a farming family with four teenage boys. Officially employed to do the housework, she soon

discovered her role was infuriatingly fluid. 'Mrs Ward would take
the cream to Lincoln market and I'd be left pulling the milk separator
to pieces and washing it all. I had enough to do in the house.' Edna
did what she was told. 'You just accepted it. I got on well enough
with the boys. They liked my cakey pudding.' Apparently, that wasn't
all they liked. Amidst four strapping lads, all at different stages of
adolescence, Edna's buxom presence in the kitchen ('Oh yes, I was
a healthy lass by then!') was deemed an unnecessary distraction. 'I
think the parents realised it was a risk cos, well, you never know.
And I was living in their house so, yes, I was got rid of.' Silent service,
cakey pudding, a gleaming milk separator, none of it was enough to
save Edna; she was sacked for becoming a woman.

Had there been any impropriety in the Ward household, it certainly didn't come from shy Edna. Like most girls of her generation,
she lived in absolute terror of becoming pregnant. 'I did know
what sex was but you didn't do things like that. Oh no. It was very
frowned upon if you had a child that was a bastard. They were
usually brought up by Grandma or an elder sister or taken away.'
During her childhood, Edna had been aware (as had the rest of the
village) who the fallen women were. They served as a warning to
the rest of Denton.

> Next door but one to us there was one. Her daughter was brought
> up by her sister, who was married and lived away. The baby didn't
> discover until she was grown up; she was told on her wedding day.
> It was kept a secret all that time! Yes, next door but one, she was
> an example of what not to be. It was drummed into you, you don't
> do that! You don't want to end up like Linda.

Social disgrace was not the only worry. Edna felt a deep loyalty
towards her worn-out, widowed mother. As the eldest child, she
understood the pressures that existed to simply make ends meet. 'If
I had got pregnant it would've made more work and more worry for
my mother. She'd enough as it was, she would've been even more
downtrodden. I couldn't have done that to my mum.' Fear and

responsibility were the twin pillars that guided Edna's response when meeting young men, of which there weren't many. 'Well, I knew all the boys growing up in the village, and they weren't particularly interesting. And I didn't really have any time to meet others. I worked every day and only had two half-days off.' In that rare free time, Edna was focused on returning to Denton and helping at home; boys were low on the list of priorities.

Nonetheless, there was a boyfriend of sorts for a couple of years. 'He was the butcher's lad, called Walter. He used to deliver to the bakers that I was working for. We cycled on a tandem sometimes and went for walks up Hall's Hill.' Two shy sweethearts hand in hand, tentatively talking, admiring the bluebells and the buttercups. 'No one ever told me I was pretty, I was very ordinary-looking in fact, but I think I had a kind face if you know what I mean.' Occasionally, Walter and Edna would risk a cuddle and a kiss: 'Oh yes, I definitely kissed him. And I met his parents; they lived down the Horse and Jockey yard, and they were poor, exactly the same as mine.'

And then, as inconclusively as it began, the relationship fizzled out. Walter wandered off. 'I still saw him cycle by on a Monday but no, I didn't see him any more. I suppose I did feel sad for a bit but there we are.' Edna isn't entirely sure why the relationship ended, but marriage had never been an option. 'It didn't get that far and, even if it had, we'd've had nowhere to live.' Perhaps Walter wanted more physically? 'Perhaps,' she concedes. 'But as I said, you didn't do things in those days that you do today, dear.'

HELENA

'You can ask anything you like, there are no secrets in my life.' Today Helena is making up for lost time. She can't believe how little she once knew. It turns out her painful discovery of the menstrual cycle at county school did not open the floodgates to biological learning. 'My father always threatened us when we went away on a Sunday School trip: "Now, if you get into trouble don't come back 'ere! There'll be no help for you 'ere!" That is what we were always warned. "You keep OUT of trouble!"' The consummate wide-eyed confessor, she drops her voice to a virtual whisper. 'Do you know, for a long time I didn't know what he meant, what *trouble* he was talking about. For years I didn't know what was what! I wondered what it was I was supposed to be doing that was so wrong?'

She laughs. 'I know, extraordinary now to think. I suppose I could have got into trouble, not willingly but . . . I think my mother should have . . . ' She trails off, aware there is no point in regret, it's in the distant past now, a place where for teenage Helena there was no sexual activity, not even in her imagination. 'Well, I suppose if you asked me about where babies came from, because I lived on a farm, I suppose I'd say from the tummy but how they got there and why? No idea!' Helena giggles.

> It was my younger sister Connie who told me what actually happened, when I was about nineteen. I was really shocked, you know. My sisters knew more than me because they stayed on at the local school and in the summer the boys and girls went swimming together in the local river and got up to all sorts of high jinks.

Armed belatedly with a few facts, Helena could at last make sense of the men who expressed an interest or tried walking a little too close.

> I'd brushed them off anyway, it was intuition I suppose. They soon realised there wasn't any hanky-panky, if you know what I mean. It wasn't that I was good or holy, it was because my father always threatened us – 'Now, if you get into trouble, don't come back 'ere!'

A bright girl with an eager face, from an early age Helena gave the impression of a woman on a mission; that had a special appeal in slow-paced Brecon. 'I can tell you this, I went with a few boys.' (To clarify, that means Helena walked home with a few boys, perhaps they occasionally held hands.) The local hills were full of young lads on the lookout; the walk home was long and the Jones sisters attracted their share of suitors. 'Me and my two sisters would be together and the boys would sort of come with us; perhaps there would be four or five of them so three quarters of the way we always had company.' Out spills a story of the Moses brothers, whose mother owned the local post office in Trallong. Basil had a crush on Helena's sister Glenys, and as one brother walked Glenys home against the weather and the hill's incline, the other brother, David, thought it more than his duty to escort Helena – he desired her (although Helena doesn't put it like that). Basil's courting was successful – he'd married Glenys by the time she was eighteen – but Helena was not won so easily, her nonchalance no doubt adding to her allure. 'Well, you know, I think he did find me attractive, I think he liked our chats and to hear about the books I'd read. I suppose he was my boyfriend but I never fancied him as a boyfriend. Heavens no!'

Unlike her sisters, for whom early marriage provided an escape route from domestic service, Helena's eye was fixed on a teaching career and she knew girls couldn't have everything, at least not all at the same time. Boys would have to wait.

CHAPTER SIX

WINBERRIES AND LIPSTICK

ANN

Ann was just sixteen at the beginning of the 'devil's decade'. Economic depression, fascism, appeasement, war – the 1930s began in the immediate aftermath of an almighty financial crash and ended with the outbreak of another global conflict. The myth of 1919, that 'sacred year' (so-called by Virginia Woolf) famous for opening the professions to women, has burnished the interwar period with a progressive female sheen it doesn't deserve. The Wall Street Crash of 1929 and subsequent economic downturn were inimical to women's aspirations; jobs for men were always the priority, few worried about a glut of unemployed middle-class girls. Although the country's industrial heartlands were worst hit, a lack of financial liquidity affected everyone, Ann and her family included. 'There was a great slump and my father was extremely anxious about the survival of Sidgwick & Jackson, his publishing firm on which we all survived.' Six children and Missy, her mother and father, a maid, sometimes a gardener – these were unexpected, reduced times in the large, loquacious Kent household.

Ann's elder sister Elizabeth was by now an undergraduate at Cambridge. 'I knew that when Elizabeth went up to Newnham she was fitted out with a tailored suit and at least two long evening dresses. I wasn't, there was so little money. I didn't enquire but it worried me.' Ann visited her sister at Cambridge; she was impressed by Elizabeth's friends and enjoyed the May ball and her first outing in a gown that fell all the way to the floor, but university and its trappings were never destined to be part of Ann's world. 'I don't think my parents minded, they decided I had had enough of education and took me away from school at about seventeen. But it felt uncertain, I didn't know what to do.' Ann was packed off to France, Rouen more specifically, to brush up on her French. She spent a pleasing few months with a middle-class family who had a daughter her age and then returned to England, still none the wiser as to what path to pursue.

This was bothersome, since Ann has always been a doer – our simple lunch is offset with a beautiful coral-coloured japonica jelly. Ann 'steals' the japonica from local bushes (she won't say which) and pushes their pulp through an old net curtain. Perhaps at 103 Ann can (almost) be contained with effortful jelly-making but such domestic pursuits were not sufficient for a seventeen-year-old, keen to savour experience. However, her options were limited. Cambridge established what eventually became a Women's Employment Board to help their students into a variety of work, but Ann wasn't at Cambridge. Her background and interests precluded elementary teaching and nursing, and while 'girls of twenty did sometimes do shorthand and typing', Ann didn't. If this saved her from the boredom of secretarial work, it also ruled out the last option in the standard triumvirate of middle-class employment for women.

She was still young and by her own estimation far too young to contemplate settling down with a man. 'There weren't any men around and anyway you weren't immediately expected to get married, and certainly not in my family.' A period as an independent 'Bachelor Girl' was *de rigueur* in London society, (although this was only ever regarded as a temporary state before young women got down to the essential business of marriage and children). With idle hours to fill, in the attic of their Keston family home, Ann whiled away the time experimenting with colour and design. If in childhood she had mastered the art of printing with cork stoppers and a handy penknife, now she 'drew up different coloured paper, created patterns, that sort of thing.' Her designs were good enough to impress Marion Richardson, the esteemed Hayes Court art teacher and a colleague of artist Roger Fry, (here Ann gives one of her nods to the Bloomsbury movement). Marion recommended that the eager teenager pursue her talent at Chelsea School of Art. Ann smiles. Her young self had just found a first footing in the precarious London art world. The alternative Sidgwick daughter had created her own silver lining at the beginning of Auden's low dishonest decade.

HELENA

Unlike Ann, Helena always had a clear idea of what she was going to do. Head down at Brecon County School, it was simply a matter of time before she acquired her school certificate and headed to the teacher training college in Barry, Glamorgan. The college was single sex, ruled over by an indomitable martinet and nicknamed the nunnery. There was a brown and cream uniform, complete with blazer and ankle socks, no make-up was permitted and the curfew set early at 8pm. Helena was oblivious to the restrictions. She has fond memories of the girls' dormitories and came away with a life-long friend in fellow trainee teacher Myrtle. More importantly, she graduated within two years, having already completed a year as a student teacher at the local Trallong Elementary School. She had deliberately focused on minimising the time she spent away from home for good reason; ever since the death of her sister Vanu, Helena had been the mainstay for the entire Jones family. 'Losing Vanu destroyed my mother. My father thought having another baby would help, so aged forty-two she had my brother, Eirvil, who was sixteen years younger than me.' Doubtfully Helena adds, 'I think Father said it would make up for the daughter she'd lost – years later he said something like that. And we moved after Vanu died; Father bought a farm miles from the village, called Pengarn.'

Helena worried. 'I was complaining about it being so remote – three miles to go for a doctor. I asked, "What if this baby was ill?" "Well," Father said, "I thought it would help your mother." I suppose it did in a way, I don't know.' Her concerns about access to a doctor weren't without substance; baby Eirvil wasn't ill, but his mother was. Incremental blindness was slowly gnawing at Ada's ability to run the homestead. Bathe the baby, bottle the fruit, churn the butter, grow the vegetables, mangle the clothes, bake the bread – the list was never-ending and Ada, a woman in her mid-forties with a sight disorder, who had borne eight children and endured at least one miscarriage, was physically depleted. Whenever possible, dutiful Helena picked up the slack. The three-year teacher training course was potted in two and soon the eldest Jones daughter was back, helping at distant Pengarn.

'Why not! I've never learnt to say no!' Over eighty years later and just two weeks shy of her one hundredth birthday, Helena agrees to a mini road trip to visit the old homestead.' She's not sure she remembers exactly where it is, but emboldened by memories, soon we are out of Brecon and zipping across a plateau that serves up a majestic view of the beacons. 'That mountain is Pen y Fan and the flat black one is Corn Du. Yes, that's right, bracken grows up here and the farmers used to cut it for the cattle to sleep on in winter.'

The colours, the sounds, the handsome landscape trigger emotions and thoughts flood back. But hedgerows have grown, additional lanes have been added – 'My God, I don't know where we are now.' Changes are distracting. Pengarn is remote but perhaps we've gone a little too far? We ask at the next farm. A large man pushes a red, working arm through the window. 'Hello, Phil Davies!' He's delighted to see Helena Jones: 'All Sennybridge people think a heck of a lot of Helena Jones. And I gather you have a significant birthday this month, Mrs Jones?' Helena is bemused but flattered. A whole farming family tip out to have a look. 'Ooh, it's Mrs Jones.' She nods and tries to resist his offer to lead us to Pengarn. Regardless, Phil shows the way in a silver Mercedes (farming these parts has much changed).

We are tracking back the way we came. Flanked by tangles of blackthorn and hawthorn, velvet foxgloves, and pungent honey-suckle, Helena relaxes into the afternoon.

> Aren't people kind. They did seem to know me, didn't they? I mean, I didn't know them but they seemed to know me.
> There's Cwm Camlais Chapel! We used to walk there, through the fields about three miles. That's where I performed my first eisteddfod. I taught Sunday school there. It's a tidy chapel, isn't it?
> That poor man, driving all this way.

With a broad smile and a honk of his horn, Phil leaves us to manage the final ascent. Pengarn was built high up, into the side of a valley where Suffolk sheep now graze. Exposed to the elements, winters were relentless, with sharp winds and buffeting snow; in contrast, our August day is balmy and full of surprise. A swimming pool and an ersatz house confound their ancient visitor; her father's dairy and outhouses are now home to a burly transportation entrepreneur and his young family. It is beyond the barn conversion that Pengarn, with its sombre stone exterior, is finally found. A fat sleeping tabby cat is the silent sentinel, and the black framed porch sits behind, where once the postman left Helena's (many) letters.

A young girl with whitewashed hair pokes her head out of the porch. It's Eden, daughter of Clive Jackson, lead singer of the one-time glam rock band Doctor and the Medics. Living here for the Jacksons is a lifestyle choice, it bears no comparison with Helena's day. Helena and Eden chat together about the house, but Helena doesn't want to go in – she might not find the bed on the landing, perhaps the parlour has had a makeover. 'That little shed there was the cart house, where we kept the farm cart. Well, I'm glad we made it. That's good, isn't it?'

Helena settles back in the car with an abiding sense of

achievement. Back on the old Warren Road, steadfast in the certainty that Brecon lies ahead, she considers the two competing pressures that defined her young adult life: starting out as a teacher and familial duty at Pengarn. Her mother and father needed her. But Pengarn was isolated and teaching options in the surrounding area limited; fresh out of college, Helena had to confront the uncomfortable reality that there was a glut of teachers in Wales. 'They were two a penny in those days.' Thousands of like-minded parents had identified the profession as a way out of working-class poverty for their children (especially girls). As early as 1928, the vast majority of newly trained Welsh teachers had left to work in England, and with the desire for teaching posts in Wales so strong, people were prepared to pay for them. Not Helena. She shakes her head. She didn't contemplate leaving her beloved family and country full time, nor would it ever have occurred to her to bribe. But by the early 1930s the pall of economic depression was widespread, agricultural prices were in the doldrums and Pengarn's overheads high. A distant economic crisis had become personal. Helena sighs, a wage was imperative.

I moved to Harrow to be a companion to a lady there. I saw the job advertised and I thought I would take it until a teaching job came up at home. Yes, that's right, Harrow, on the outskirts of London in England. I suppose I would've been about twenty, as it was the mid-'30s. No, I didn't like it at all, but it was only for a few months.

Helena had landed a stop-gap job in Harrow on the Hill. Just shy of London, and home to one of the oldest public schools in the country, this Middlesex suburb was cold comfort for a homesick young Welsh girl. 'It was the only time I have not lived in Wales and I didn't like it.' Helena refuses to remember the name of her employer and landlady. 'She was a writer, I think, and a widow. I think she wanted company, that was it. I was her companion.' Helena recalls doing the odd spot of shopping and perhaps a little light dusting in between chats and letter-writing duties for her hostess. 'The lady of the house shall we say, she used to take me out. It was such a shock to see all those buildings.' London's 'octopus' had begun to stretch its tentacles and lay claim to many of Middlesex's rich pastures and leafy lanes.* Helena was used to rolling greens, not relentless grey. Despite an abundance of Georgian architecture amidst the urban creep, Harrow was not to her liking. Regrettably the companionship between employer and assistant did not extend to sightseeing in neighbouring London, and Helena was too unsure to go it alone, so instead she stuck it out in the English suburbs. 'I was *very* lonely. I didn't have any friends there.'

Emotional longing went both ways; Pengarn wasn't the same without knowing, hardworking Helena. Despite poor sight, her mother walked the hills for winberries to send to her daughter. A parcel arrived wrapped in brown paper and Helena made the fat blue fruits into a tart for her landlady. 'Oh she loved it, she had never enjoyed anything so much in her life.' The affection was there, certainly on the part of her isolated elderly employer ('she was very upset when I did leave'), but for Helena, one English woman was slim pickings. 'It felt different living in Harrow, there wasn't the same warmth and comradeship. I missed the company and the affection that you get from your friends and the interest you get too. We care in Wales, don't we?' Was it Wales generally, or Helena's Wales? She's unsure. The depression post-1929 had hit the country's already struggling industrial heartlands hard. With the market in primary products depressed, rural areas fared little better. Between the wars, there was a mass exodus of nearly 400,000 predominately young workers. The majority emigrated to south-east England and many never returned to their Welsh homeland.[1] Unlike Helena, they didn't find a job to go back to.

---

* This was the description of London's growth given by Lord Curzon in 1913 when he opened a National Trust property. It was subsequently used as a book title, *England and the Octopus*, in 1928 by architect Clough Williams-Ellis, which decried the urbanisation of the English countryside.

ANN

Infamously associated with 1980s Sloane Rangers, during the inter-war period Chelsea had an exciting artistic reputation. In Victorian London, painters Dante Gabriel Rossetti, J. M. W. Turner and John Singer Sargent had all called it home; this was a well-established bohemian quarter with writers and poets adding to the vibrant atmosphere. Founded in 1895 as a faculty of the polytechnic, the Chelsea School of Art capitalised on the area's pedigree; by the 1930s, it was a prestigious college focused on illustration, textiles, etchings, craft, sculpture and architecture.[2] Ann had found the perfect home, but someone had to pay for it. 'I was dependent on a stipend. Father paid my fees for college and my mother gave me 10 shillings a week for the train fare. That was about fifty pence in today's money.' Three days a week, this contemplative teenage girl, certain in her artistic endeavour but neither gregarious nor showy, commuted from Kent into the artistic quarter of 1930s London.

Ann makes a second reference to her straitened circumstances. 'I had a simple lunch. I didn't socialise much. It was restrictive, I lived modestly.' However, she also concedes that poverty is relative. She and her friends had a knack of eking out their weekly allow-ance – there is more than a dash of urbane sophistication to her tales of student living. Ann, desultory and pale-skinned in the two photographs she produces, was familiar with the Café Royal on Regent Street – then the epicentre of fashionable London ('we only ever had a coffee') – and Lyons Tea Shop in Piccadilly. There were trips to the Dominion Cinema on Tottenham Court Road amidst pink lampshades and the standard crush that accompanied any new release. She considered live theatre more of an event.

> I remember the Old Vic. You sat right at the top in wooden seats; it was very uncomfortable and I think it cost about four pence. And there below you on the stage was *Romeo and Juliet*, with Laurence Olivier and John Gielgud alternating between Romeo and Mercutio, night after night.

A conversation with Ann which doesn't involve a name from twentieth-century history that's worth dropping (or *Googling* – although Ann refuses to recognise the term) is extremely rare.

> Oh yes, didn't I mention it, I knew Henry Moore from the age of eighteen? He was at Chelsea, yes, he taught sculpture. So was Graham Sutherland. I was never taught by either of these artists but their influence was felt throughout the school.

Slap-bang in the heart of edgy, uncertain 1930s London, Ann was inescapably part of an artistic literary world where the connection to and the support of others was a means of survival. Chelsea School of Art's reach crossed London society. For pin money, Ann and her good friend Elizabeth were recommended by their well-known teacher, the painter Robert Medley, to the famous literary figure John Hayward. In Hayward's home off Old Brompton Road, the girls discussed the latest Auden/Isherwood plays and René Clair films while painting his bookshelves to resemble carved marble ('a convincing *trompe l'œil*'). The servant quickly learnt that Ann and Elizabeth were not to be served *Indian* tea in the kitchen but rather *China* tea in the drawing room with their host.[3] They were young ladies after all. John Hayward was charmed.

'I had flair, yes, I put things together well.' Ann is modest but honest, so yes, she will admit to being stylish (despite the absence of a clothing allowance). If anything, her student penury encouraged creativity.

> I can remember myself in a long sea-blue-green silk and velvet dress, very ruched down the front and tight fitting. It had pale pink chiffon shoulder straps and I made it in order to sell catalogues at the exhibition in Burlington Street where Picasso's *Guernica* was first shown. The painting showed the bombing of Bilbao during the Spanish Civil War.

Well over a hundred years old, Ann is a splendid remnant of a pre-war culture that was saturated in depressed literature, angst-ridden paintings, old-fashioned etiquette and vintage style. The 1930s flirted with fascism and communism, and art reflected the disturbing new reality that was pressing its way across the Continent. Fashion, meanwhile, shrugged off this uncertainty with elegant, figure-hugging glamour; floor-length gowns in pastels and jewel colours on silks and satins were bang on trend. So was Ann. 'Oh yes, the aim was to look good, I wore make-up – foundation, face powder, my eyelashes were black, my eyelids were blue. Everything . . . ' When, a few years earlier, her younger brother Jeremy had watched his sister applying lipstick, he'd accurately predicted that Father wouldn't approve. Her retort was uncompromising: 'Well, he'll have to put up with it.' Ann went further and let it be known that she had walked with painted lips up Burlington Arcade, by then a shopping centre, 'but in the past it had been a rendezvous for prostitutes and to wear lipstick was more or less an indication that you were on the market, at least so he thought'. Ann knew she was goading her beloved father, but fashions changed at breakneck speed, and he really ought to keep up. By the 1930s, lipstick was everyday wear for almost every girl. Acknowledgement of this change came during the Second World War, when the Board of Trade considered make-up to be a necessity rather than a dispensable luxury.[4] Ann sighs thoughtfully, 'I did take a lot of trouble.'

For as long as she can remember, art and the visual world have been driving forces in her life; wardrobe and style were (and still are) a vital extension of that aesthetic instinct. The question, 'Who did you take a lot of trouble for?' meets a nonplussed response – 'For myself, of course.' Trying to understand if there were any men who occupied the thoughts of this unusual bohemian twenty-something is hard to ascertain. She insists, 'There were very few men,' but does admit to a brief crush on her course leader at the art school.

I was his star pupil in the department of design. I hope he didn't know I had a crush. He had been a student at Chelsea and was three or four years older than me. I used to look forward to seeing him, that sort of thing.

But the pipe dream was quickly snuffed out when she discovered he was married. 'It was quite a shock when I discovered, yes. I was temporarily upset but hardly surprised.' Ann is brusque, this was a long time ago. Of course, liberal views abounded in the art world's unconventional circles and Ann's young coterie believed they knew better than their elders. 'I do remember my friend Elizabeth and I discussing the social problems of the day with John Hayward.' He mentioned the many letters agony aunts in the press received from 'barely literate' girls – 'Should they sleep with their boyfriends or not?' Sexual behaviour was changing, but public opinion would take decades to catch up. 'One must remember that then it was almost impossible for unmarried women to get contraceptive advice.'[5] But she admits

> there was a female doctor whose name we had. It was common knowledge among some. I mean, there was contraception but it was very difficult contraception. I know some of the people who applied and got a French letter, that's what they were called then.

Ann didn't apply, she didn't have a boyfriend and, as she pertinently points out, having liberal views was one thing, behaving in a sexually liberal manner was quite another.

> I had no opportunity or inclination to behave in that way, but one felt one didn't condemn women whom you knew were living with their boyfriends.
> Yes, I think my parents would have condemned them. There was a gulf between much of our thinking. They were advanced liberals, believing in trade unions and Lloyd George's health insurance and such things, but they were from a different generation.

In the 1930s, the Edwardians – those who had lived and fought through the First World War – desperately clung to old norms, retailoring their tweed two-piece suits accordingly. The vast majority shrugged off the mass unemployment that stained the decade, continued to take their moral lead from the Anglican Church, enjoyed Stanley Baldwin's reassuring broadcasts and above all else turned a deaf ear to the ugly noises coming from the Continent. They insisted there could never be another war. Not for the last time in Britain's history, the old were out of step with their young.

CHAPTER SEVEN

BUT TODAY THE STRUGGLE

JOYCE, ANN

'I can remember my mother voting in 1929 – she went to the voting booth in tears, which I didn't understand at all of course, because I thought she had a vote just like my father.' Joyce, born in the year when the first women were enfranchised, was ten when the 'Flappers' Vote' passed into law in 1928. Finally, women had secured the franchise on the same terms as men. Participating in her first election a year later, Joyce's mother, Nellie, was understandably moved. After all, the Enfranchisement Act of 1918 had met with 'ravenous expectation' and yet deliberately failed to give women under thirty (who'd carried the war effort at home) the vote. The political Establishment feared that the 2 million 'surplus women' in the wake of the First World War would outvote men. Nellie's generation (nearly 5 million of them) had to wait another ten years. When it came, the 1929 general election was memorable not for the second Labour government it produced, but because this was the first time in Nellie's life she had equivalent political clout to her husband. That meant a great deal. But evidently it didn't mean as much to her young daughter, who couldn't under-stand her mother's emotion at all. The gulf between Nellie, who had lived through the violent, frantic final years of suffragette protest, and her daughter, Joyce, born in 1918 when the first British women had just crossed the political line, is a subtle example of intergenerational difference found more broadly in society. Many feminists felt let down by 'modern young women' who knew 'amazingly little of what life was like before the war' and showed 'a strong hostility to the word "feminism" and all which they imagined it to connote'.[1]

Old-school suffragettes were frustrated by the complacency they had gifted the younger generation (at least at the ballot box). Joyce reiterates her ambivalence towards the word feminism.

> It is a formula I would never have thought of using. I don't think it was in common parlance. I was concerned women should be educated. I suppose I was a feminist, but I wouldn't have thought of calling myself such a thing.

Receiving minimal reverence and recognition from young women, the old brigade huffed and puffed, with one former suffragette guffawing, 'Girls today? I cannot see much of the old spirit about now but of course there is nothing to fight for.'[2] This myopic comment says more about the entrenched attitudes of the pre-war suffragettes than it does about girls between the wars. Born in 1914, Ann was the only woman in this book old enough to take part in the 1935 general election* (after which there wasn't one for ten years). She admits she took her vote for granted, 'absolutely, yes', but she did not waste it. However in 1935, turnout was proportionally its lowest since 1923; for many young people, the national government fudged together in the wake of the global depression of 1929 had no answers to the two great crises of the decade – long-term unemployment at home and rising fascism on the Continent. Compared with these bogeymen, feminist causes were diffuse and many, and young girls could be forgiven for not caring hugely about widows' pensions or family allowance proposals. The old suffragettes were wrong; girls hadn't given up fighting, they were just fighting for different things. In 1935, only one victory really excited Ann's friends and that was

---

* From 1928, the universal voting age was twenty-one; it wasn't reduced to eighteen until 1970.

the election of William ('Willie') Gallacher; the Scot was the first communist to sit in the House of Commons. 'Yes, it was trendy, I suppose you would say, to be a communist.'

Elizabeth, Ann's eldest sister, was the Sidgwick's first communist. She left Cambridge in the early 1930s with a first-class Classics degree, a broken heart ('she had a boyfriend but he ended it and she became terribly withdrawn') and a keen interest in far left politics. By this time, Cambridge University was a hotbed of left-wing thinking, with students spearheading a nationwide, poet-led movement (Auden, Spender, Day-Lewis). The systemic problems of the 1920s – uneconomic industrial heartlands, falling international demand, rising poverty – had not gone away and conditions were ripe for extreme ideological thinking. In January 1933 unemployment reached its peak at just under 3 million; mass destitution saw people take to the streets. The indignity of the means test and a cut in unemployment benefit brought debilitating poverty out of the more remote regions of Britain (Lancashire, Tyneside, Wales, Scotland) and into the full shameful blare of cosmopolitan London's public and press. Joyce was a London schoolgirl (and a privileged one at that), but she confidently insists that while her upbringing was sheltered, she was 'not all that sheltered. There were things in the newspapers; then there was the Great March down from Jarrow when the poor marched from the north, and the strikes, yes that's right there was a constant bubbling.' A year after the Jarrow March, in 1937, Joyce entered Oxford's girls' college Somerville to study her lifelong passion – the Classics (or 'Greats' as they were known at Oxford). There she was struck by the radical element in student life.

> I have sometimes said, 'Everybody in my year joined the Labour Club,' but that's not quite true. I can remember two members of my year who joined the Conservatives – they stood out. I joined the Labour Club.

Six years older than Joyce and considerably more flamboyant, Ann's sister Elizabeth went several steps further. Having caught the communist bug at Cambridge, she attended a local Communist Party meeting back at home in Bromley in the mid-1930s. There, she not only acquired Communist Party membership but also a working-class, Communist Party boyfriend, whom she married, much to the chagrin of her parents. 'Yes, Mother and Father were very upset at the time.' Little sister Ann was considerably more sympathetic.

> When we arrived at ... young adulthood and looked around at the world, we saw terrible, worldwide unemployment, which in those days meant near starvation. We saw the rise of fascism in Italy and Germany, the invasion of China by Japan ... We knew that our parents, obliviously or deliberately ignoring the growing menaces abroad, had deceived us (and themselves) when they said war *could not* come again. Patriotism, which they had valued, was to us an attitude to be mocked. It was only through international co-operation could we be saved from war.[3]

Ann is also nonchalant about 'the set' her sister mixed with at Cambridge.

> Guy Burgess, Donald Maclean – Elizabeth knew the Cambridge Spies. I remember finding a letter not long ago from her when she was there, saying she couldn't return a book I had lent her because she had lent it to somebody called Donald Maclean.

Post-war, these men were infamously known for their respective roles in the Cambridge Spy Ring, a clandestine group who passed information to the Soviet Union during the Second World War. But Ann's long view of their lives and the 'devil's decade' which informed their actions stops her passing judgement. She remembers the appeal of Russia in the 1930s, when that giant country was held up as a means of both escaping the evils of capitalist anarchy and resisting fascism. The advent of the Spanish Civil War gave additional romantic impetus to the communist cause célèbre. Fascist Italy and Germany funded Franco, and the Soviets responded by supporting the republic – suddenly a Spanish scuffle was a question of international significance. British politicians opted for inaction, leaving a vacuum for left-wing idealists to fill. Poets left for the front line and students dreamt of sabre scars on their cheeks – to have supported fascist Franco would have been unthinkable.[4] Young idealists and communists surrounded Ann. 'We all knew the poet John Cornford. He was at Cambridge, but he was killed in Spain.' Standing up for a utopian future was a serious, potentially fatal business.

Younger than Elizabeth and at Oxford not Cambridge, Joyce did not know any of the Cambridge Spies when they were students, but years later, after the war, on a research placement at the British School in Rome, she met an impressive art historian – Anthony Blunt. They mixed in common circles; a black and white photograph catches the pair enjoying the Italian sunshine in a trattoria; Blunt is handsome in side profile, looking relaxed with clothes to match, Joyce sits across the table in sun specs, wearing a broad smile. 'He was a fairly tall, considerate man and a very good academic.' Joyce didn't know him well but recalls a shared car journey to a gathering in the Italian countryside. 'We talked about pictures and sculptures and gossiped about people we knew and the weather. His Russian liaison was a wartime thing. I knew him after he ceased to be ... ' She doesn't use the word. Joyce is a discreet woman who liked the man she remembers. Much later she would discover their meetings in 1950s Rome coincided with the initial unravelling of his identity as a wartime spy. 'He had a long and no doubt distressing interrogation. And then they let him go and he came back out to Rome but he was ... ' Again, she doesn't finish the sentence. Vulnerable? Perhaps. With the defection of Burgess and Maclean to Moscow in 1951, Blunt came under suspicion; he was interrogated by MI5 a year later. It would be another decade before the Security Service understood the extent of his espionage (several years older than Maclean, Philby and Burgess, Blunt had acted as a recruiter for most of the group). And it was almost twenty years before Margaret Thatcher blew his immunity with a declaration of his wartime role to the Commons in 1979, after which he was hounded by the press. Joyce was astounded by the revelations. 'Oh yes, yes! I didn't ... I couldn't believe it when it was first ... No, I didn't believe it.'

In the 1970s, Ann also came across Anthony Blunt in his capacity as Director of the Courtauld Institute of Art. Unlike Joyce, who had no association with communism in the 1930s, Ann is more dispassionate about Blunt's late unmasking. 'Apparently he was an intensely conceited man. No, I wasn't surprised when I heard what he'd done. One knew that these people ... ' She doesn't finish her sentence either, preferring to provide more context.

It had become a great dividing line during the war, but before the war, people would become a member of the Communist Party – how else could one hope to influence our head-in-the-sand rulers? Then, when the Hitler–Stalin pact came about in '39, people thought, 'This is ghastly', and got out of being a communist and so on, but some didn't.

Ann, who only ever dabbled at the red edges, including reading material from the popular Left Book Club in the 1930s ('I was never a card-carrying communist'), deftly captures the idealism of her generation and the cruel realities of international politicking that ran it asunder. There is a lingering sense that those Cambridge Spies, they got in too deep, that's all. Ann can understand that. 'For us *anyone* who would fight fascism was our friend.'

For Ann, the painful political confusion of the 1930s – appeasement and a hatred of war versus rising fascism and rapid rearmament – was exacerbated through her personal relationships. Elizabeth Edwards, Ann's best friend at Chelsea School of Art, introduced her to a growing community in north London. 'Elizabeth lived in Hampstead with her parents and she was all mixed up with the Jews there. She was a quarter Jewish herself and she'd say, "I am the go-between between the German Jewish Hampstead girls and the

English ones."' There had long been German Jews in north London, but anti-Semitic violence and discrimination under the new Nazi regime saw their numbers rise dramatically. Many who found sanctuary in England left educated, moneyed lives behind. It was within this exciting cosmopolitan milieu that Ann mixed. In the late 1930s, she even sat for the famous German-Jewish artist Ludwig Meidner in a tiny attic flat in Golders Green. Ann loathed the resulting portrait ('I later tore it up. I looked sixty') but has never forgotten the exotic arguments that flew over her head in German (once accompanied by a flying orange enamel teapot), the bar mitzvah in a room with strange cakes and the artist's penchant for quoting bits of the Ossian poetry.[5] Historian A. J. P. Taylor later concluded: 'Every refugee was walking propaganda against the Nazis, even if he never opened his mouth.'[6] And Ann was socialising with the very best of them. Early on, that placed her among British exceptions who knew and cared about the Nazi's treatment of the Jews. Elsewhere, large sections of society still harboured a latent whiff of anti-Semitism. Golf clubs occasionally barred Jews, and famous British public schools weren't always as inclusive as they could have been.

At the vanguard of contemporary political protest, surrounded by ideological students and cerebral German refugees, Ann was out of step with much of the country. All these years later, she still finds the memory of their collective impotence frustrating.

> As the 1930s proceeded, the inevitability of another world war increased. We, those of my generation, mostly too young to have voted in any general election, were in the hands of older politicians – those who could not face another war.

War costs lives and money, and more importantly from a British point of view it gummed up financial markets and imperilled trade – the very lifeblood of the nation's international economy. Hopes were pinned on a rosy future; in September 1931, Lord Robert Cecil, speaking at the League of Nations assembly, declared, 'There has scarcely been a period in the world's history when war seems less likely than it does at present.'[7] A week later, the Japanese entered Chinese Manchuria and by early 1932 the region had been brutally conquered. A year later, much closer to home, the leader of the right-wing National Socialist German Workers' Party, Adolf Hitler, was appointed Chancellor. Italy already had a fascist dictator, Benito Mussolini. British politicians talked up democracy but friendly gestures towards their new fascist friends were plentiful. MacDonald wrote chatty letters to Mussolini, Austen Chamberlain exchanged photographs with him and Churchill wrote effusively of both Mussolini and Hitler in newspaper articles.[8] In 1934, preparations for rearmament were still mainly on paper. Prime Minister Stanley Baldwin, later branded one of the 'guilty men' for failing to prioritise war over prosperity, rightly pointed out that both the ruled and their rulers wanted the same thing. Beyond the unemployed mass, in the 1930s the majority of Britons were enjoying a higher standard of living than ever before – cars, holidays, electricity, even the odd vacuum cleaner. Peace was in everybody's interest – wasn't it?

Ann shakes her head and tells the story of how her irate father sat in his Kent home, near Biggin Hill Aerodrome in 1938, and listened to the fighter planes practising overhead. 'Even then he'd complain about the cost of the petrol and the noise. And then a year later . . . '; she raises her eyes skywards. It's easy to be wise after the event; evidently Ann was wise long before it. Others, meanwhile, were simply getting on with their lives.

OLIVE

'Where you been, eh? Let me tell you, my Ray since he gone, I've no one 'ere to chat to.' Olive sits in the reclining chair in her north London home, holding a small hot water bottle against her stomach with an arm covered in thin, rose-gold bangles. Olive likes to talk, she likes an audience and she likes to be in full control of the discussion. Best of all, she likes to reminisce about her late husband, Ray. When she gets excited, she gesticulates and the gold bangles tinkle and rustle. Ray died eight years ago and talking about him,

indulging in rich, crazy, deliciously inappropriate anecdotes, keeps
him alive. He bought her a lot of jewellery. 'I was his illustrious
wife!' But Olive didn't meet Ray, her second husband, until she came
to Britain in the 1950s. She avoids memories that might complicate
her narrative of their time together. But Olive is also a natural
storyteller and understands that the little girl born and educated in
sunny imperial British Guiana needs a back story. It turns out she
has a rich one.

The 1930s were a particularly busy time; young Olive left school,
acquired a trade and had three children. She also got married.

> I wasn't in love. At my school, boys were der and used to talk
> about when dey get big and studyin' dey're going to marry me
> and all dis kinda thing. Yeah, I was pretty. But den my husband
> comes and his position and everyting. My moder put me, my
> moder put me ...

Olive's mother organised her daughter's marriage when she was eighteen. It was the mid-1930s; not only was Rosalind a single parent, she
was also technically a widow. Mr Higgins, always entrepreneurial,
had invested poorly at a time when Guyana's economy was in dire
straits. The indignity of failure led him to take his own life. Olive is
matter-of-fact: 'So dat was dat.' When he pops up in conversation,
her father is a pleasing memory, but only a fleeting one – 'sometimes
we went in car to de school, my father drivin'.' There were flash
gestures and the odd appearance with his new family and then he
was gone. Rosalind and her two girls had to fend for themselves. The
obvious answer was for her daughters to marry well. One fellow in
particular had all the right credentials; Sigismund was a handsome,
older man. 'Yes, he was black', and crucially he had a reliable, public
sector job. 'A sanitary inspector. It was a good job, he used to go after
dey kill de cows, he used to go and examine de meat and so on.' Paid
to maintain food hygiene standards, Sigismund was a government
employee. That meant status and security and money in an economy
badly affected by the global crisis. Having siphoned off any capital

in Guyana's good years, by the 1930s, after two royal commissions, the British government was reduced to propping the colony up with financial aid. Sigismund was a good bet in tough times.

The wedding was a big one. Olive doesn't dwell on it, but she can recall the ceremony's outstanding features. 'It was mostly a Hindu marriage, cos of my father's background. It was a big, big wedding. You know why you marry like dat? Cos you get money, everybody throw money at you!' Unlike Guyana's African descendants, who'd comprehensively converted to Christianity, many Indians tenaciously held on to aspects of their religious culture. It wasn't uncommon to find Hindu gods in grandmothers' houses and a reverence to a mythical Indian land.[9] In British Guiana, Olive had a Hindu wedding and made a profit too. Then came the honeymoon, when the teenage girl got to know her older husband. Anxious, brave and beautiful, she set off for a week in the countryside, where they stayed with a cousin. 'A whole week!' Olive pulls a face. 'A whole week! Because when I saw, when I saw dat ting! Oh my Lord! Oh God!' She takes my hand and she laughs and she laughs.

But I saw dat ting! Hahahaha. Dat ting!! Hahaha. Dat was dat. A week and den I come back. Moder never tell me *nothing*. Yes, de friends, we talk and we talk about what is going to happen. And den I have baby Terence. He is dead now.

Olive loses her virginity and outlives her son in one long, emotional breath. Marriage, sex, birth, death – just like that. Passionately connected to her own womanhood and female instincts, Olive always grabbed life with two hands. Guyana's strained colonial status, the impoverished state of the country, no universal franchise, the ultimate unaccountability of the Governor – Olive shrugs. In early adulthood she had more important things to worry about. 'I had my babies at home, I paid a nurse.' Young, healthy Olive, flanked by her mother and her sister, was fully prepared for labour. Complacency was not an option. In the first half of the twentieth century, everybody knew about death in childbirth. It was one of the few conditions that could kill a previously healthy young woman. Only recently has the Church of England prayer book removed the service for postnatal mothers, which started by giving thanks to God for 'the safe deliverance and preservation from the great dangers of childbirth'.[10] Olive and her diligent mother took no risks. Under instruction from the nurse, they had bought a big tin of olive oil.

> When you havin' de baby she help you to pour de oil and she take her finger and open you! And tell you when to push! And she put de oil … I wasn't conscionable of what she was doing because I was in pain. Oh God, oh! Not again. Hahaha. Never again!! Hear me, never again, oh my God!

But there was a second time and a third time in quick succession, and by the age of twenty-five Olive had three children, Terence, Joye and Gloria. Labour never got any easier.

> In de night the nurse said, 'Put a brick on your head!' cos de pain would knock me. Yes, I put a brick on my head! Delivery was always good. De nurse tell me, 'Wait wait, I'm goin' tell you when to push!' Oh Lord! When it come, den she come every morning and bathe me, she bring a tub and boil a lot of bark and coconut tree roots and it go black, and she put you down in de water.

With bright expression, Olive relives the arrival of all her babies. By the time number three had come along, Olive found the birthing practices familiar, reassuring even. 'After nine days, de nurse take a long pepper and she put it with soft grease and she roll it and push it up your bottom! She says, "Dat kills de sore in your back." Hahaha!' Eighty years later, the rituals are also very funny. 'Hahaha.'

~

'But you are not to put about my marriage. I did not marry for love.' And so, the story unfolds without Sigismund, who was absent much of the time. The children were primarily looked after by their grandmother, while Olive, in the same house, established herself as an accomplished dressmaker. When she was fifteen, Rosalind had removed her daughter from school and sent her to a seamstress, whom she paid a small sum to teach her how to sew. Within a year, Olive had a trade for life and was soon established as a dressmaker, employing her own 'sewing girls' and working long hours on a pedal-powered sewing machine. Her mother fed and washed the three children before they tripped off every morning to their private day school, the British Guiana Education Trust. 'Yeah, der were two salaries. Me and my husband's.' Olive was a very proud mother, stringently adhering to the snobbish and nuanced rules that riddled colonial Georgetown's social hierarchy. Her immaculate children wore blemish-free, knitted white socks and crisp dresses and shirts. They were delivered to school as pretty as pictures, with bows and buckles and large alert eyes, and a stern warning ringing in their ears. 'Remember, I don't know no letter below C! A, B, C is all I know, and I can't count above five! One, two, three, four, five!' Any grade or position received at school that wasn't ranked in the top few, Olive did not want to know about. She expected the best. To underline this point, she breaks into song:

We go to our places,
With clean hands and faces,
And pay great attention to what we are told,
Or else you will never be happy and clever
Cos learning is better than silver or gold.

Pounding away on her machine, in her little wooden house, Olive led by example – she worked consistently and hard. Her reputation as a talented seamstress grew; rarely were obstacles allowed to disrupt her schedule. 'I got sick. My cousin was gettin' married and I had to make her wedding dress and I hadn't de power. I had a pedal but I was too sick to use it.' Sweating profusely, she cut out the dress in downy white satin and each of her children in turn worked the pedal on her machine, pushing and panting, little legs straining with the effort. 'Dey were so proud to do dis ting, you know! "My turn! My turn!"' The bridal dress was duly delivered and more commissions rolled in. Olive was happy at work. She enjoyed the fabrics and the beading, the smocking and the small detail that could set off a dress. And she loved the gaudy bright colours that sashayed down Georgetown's regency streets. 'In Guyana, dey wear dresses and everyting just like here, but I think dey are more stylish dan England because you don't have winter, you only have rain and sun and lots of holidays, and dey will come to you to make dresses. Dat is it.'

With a dead father and distant husband, Olive was growing into a strong, independent woman. 'I only trusted in de one man, and dat was God. De good Lord.' She believes it was God who oversaw her family life and protected her mother and three children, it was God who kept the tumult of unemployment and desperate poverty from her door and God who gifted her a trade that would stand her in good stead for the rest of her life. 'Der was dat king who came and went, yes I think I remember dat.' Gadfly Edward VIII's abdication in 1936 proved that even the pinnacle of imperial righteousness – the British monarchy – could blow off course, but not God. 'It was God who showed me de way.' Olive kept her devout head down in the devil's decade. With Guyana's rising sun, daily she sat stitching, cutting, tucking, pedalling and praying. *Be present at our table, Lord. Be here and everywhere.*

PHYLLIS

Of the six women featured in this book, only Olive was married before the outbreak of the Second World War. In 1930s Britain, just one tenth of wives were in employment; prolific marriage bars often blocked those willing to stay in work. An equivalent statistic is harder to glean for the disparate empire community, but anachronistic colonial habits ensured that married women in the higher echelons of society tended to stay at home. Olive, a black, Guyanese,

self-employed wife sewing in her front room, avoided social oppro-
brium but amidst the snobbery of India's British Raj, working wives
attracted more attention. A hangover from the late Victorian era,
with its emphasis on racial purity, the 'management of sexuality,
parenting and morality' lay at the heart of Britain's most treasured
imperial project.[11] Married white women, who were known as
'memsahibs', were entrusted with 'upholding the domestic regime
that prevented men from "going native" and allowed the European
population to reproduce itself, literally as well as figuratively'.[12] In
other words, memsahibs were expected to stay at home, manage the
servants and produce (white) children.

Phyllis Gargan's mother, Irene Drummond, had an Indian grandmother. 'Well, we think she was Indian; she was the only person not
named in the family tree. My great-grandfather went out to India at a
time when only the officer class were allowed to take their wives. So
we presume ... ' But the Gargans were not classified as Anglo-Indian
(a lower status, mixed-race section of British-Indian society). Phyllis
is quite sure of this. She explains that her own sandy complexion
'is only on my face, and only when I've been in the sun. We weren't
the ruling class but we weren't Anglo-Indians. We were somewhere
in the middle. There were many layers in Indian society.' With just
one distant Indian relative, the Gargans belonged to a large group
of racially ambiguous, poorer whites. Phyllis's mother, Irene, who
was a nurse, had done well to marry a white British boy, albeit from
Ireland. Their partnership, sealed the year before Phyllis's birth in
1916, allowed her to give up nursing (true memsahibs did not work),
focus on the home and have six children.

Phyllis is matter-of-fact about her own relationship with her
mother. 'We were never close, she was only interested in babies.
That was it. She had fallen out with the rest of her family so we
didn't know about them.' In the brusque analysis Phyllis offers,
the death of Irene's mother when she was only two or three had a
significant impact on a woman destined to grow up 'with a chip
on both shoulders'. Phyllis believes a poor relationship with a subsequent stepmother and a childhood shelved into boarding school

explains her mother's antisocial behaviour as an adult. She has less truck with the suggestion that a hierarchical British-Indian society obsessed with racial nuance and social fripperies may have left Irene feeling inadequate or, at the very least, judged. Perhaps her offish character was a mixture of the two; either way, it took its toll on the Gargan marriage, the breakdown of which Phyllis identifies as her mother's doing.

It was 1933, and the family had just returned to Burma from their prestigious visit to the Mother Country, but now the atmosphere was sullied by family discord. Phyllis, a happy-go-lucky sixteen-year-old, was unprepared for the fallout. Otherwise seemingly impervious to difficulty, she felt profoundly the impact of her parents' separation.

> It was very painful when my parents split because of my mother's bitterness, and it was pushed down our throats all the time. She was very jealous and I couldn't see why she was being jealous. My dad mixed with the sergeants and people like that – never the officers – and mother would never come out, she would never mix or come even to Christmas parties and things like that.

Desmond, Irene's second son and Phyllis's baby brother, had died of meningitis in 1932, when he was less than a year old. At the time, Irene had been in hospital having a hysterectomy; the double trauma exacerbated her antisocial tendencies. In pain emotionally, she removed herself and her remaining children from William Gargan. By the mid-1930s, the marriage was dead, and the fatherless family had left Burma and were living in a small cottage in India's Bangalore. 'All our furniture was rented and very basic.' The girls returned to a convent school they'd attended some years earlier. Almost a century old, Phyllis says that she has no regrets about her life, but then she will pause, look out of the window at Edinburgh's chimney pots and confide, 'I regret my family's split up, I regret that.' In her handwritten memoir, she deals with the issue in one sad sentence. 'Broken marriages usually do affect children in spite of what people say.'[13]

Financially straitened, her mother returned to work as a nurse – 'That was what she wanted,' insists Phyllis. She refuses to countenance the idea her father might have had an affair. Phyllis desperately missed gregarious William Gargan; his physical absence throbbed like an open wound. There was no question of her staying with him in Burma. She was the eldest daughter, her mother needed Phyllis to look after the younger sisters. 'As a moral guide, I suppose you would say.' Like Helena, miles away in Wales, being the eldest daughter of a large brood came with considerable, uninvited responsibilities. Phyllis wouldn't see her father again for over a decade. No more shooting for the pot, climbing in the jungle, swimming in the river – her childhood was over just like that. Judgement and stigma inevitably surrounded a fatherless family, but Phyllis just shrugs. The worst had happened, her father had left – people could say what they liked.

Given the eggy mess flummoxing her family life, it is hardly surprising that the seismic changes which ruptured and frayed British India's imperial structure still went unnoticed by Phyllis. The relationship between mother ship and colonial protégé was strained to breaking point. Nehru was a Harrovian schoolboy and studied at Cambridge; both he and Gandhi attended London's Inner Temple, where they trained in law, and Ali Jinnah became a barrister at London's Lincoln Inn* – here was the English-educated, Indian elite the British Empire had once dreamt of but, now a reality, these men were underestimated by the British government. Dominion status was promised to India but titbits of delegated power were an insult to the sophisticated independence movement. There were old romantics like Winston Churchill who made a hullabaloo about preserving the Indian Empire from the back benches, but on the whole Britain knew the game was up. Nonetheless, clumsily they fudged and prevaricated

---

* Jawaharlal Nehru led the Indian National Congress between the wars and became the first prime minister of India. Mahatma Gandhi was the pre-eminent leader of Indian nationalism in twentieth-century British-ruled India, and Muhammad Ali Jinnah was the leader of the All-India Muslim League and first governor general of Pakistan.

(India had been a valuable source of soldiers in the First World War,* and they might be needed again). The marriage was over, but the predicted break-up – white Britain torn from brown India, Hindu pitched against Muslim, north divided from south – was too painful to bear. In its final years, the Indian Empire was kept going by habit alone. Phyllis laughs. 'We just carried on as normal.' Or at least as normal as life could be without her father.

⁓

Between the wars in Britain, young women with aspirations often ended up teaching or nursing. Likewise, in India, for those single white women who did work, becoming either a governess or a nurse was the most respectable option. Once Phyllis left her convent education, in proud possession of a School Leaver's Certificate, she followed her mother into nursing. 'There was nothing for me at home, I wanted to get away so I went to train at St George's Hospital in Bombay.'

In 1935, Phyllis started work, secure in the knowledge that she was part of an impressive nursing pedigree. 'We "probationers" lived in a small building – single rooms – locked by a night sister at 10pm. Started at 8am ... Worked two shifts a day.'[14] Today she remains sure that her style of nursing outstripped British methods both then and now. 'Over here, you have too many technicians, they have too many books to fill in. In India, when you nurse a patient you do everything, you feed them, you care for them, you wash them.' Smallpox, typhoid, tuberculosis, plague – killers stalked the wards, but nothing was as terrifying as Matron Miss MacFarlane; a sister in Mesopotamia in the First World War, she kept strict control of her starched charges. Pressed in dazzling whites, with an ostentatiously large cap and rubber-soled shoes, probationer Phyllis disinfected hands with carbolic, fed morsels of fried liver to the pallid, applied

---

* India made a bigger contribution to the First World War than Australia; over 60,000 Indian soldiers were killed in foreign fields.

linseed plasters on rattling chests, used brown soap and sugar to pull puss from boils, and prepared boiling sponges to stem bleeding. 'That's why I can carry very hot things.' Death was a frequent occurrence: 'You would lay them on a raised marble slab and put a cage on top to stop the rats. The hospital had a small mortuary and burials were within twenty-four hours because of the climate.' Phyllis discovered she thrived in the operating theatre. 'That was my particular passion. I had no qualms about the messy side. Nothing fazed me.'

No reminder is needed that she has always been 'tough'. But she was also naïve. Growing up, Phyllis had been cloistered among immediate family or restricted within a convent school; she was wholly unprepared for the intimate exposure to the many faculties of the human body that came with nursing.

After I qualified, I was sent to a big maternity hospital. I had to take this message into the sister, who was in obstetrics. I went in and I just gawped. I gawped. I had no idea where a baby came from. I had no clue a baby came from there.

Pulled, hot and pink and steaming, from the bright private gash of a heaving woman, the arrival of a brand-new life stopped Phyllis in her tracks. The staff nurse picked up on the young girl's stupefaction.

'Wait outside the door, dear.'
'Do you know nothing about babies . . . ? But your mother had so many?'
I don't know what happens to them. Mother went to military hospital, we were always with the military. I didn't know . . .

Today, Phyllis admits that babies have never interested her. Regardless, the quaint idea that 'the line down from the centre of a woman's belly button opened up and the baby popped out' was fantastical. Echoes with Helena in Wales are prevalent. Fecund mothers, so many siblings and a dark ignorant hole at the heart of their respective upbringings. Girls were excluded from so much on the basis of their gender, and they were also excluded from the most primal connection with their own femininity. 'Mother just said, "Keep your legs crossed!" That's all she ever told us.' Phyllis insists it didn't matter, 'I was a tomboy.' Born into a culture where being a girl meant restrictive clothing, restrictive activities and restrictive socialising, Phyllis claims her tomboyism with pride. Her only surviving brother, Terry, received preferential treatment and went to boarding school in England but at least her father had taught her how to fish and shoot. 'Yes, I was always a tomboy.'

During her training, tomboy Phyllis received a rude awakening on the men's ward at St George's Hospital.

> Well, I got into trouble. The matron was strict. The curtains had to be straight and the bed clothes straight and so I went down the ward before inspection and got men to put their knees down. I walked along and I slapped down one of the men and the staff nurse suddenly called me away and said, 'Stop doing that!' and I said, 'Why?' and she said, 'That's his dickie standing up.' Well, I didn't know, I didn't know that a dickie could stand up. I knew nothing about that. I hadn't seen a dickie stand up!

Olive on her honeymoon, Phyllis in the men's ward – girls were in the dark, enfeebled and disempowered through their needless ignorance. It's shocking and it's funny, shockingly funny. Phyllis is giggling, we both are – uncontrollably. A tomboy nurse, pristine and prissy, sweeping across the ward, smacking down an unsuspecting erection lest the terrifying matron launch an attack.

CHAPTER EIGHT

STORM CLOUDS

National identity comes in many forms. In the mid-twentieth century, Britishness was like an onion, it had numerous layers; it mixed well and it could stand alone, it made eyes water and it was still strong. Olive, a Guyanese woman, and Phyllis, born in India, were British by proxy; they lived a long way off but Britain was always 'there'. They believed in British invincibility. 'Hitler?' Phyllis shrugs, 'Well, yes, I suppose later on in the 1930s in the press there was talk about him, but no, it didn't worry us.' Phyllis is not a complacent woman but, frankly, why would a young girl worry about a European scenario thousands of miles away that even the British Establishment were slow to confront? Germany rolled into Austria in March 1938 and *The Times* found an improbable parallel with the unification of Scotland and England nearly 250 years earlier. Months later, a repeat procession of Nazis into Czechoslovakia saw the British prime minister, Neville Chamberlain, on the steps of Downing Street promising 'peace for our time' before encouraging his audience to 'go home and get a nice, quiet sleep'.

EDNA, ANN

Edna nods, she remembers Prime Minister Chamberlain but preferred his Conservative predecessor, Baldwin. 'That's right, I didn't worry. But I did know there was going to be a war. Oh yes, I knew all right. I'll tell you how.' From 1935, Edna worked for Granny Parks in Grantham (the baker sacked her when she went home to bed with tonsillitis). Well into her nineties and once in service herself (before marrying her way out), Granny Parks had a profound impact on young Edna. 'I loved her as much as my own mother. She was very wise.' Granny Parks reciprocated Edna's love, entrusting her young servant with paperwork, visits to the solicitor and the charge of her beloved dog.

> Paddy, he was a terrier. He would go and sit underneath his collar when it was time for his walk. I took him home with me when Granny Parks died; she bequeathed him to me. He howled for days when she died. Oh, he was lovely! Unfortunately, my sister took him for a walk and a car ran at him on the grassy verge and killed him.

Edna's preamble concerning Paddy is an important part of the story. It's all about trust. Edna and Granny Parks trusted each other – Paddy was a living embodiment of that trust.

> I loved Paddy and I loved Granny Parks. One of the things she said was, 'There will be a war after I have died, and it won't be very long after.' It was a year in fact, as she died in 1938. But she said, 'Edna, you need not worry, because we are going to win that war!' So I never worried.

So Edna knew what Ann knew – war was inevitable – but, unlike Ann, she didn't worry. 'There was no need, you see, I knew it was going to be okay. Granny Parks was good at predictions.' Perhaps to underline her lack of anxiety, Edna returns to the story of Paddy the dog, explaining where he slept (in her bed), and where he was buried (in Denton's orchard). Firmly embedded at the bottom of the social hierarchy, like Granny Parks before her, Edna had unwavering faith in Great Britain. Much-anticipated weekly visits to Grantham's picture house, where swashbuckling epics were standard fare, reinforced a fanciful idea of gung-ho fortitude and national greatness. In liberal London, Ann railed at the stupidity of the politicians and their supine treatment of Hitler. 'Despair is what I felt. Yes, despair! I was horrified when Chamberlain came back from Munich!' But Edna did not lose sleep. No need, and anyway she had more than enough on her plate organising Granny Park's funeral.

> Her sister's family, they had been waiting for her to die. On the day of the funeral, I stayed to prepare the food and I went into the sitting room and they'd had every picture off the wall. I just sat down and cried. Luckily, I'd been warned and I had already taken home what Granny Parks had given me. She gave me the chest she had when she first went into service in the nineteenth century. My grandma and grandpa had them too, cos they were both in service. It had a little container at the end that held all your little private bits and pieces, and the rest was for your clothes. I got a travelling bag as well. I think she must've loved me for what she gave me.

Edna is comfortable talking about Granny Parks; her three years with the old woman from 1935 were some of the happiest of her working life. The former servant treated Edna with respect, and she loved chatting and sharing opinions with the young girl. Arterial roads and petrol pumps, wirelesses and Kodak cameras, cinemas and dance halls, the trappings of emerging modern England were shocking to a woman born in 1847. Draped head to toe in widow's black, she'd shake her head and assure Edna, 'They will get so clever they will end the Earth.' 'Oh yes, she was very intelligent, and now you haven't asked me about Edward VIII, who was the biggest scandal of them all before the war. Granny Parks always said he would never be king. She prophesied it.'

In fact, Edward VIII was Britain's king for eleven months in 1936, but he abdicated in December five months before his coronation, so Granny Parks had a point. His modish arrival at Daddy's (George V's) deathbed in his own plane, 'hatless from the air' as John Betjeman put it, was a harbinger of things to come. Edward's

antics were a catastrophe for the monarchy. Edna was all ears; this
was a public scandal that even resonated in Lincolnshire – it particularly resonated in Lincolnshire. 'You see, he had a house in Melton
Mowbray and, as prince, he rode in the next village. We used to see
him coming through with the Belvoir Hunt. I suppose he was quite
good-looking but he wasn't very stable.' Edna stops to whisper something inaudible about Edward and two sisters. Eighty years on she's
still full of the gossip; *The Times* was tactful enough not to print it,
but everybody knew that Edward had enjoyed plenty of affairs with
(invariably married) women. Wallis Simpson was one of many, but
now Edward was king and this was the woman he wanted to marry.
Edna tuts. 'She was a dreadful woman. An American, she wanted to
be the Queen of England!'

Before the storm burst, Prime Minister Baldwin conceded that, at
forty-one, 'it's a tragedy he is not married'.[1] A 'bright young thing'
from the preceding decade, Edward was out of touch with the sensi-
bilities of middle England. 'Edward and Wallis were both a bloody
nuisance. He was a devil of a ladies' man.' Edna is warming to her
theme: 'Thank goodness that man, what's he called? Yes, Baldwin,
that's it. Thank goodness Prime Minister Baldwin put a stop to
it.' The trendy young, including a smattering of communists and
fascists, marched in favour of Edward outside Buckingham Palace
and Churchill believed the King should marry whom he liked, but
provincial, reassuring Baldwin thought otherwise. The decline in
moral standards had been exaggerated. Divorce and public life
did not mix, nor did Anglicanism and divorce, and the King was
Supreme Governor of the Church of England. The matrimonial
union of Edward and his American floozy threatened the façade
of decent, upright England. The King must accept the advice of his
ministers; MPs returned to their constituencies and were struck by
the strength of opinion they found there. Edward could not marry
Wallis Simpson and be king. Edna nods. Quite right too.

We didn't want this American woman, who had been married
twice, but she, the horrible so-and-so, was determined she was

going to be Queen. I always thought it was a jolly good thing he abdicated. I was not interested in politics but I did mind about that.

Liberal Ann, a couple of years older than Edna and living in louche London, was of the same opinion. She sighs. 'It was all rather ridiculous.' Ann and her friends were highly critical of the government's foreign policy but she is adamant they agreed with Baldwin on the subject of Edward. 'Everyone I knew thought the pair highly unsuitable. I think when he abdicated, most people felt it was rather a relief.' Edna has always been a monarchist – as an impressionable girl she liked the idea that her king was unimpeachable, perfect even, a beacon to revere and trust. Wallis Simpson simply would not do. Ann was more practical. She resented the attention the subject received in the 'gutter press'. She laughs and retrieves a newspaper clipping. The scandal created such a stir, an old woman in an alms house sat up and demanded her teeth, keen to have a say. By the end of 1936, Edward's brother Albert (George VI) had become king. Ann approved. 'It was the right decision. Wallis was highly unsuitable and on the other hand you had Elizabeth, the wife of his brother, who was more appropriate. She was a Scottish aristocrat and a well-liked mother of two; she was an obvious assistance to her husband. Wallis was none of those things.' Ann is unrelenting. No matter that Edward's reluctant successor George was painfully shy, the hoo-ha had gone on quite long enough and needed urgent resolution. Britain really should be focusing on other matters.

> Although it all worked out rather well for me, because I got an interesting job decorating a shop window on Charing Cross Road off Trafalgar Square for George's coronation. It was a travel agent and we filled all the windows with Union Jacks and painted backgrounds. Yes, it was rather fun.

The coronation went ahead as planned on 12 May 1937; the cosmopolitan bustle showed off Britain's imperial status – prime ministers from the dominions, native African royalty and Indian princes joined the procession in a final shuffle for empire. Times were changing. The same year, a Private Member's Bill was introduced that relaxed the divorce laws. But kings play by different rules and a delighted Granny Parks lived to see her prediction come (partially) true. Edward was never a *real* British king. Edna was chuffed to bits. 'It was very hard on King George because he had that dreadful stammer, but he had to get over it and he did very well. He was a very good king. He led us very well in the war. Did I tell you that Granny Parks predicted we would win the war?'

JOYCE

Before the Second World War, Oxford University remained a very male institution, with just five colleges for women.* Established in 1879, Somerville was one of the original two and by the time women had been granted full university membership in 1920 it had acquired a considerable reputation for nurturing highly intelligent girls. Former student and writer Winifred Holtby playfully noted: 'LMH† for young ladies, St Hilda's for games, St Hugh's for religion, Somerville for brains.' (A less kind version preferred by some men's colleges included 'Somerville for freaks'.²) St Paul's schoolgirl Joyce Reynolds tactfully justified her choice of Oxford over Cambridge on the basis of the former's more generous exhibition award, but in fact she preferred erudite Somerville and the Oxford Classics course.

Arriving at Somerville in 1937 aged eighteen, Joyce thrived on the serious academic schedule. There were daily lectures and weekly tutorials, some in college and others elsewhere in the university: onto her bike, down Woodstock Road and into the world of Horace, Tacitus, Virgil, Plato ... then back to Somerville Library, teasing

---

* Although St Anne's, which originated as the Society of Oxford Home Students, catering for women who lived with private families, wasn't incorporated by Royal Charter until 1952 and all five female colleges were only granted full collegiate status in 1959.
† Lady Margaret Hall – one of the five Oxford girls' colleges between the wars.

her mind around Greek prose, translations and poetry. She soon overtook the other students in college, many of whom had 'much more social confidence than me. I remember one in particular, for her it was all about having *fun*.' Joyce did not let (social) fun get in her way. 'No, I didn't drink alcohol. That and smoking and putting your hair up in a bun or roll – those were the things that indicated you were grown up.' Joyce saw no need for adult gimmicks.

I wore my hair in a bob and always short.

No, I didn't smoke. I gave it a go, but I didn't like it.

I remember the first time I went to a college dance, my partner took me out to dinner first and yes there was a drink. I was a bit surprised, but I wasn't going to show that I was surprised so I drank it!

No, no, no! Women didn't go into bars.

I don't think all women were as naïve as me. It was partly my parents' influence and partly my personality.

Between the wars chaperones became obsolete and there were greater social freedoms for women within the university; however, Joyce was a reserved, unsophisticated girl. A few months before she went up to Oxford, her final recollection from St Paul's was a post-exam bubble-blowing session on the rooftop of the school.

A member of staff came up to *request* (*not* instruct) the prefects not to blow them so that they descended over the classroom windows . . . so we blew them over Brook Green instead, and I have a visual memory of the driver of a horse and cart looking amazed as a series of bubbles descended before his eyes.[3]

An age of innocence permeates the anecdote; Joyce tailored her life at Oxford accordingly. Others remember a hive of protests, Socialist League pamphlets and meetings in the tense atmosphere of the late 1930s, but Joyce didn't particularly enjoy debating and never went on a demonstration – Labour Party membership and meetings sufficed politically. She devoted the vast majority of her time to the study of Classics. 'It wasn't all-consuming but it was very engaging.' Fifty years later, her Somerville contemporary, the writer Iris Murdoch, remembered that as an undergraduate one's 'social life was overcast by wars and rumours of wars'.[4] Joyce shakes her head. 'It's not true for me that it was overcast. Not really.' With her acute mental economy, she does not allow a retrospective understanding of 1939 to muddle the memory of her young self.

> Yes, we knew what was happening. I saw the war coming, I hoped it would not, but I was pretty sure it would. But I was more interested in my work, I regret to say. One probably ought to have been more balanced between public affairs and one's work.

In 1938, the Sudetenland in Czechoslovakia was gifted to Germany for 'peace' in Europe thanks to the Munich Agreement; by March 1939, Hitler mocked that pact and triumphantly entered a denuded Prague. Thuggery and discrimination followed. Joyce recalls meeting Czechoslovakian exiles in London. 'My parents were very enthusiastic members of a League of Nations society, and their friends organised events for refugees.' Talking to interesting Czechoslovakians in Putney saddened her: 'I felt sorry for them, and it made the prospect of war seem more real.' The noose was tightening across Europe and she knew it. Miffed by Hitler's land grab in Czechoslovakia, Mussolini occupied Albania on Good Friday, 1939. For Joyce, the timing was distressing. Coming to the end of her second year at Oxford, that same month she had been enthusiastically organising a study trip to Rome. 'Three of us from different subjects wanted to go to Italy, mainly for archaeological and historical reasons. We were due to go during the Easter vacation.'

However, unfolding events didn't bode well for safe passage. *The Times* warned that, minus action from Britain, both Hitler and Mussolini would strike again.[5] In fact, the Führer was planning an Italian trip to formalise the Axis agreement of 1936 with his fellow fascist leader. Joyce can't remember exactly what or when the tipping point was, but around this time she took the decision that a trip to Italy was too risky. 'I worried that there might be danger, or that Italy might start fighting and we wouldn't be able to get home. I was very disappointed.' Her calculation was a wise one. By 22 May 1939, the cat-and-mouse game between the two dictators ended with the signing of the Pact of Steel. Hitler's vast entourage landed in Rome to stay with the Italian king and outshine Il Duce, Mussolini. A military and political alliance was duly agreed.

Europe held its breath, but Joyce was undeterred. She recovered from the disappointment and began reorganising her study trip. 'We went as soon as the vacation began, so it must've been June or July.' Rome, her destination, was full of Mussolini's Blackshirts parading around with a farcical goose step, vainly trying to enforce anti-bourgeois measures. Regular Italians were nonplussed by their country's increasing alignment with Nazi Germany; people wryly remarked, 'You know, we were better off under Mussolini,' and wall writings appeared in Turin with caricatures of Hitler alongside the phrase 'Behold the Führer, Duce of the Duce'.[6] Arriving in the Italian capital by train, Joyce does not recall feeling afraid of the fascists. 'They were rather handsome! Very pretty.' Like so many, Joyce struggled to take Mussolini and his men seriously. One English visitor recalled 'Musso' – 'He was rather a figure of fun ... He would put on a face, throw out his jaw and march about, which was ridiculous.'[7]

The trio of Oxford students stayed in a lodging house run by a charming, middle-aged Italian woman. Joyce had been in charge of booking, cancelling and rebooking their reservation. When they arrived, their hostess surmised, 'You cancelled, didn't you, because you thought we were going to war?' The pertinent observation embarrassed the English girls. 'I can't tell you why we were embarrassed, we just were.' Perhaps Italian hospitality made the idea of war seem utterly ludicrous. 'They were all so friendly. It appeared less worrying than in the news.'

Joyce walked easily among the 'pretty' fascists on Rome's sun-baked streets, the Tiber River slipped timelessly through the city and the girls split off to nourish their respective historical interests – the trip was proving a great success. But . . . 'I don't know whether to tell you this.' Now in her ninety-ninth year, Joyce weighs up the odds. And makes her decision. 'The other two girls were interested in medieval and modern history, whereas I had an interest in the ancient world, so I was alone in some room in the Vatican Museum.' Minutes from the Sistine Chapel, cloistered in a gloomy hall, surrounded by the ancient and immense collection built up by popes down the centuries, Joyce was revelling in her passion for the classical when, quite suddenly, the man employed to protect the artefacts and their visitors came at her. 'The museum guard decided he wanted to kiss me and he seized me and he did, he kissed me!' There is horror in her voice, her arms motion to push him from her chest; she can still feel him there. 'I was really very upset. I was really *very* upset.' Joyce struggled free and fled the museum, but the repugnant impression remained. A modest twenty-year-old woman, her first kiss with a man was an act of sexual violation in a foreign land.

'Hardy' is a word Joyce's now elderly pupils use recurrently to describe their former tutor. Nearly one hundred and still at work, the label is an obvious one. But Joyce has always been hardy. She was hardy – fearless, even – aged twenty when, bolting from the Vatican collection, she immediately shared the horrific encounter with her friends, and together they took matters further. One had contacts with officialdom, and sporting the qualm-free righteousness possessed by extreme youth, they reported the errant museum guard. For their part, fear of retribution did not feature. And Joyce is sure the guard was reprimanded. 'My guess is he may well have been sacked. It was the Vatican Museum after all.' Whether he lost his job or not is now academic, but what's significant is Joyce's certainty that the right thing would be done. In 1938, women were not regularly levelling with the opposite sex in the workplace and in courts about inappropriate behaviour. Joyce was not inhibited by a track record of failure. And she was hardy. The violation took place midway through her Italian trip. 'No, of course I didn't go home. No, it didn't change my opinion of Italian people, but it was my overriding memory of that trip.'

CHAPTER NINE

THIS COUNTRY IS AT
WAR WITH GERMANY

It was Germany's entry into Poland that finally saw France and Britain declare war against the Third Reich on 3 September 1939. Within two years, the conflagration would spread with terrifying contagion. Global, total and indiscriminate, people died on the front line, in the air, at sea, in gas chambers, at work in factories and offices, and at home in bed. The millions of dead over a six-year period were unprecedented, nations were pulped and generations traumatised. The world would never be the same again – *lest we forget*. Britain had belatedly woken up to the danger of Continental fascism to fight comprehensively and vigorously. Total war required total national commitment – the Celtic fringes, the empire, women – no group was exempt. Young men fought in the Middle East, the South Pacific, fascist Italy, North Africa – they saw a world they never knew existed. As for women, they put on uniforms, read cipher codes, reared livestock, built fighter jets and filled in forms. Great Britain stood together, united by a common enemy and a shared sense of purpose.

Hindsight and historians frequently reiterate the feats of this 'great generation', who saved the country from the jackboot. The story is glorious but a nation's glory does not necessarily translate into individual victories. Girls who had never worked before or left home found their lives changed, but not always for the better. Generalisations about a new-found freedom and independence are dangerous. Young women from different ends of the class system rarely experienced the same war. And no one had a crystal ball. In 1939, glory and victory, female conscription and total war, were in the future. Chamberlain's announcement on 3 September upped the stakes in a grisly international game, but life went on.

JOYCE

By the summer of '39, Joyce had returned from Italy and was at home in south-west London for the last month of the vacation. The atmosphere was sombre; nightly, the Reynolds family sat around the wireless. 'My parents had lived through a war, they knew much more than me exactly what it could mean.' In London, trenches were burrowed in parks, gas masks handed out like sweeties and air-raid shelters mushroomed overnight. The lights went off and petrol rationing came in, people waited for something to happen. Joyce nods. 'I was to have had a gold ring given me for my twenty-first birthday but when my birthday came that December I wasn't given a gold ring, not a new one anyway, because gold was very difficult to get.' A significant birthday lost out to the damp squib of the phoney war. Twenty-firsts and rings and things mattered to young girls, even ones who rarely fussed over appearances. Joyce pulls a ring from her long, thin finger and hands it over. 'Instead, my mother presented me with a box and in it was the ring she had received for her twenty-first. If you look closely, you can see her initials. It's probably only rose gold, her family didn't have much money.' The ring is cut in the shape of a shield and rubbed almost to obscurity are the initials of Nellie Farmer. A faded offering in the palm of Joyce's hand, it has a touching appeal. 'Well, I suppose I was touched later but 21-year-olds are less susceptible to being touched. I never got my own gold ring, after the war they all forgot.'

Uninvited war arrived, bumping clumsily into the minutiae of people's lives. It is typical of Joyce's uncompromising style that she tells the story of a ring when asked about the first months of the conflict. Many in the British Cabinet were only just beginning to comprehend the implications of a war they weren't ready for. Conscription had started for a quarter of a million men but the means to process even this scale of call-up were not in place. Many well-intending, middle-aged women volunteered to ready their country for action. Tens of thousands belonged to the Auxiliary Fire Service (including Joyce's mother) or the Women's Voluntary Service, which co-ordinated the evacuation programme before the conflict even began. Some young girls were excited by the idea of wearing a uniform and serving in the armed forces, but in 1939 the British government didn't anticipate needing their assistance. A semblance of normality remained a national priority. *Women's Own* reminded its readers, 'We are standing by our posts as men are standing by theirs.'[1] For the time being this was still a man's war, albeit with very little fighting. After a spurt of preventative activity and dire warnings, sandbags soon began dribbling their contents onto paving stones, evacuated women and children got itchy feet in the countryside and Britain sent a 'symbolic' expeditionary force to France. Action was limited. Small wonder Joyce felt the absence of her long-promised gold ring.

She had returned to Oxford in October 1939, where change was incremental. One writer later opined of 1940 that 'if an old Somervillian were to wake up in the college precincts, it might take her several minutes to deduce the fact of a European war'.[2] College food, already simple fare, got thinner – kedgeree less fishy, stew less meaty, pudding less creamy – and Joyce, with other Somervillians, made way for Radcliffe Infirmary nurses by moving to rooms in Lady Margaret Hall. 'That was rather agreeable as I had a pleasant view over Norham Gardens.' Initially, the government advised women to stay the course at university and most did so, in Joyce's case with particular relish. Oxford blackouts were manageable (in the dark, she reassured herself that 'all the young men who would perhaps tackle me were in the army') and, even with no Luftwaffe overhead, fire-watching duties could prove diverting. Appropriately, Joyce was assigned to the top of the Ashmolean – the university's museum of art and archaeology. One former student recalled 'sleeping on a camp bed between a mummy in a glass case and a stuffed alligator'.[3] There were no fires, but holed up among ancient Egyptian artefacts and Anglo-Saxon treasures, the girls found a drawer full of old student reports. 'I remember somebody with great excitement discovering a report on a man who was moving towards becoming professor. It said, "He has not worked properly this term, his work has been late in coming in and is careless." We were all frightfully thrilled.' A yet-to-materialise Nazi incendiary could not compete with an indiscretion concerning a Classics tutor. The phoney war enjoyed an extended honeymoon for Joyce and her undergraduate friends in the city of dreaming spires.

HELENA, EDNA

A year after Helena returned from Harrow on the Hill, she got a job in Elan Valley, Mid Wales, and is quite certain that her two stints teaching there were among the happiest times of her life. That the first three years coincided with the beginning of the war did not diminish the joy she felt as she grew into her role as a teacher, found her feet in a new community and fell in love. A prolific writer, Helena kept a daily diary in which she jotted down thoughts, itineraries and events. The year 1939 was fraught with international tension but on paper it had to compete with Helena's full life. On Easter Sunday of April 1939, she observed: *'Italy taken towns in Albania'*, but no other extract refers to the political situation until Monday 4 September, when she notes, *'We have declared war on Germany and fighting is taking place. No children in school but teacher must be on duty.'* In her diary, the Spartan acknowledgement that war was a reality and adjustments had to be made is just that, an acknowledgement.

1939

Tues, 5 Sept. Saw evacuee mothers and children arrive. Some were poor but all fairly happy. Home on Eddie's bike.

Mon, 11 Sept. Gas mask, drill etc. Wore green gym [slip] for drill.

Sun, 17 Sept. Went to church ... wore new hat. Russia marched into Poland today.

Mon, 18 Sept. Practised in school with candle at night. Bath at night.

Tues, 19 Sept. School. Air-raid practice ... Nice day.

In charge of a gaggle of school children, Helena's duty of care saw her embrace a rigmarole of procedures that accompanied the upheaval and security of over a million mothers and children nationwide. Britain's top brass had long known that a second war with Germany would come with the threat of unprecedented aerial bombing – like never before, the country's cities were sitting ducks. Fire-watching alone was not sufficient. By the end of September 1939, hordes of women and children had been evacuated from Britain's urban areas to the countryside. Elan Valley was an obvious destination. In a mighty feat of Victorian engineering, dams, reservoirs and a seventy-three-mile aqueduct had been built in the valley to supply clean water to Birmingham some fifty years earlier. A school followed for the children of the waterworks. 'It was a beautiful school! And it was huge – halls, tiled walls and toilets indoors and a big bell ... a proper school, if you know what I mean.' Having long provided the city with water, in 1939 Elan Valley now offered a ready-made refuge for some of Birmingham's children. Helena, an enthusiastic new teacher head-hunted after just a year in one of Brecon's smaller elementary schools, was an additional bonus.

Retrospectively, much has been made of the 'can-do spirit' that pulsed through the nation during the war. In 1939, two-thirds of Britain's food and many raw materials came from abroad; the shipping lanes on which this trade depended were immediately vulnerable to enemy attack after war was declared – within two months, 200,000 tonnes of British shipping had been sunk. Increased domestic production and rationing were introduced to minimise the anticipated shortfall. Across Britain, the distribution of petrol, then food and clothing, were monitored and restricted accordingly, the cutbacks necessitating a make-do-and-mend mentality which the Ministry of Information did much to reinforce. But the impact of rationing, even in the early days, was not felt evenly. Helena, brought up miles from city shops on a diet of locally sourced food and adept at managing a rural homestead, needed no publicly funded poster to lecture her on resourcefulness. Her life had been spent growing, foraging, cooking, mending, making and hoarding. In the first four months of 1939, she purchased wool for a frock, sewed buttons on a jersey, darned stockings, made two aprons, finished a green skirt, altered the hem on a navy coat and cut out of blue satin – the *pièce de résistance* – a petticoat and knickers ensemble. Helena's wardrobe was war-proof before the war began. Ditto her diet – on regular trips back to Pengarn she made sausages, marrow chutney, ripe berry tarts and jellies. In Elan Valley, she gathered nuts and received parcels of freshly churned butter; in turn, she brought her family fat salmon from the River Elan.

Domestic servant Edna was also well equipped to manage the cutbacks.

> They talk about recycling nowadays, but they don't know a damn thing. I reused everything. I bought one of the last sewing machines to be made before the war started, and for that I paid half a crown a week. I used to make all our dresses; they were simple in those days. I could turn a pair of curtains into a dress.

After the loss of Granny Parks in 1938 ('and don't forget her dog Paddy, I wept when he died'), Edna endured a couple of dud jobs before she found the Fishers. 'Mr Fisher was a lot older than Mrs Fisher, but they were a lovely couple. I stayed at home when I worked for them. Yes, I suppose now you mention it, I was with them when war broke out, but to begin with nothing really happened.' Given the extenuating circumstances, these were halcyon days. 'Mr Fisher had been a farmer you see, so we had beef.' Edna smacks her lips.

And they had a hive of bees and a very nice veg garden and a flower garden. He used to come to the back door and say, 'You'd better put a piece of paper down there, Edna, you've just washed that floor!' They were nice people to work for. I didn't wear a cap, not with Mrs Fisher. And she used to come in in the morning – cos you always had your orders every day – and she'd come in and sit on the table and she'd say, 'Well . . .' and we'd discuss what happened in the village and any news about the war and what was going on.

Fifty-seven years later, Edna will claim that the Second World War irrevocably altered her life, but in those first 'phoney' months there was little indication of the seismic social changes that lay around the corner. She didn't worry unduly – Granny Parks had told her not to – and anyway the gender divide allocated world affairs to men. Edna was just grateful for the Fishers' kindness (and their beef).

ANN

In late 1939, Edna, Helena and Joyce were cushioned from the initial upheaval of war. Ann was less fortunate. Throughout the 1930s she had continued to surround herself with like-minded young people on the far left who believed that a Soviet pact was the only way to stop Hitler. Once Britain had agreed an alliance guaranteeing Poland in the event of German aggression in March '39, even reluctant ministers were forced to decisively address 'the Soviet problem'. Ann was filled with hope. High-profile backbenchers like Churchill and Lloyd George began hitting the right note. 'If we are going in

without the help of Russia, we are walking into a trap.' But Prime
Minister Chamberlain was never convinced. 'I must confess to the
most profound distrust of Russia,' he said in March, an opinion
shared by many Conservatives, who found Germany's rampant
nationalism less appalling than the prospect of a communist creep
across Europe.[4] The prolonged negotiations between the Soviets
and the British and French were doomed to failure from the outset.
That Britain came away empty-handed mid-August was bad enough,
but nothing could prepare Ann and her friends for the Nazi–Soviet
Pact signed on 23 August 1939. Overnight, the option of an ideological people's war against Hitler had been killed. The news was
an almighty body blow. 'It was awful. A real shock. We knew what
was coming next. We had seen news films of the bombing of Chinese
cities by the Japanese, and we had seen Picasso's *Guernica*.'

Ann's pain was compounded by personal grief. Out of the blue,
her father – the exciting, intelligent, liberal-minded publisher Frank
Sidgwick – died just two weeks before the outbreak of war. Annually,
he bathed in Oxford's River Cherwell, where he enjoyed punting with
his wife. 'Father did this every year, but on that occasion he picked
up some poison from rats in the water and got what seemed to be
jaundice and died. Mother adored him, she was completely stricken.'
So was Ann. Looking down the lens of her large family some eighty
years on, she cites Frank Sidgwick as her biggest influence. He was
ripped from his daughter just as the country crashed into a war she'd
anticipated and dreaded for years. In Ann's handwritten memoirs, a
few words say it all. 'My father had just died unexpectedly at the age
of sixty, causing much financial turmoil as well as grief and shock.'

Like dominoes, the pins propping up her life fell, one after the
other. Her father was dead, war broke out and then she lost her job.
'I was teaching art at Hayes Court but the school closed down – who
would send their children to a school in such a vulnerable area as that
between London and a main aerodrome?' Like her family home in
Kent, Hayes Court was next door to Biggin Hill. Ann was matter-
of-fact about her new unemployed state.

The immediate result of the war was a marked increase in unemployment. War production was not yet in place and domestic
commerce more or less ceased. Who would buy a house which
might be soon destroyed? Who would buy a car if there would
be no petrol?

Ann's logical mind tried to make sense of this bleak new world. She
battened down the hatches in Kent. The vicious winter of 1939–40
was the coldest since 1895. The Thames froze over, an ice storm
rattled at the windows and blacked-out conditions made staying in
compulsory. Ann endured chilblains and a heartbroken mother but,
ever practical, she also invested in the future. 'I bought a strong pair
of leather shoes and some large packets of chocolate and a bicycle,
which I painted in white and gold stripes to deter thieves.'[5]

Although Chamberlain set up a war cabinet and new ministries
immediately appeared, in 1939–40 the reality was a government
backsliding into a conflict they didn't want and hadn't prepared
for. That the 'war' seemed to be running satisfactorily all by itself
in the first few months (a deliberate tactic on the part of Germany,
who were busy dealing with Poland) compounded the problem.
This complacency fed into a reticence to formally engage women in
the war effort. Long considered a man's business, there were fears
that an abundance of women in uniform was not only unnecessary
but would demoralise and confuse male soldiers. A year earlier,
during the Munich crisis when 43,000 eager volunteers descended
on the women's auxiliary services, the military weren't ready for
them.[6] Unlike most of Britain's Cabinet, Ann had long been a firm
believer in the necessity of war (and by September 1939 she needed
a job), but she had no intention of joining the forthright women
keen for a formal role in the military. 'A lot of girls went gladly
into uniform in order to pick up a boyfriend. Oh, I hated the idea
of it. Ugh.'

Instead, Ann got a job in the newly established Ministry of Food. If censorious politicians were squeamish about putting women in uniform, it quickly dawned on them that men tied to desk jobs had to be relinquished for military duties. Girls stepped into a gap exacerbated by a wartime administration that demanded additional bureaucracy on a vast scale. Swallowed up by the Ministry of Food from April 1940, Ann was a tiny cog in a giant operation designed to control, distribute and account for Britain's imperilled food supplies, the rationing of which had begun four months earlier. 'Allocating two ounces of butter, three ounces of sugar and one egg a week to everyone in England needed a lot of organising and I became one of the organisers.' Bacon was Ann's speciality. 'The work was very dull, monotonous and uninspiring, with continuous checking of distributions of quantities of bacon; all paperwork, not a whiff of the actual stuff.'[7] Vera Lynn could sing her heart out, there was nothing glamorous about Ann's war.

From the spring of 1940, newsreels recounted almost daily disasters. Ann shudders. 'The bombing of Dutch cities, the advance of the German army into France, the cutting off of the British army in the north of France and its spectacular rescue from the beaches of Dunkirk by hundreds of little boats.' Paltry British resistance wilted in the face of Germany's blitzkrieg. That Ann had long predicted the scale of the horror did not alleviate her distress. Any relief she felt from the appointment of 'the realist' Winston Churchill to the post of prime minister in June 1940 was squashed by news her department had to leave London. Two days was the notice given for cosmopolitan Ann to up sticks to Colwyn Bay, a Victorian seaside resort in North Wales. Once there, she continued to count bacon (on paper). 'Only now one had the additional worry of those you had left behind in the Blitz. The Battle of Britain had started and was fought mainly over London and Kent, where my family were.' But she didn't regret her decision to steer clear of the uniformed services. 'At least I was in charge of my own life to a certain extent, and I didn't have to go and live in a community with a lot of horrible girls and take orders. And I could wear my own clothes!'

By Christmas 1940, Ann and a selection of her colleagues in Colwyn Bay had swapped their billets for a requisitioned hotel, which gave them the privilege of one chilly bedroom apiece and a communal sitting room they could just afford to heat. By now, Ann was certain of one thing only: 'We had no future. We could only make tentative plans for the next day or the next week. We lived completely hand to mouth.' Together they made the best of a bad fist. Displaced, scared relatives who left London at the height of the bombing arrived in North Wales for a break and were treated to a 'bird of some sort (not rationed, therefore scarce)' into which the Christmas centrepiece had been duly stuffed. 'I had found one large leek!'

As soon as the bombs fell less frequently over the capital, Ann longed to return. 'I was always looking for a better job, but you had to prove the work you'd found was more worthwhile than what you were doing.' With characteristic tenacity, Ann got her way. 'I went to London on a few days' leave and managed to find a job as a clerk – a temporary civil servant – in the newly set up War Damage Commission, an organisation that paid people for having their damaged houses mended.' Even better, her old art college friend Elizabeth had a job in the same department. They rented a flat together. But any enthusiasm was short-lived – the work was stifling.

Unbelievably horrible, monotonous form checking, always on depressing subjects; crowds of peculiar, nasty and resentful middle-aged colleagues, run by civil servants of small ability who had been brought back from their retirement and resented it, to do this very dull work. The offices were ill-ventilated, mostly blacked out because the windows were broken, the hours of work very long – and there was no end in sight.[8]

By the spring of 1941, it was beginning to dawn on Ann that almost all war work, at least the sort meted out to young women, was achingly dull.

Edna

Edna's life had always been monotonous – in stark contrast to Ann, she credits the war for any positive changes that subsequently occurred. For girls, perhaps that was the secret to having a 'good war' – the absence of anything better to compare it with. 'You see, my dear, everything was shaken up in the war. Everything.' Even her employers, the Fishers, discovered that late in life they had to learn to manage their own domestic mess and free up their companionable serving girl for essential war work. 'Mind you, in the beginning I always tried to pop in and cook them their evening meal.' Come 1941, for the first time in her life, Edna's day job no longer involved demeaning scrubbing, polishing, wiping and washing.

> I became a gardener and I love gardening, so that was nice. You see, my brother Charles, when he was twenty-one, he was called up and he worked in the kitchen gardens belonging to the local manor house. So Charles came home one day and he said, 'Mr Tidmarsh' – we called him Tiddy, he was the head gardener – he said, 'Tiddy wants to know whether you would like to go and work in the gardens when I leave.'

The memory is firmly lodged in Edna's mind: her handsome brother, spick and span, all boot polish and short back and sides, ready for fighting up front, bursting into the house and asking whether his big sis wanted a man-sized job – a job that Edna had never even dared dream of. 'Too right, I wanted it!' In the absence of a father, Edna's grandfather had taught her how to plant potatoes and trim onions when she was just seven years old. 'I loved gardening. I wore a big apron with pockets. I loved being outside and we had a lovely orchard in Denton.' With another local girl, Phyllis, Edna thrived in her new role. 'You see, Tiddy, he'd trained at Kew so we were learning off the best.' Out in the air, soil between her fingers, Edna planted, weeded, dug and hoed, and took home 32 shillings a week. 'Do you know, that's twice what I was getting when I worked in service, living in. Course I gave some of the money to my mum. I liked my 32 shillings because I liked my job!'

Wartime gardening not only provided a break from the drudgery of domestic service, it also formalised Edna's relationship with the land and its abundant capacity, and that's lasted for the rest of her life. 'You see out there, dear,' and she nods her grey head beyond the plastic windowsill, 'I've a raised flower bed, so that I can reach it sitting down.' Gardening was a pleasure. Edna smiles; the war brokered change and interrupted the monotony of village life. On Sundays, she'd return to the family cottage from evensong, make a pot of tea and, together with her sister and mother, listen to Vera Lynn's *Sincerely Yours* on a battery-powered radio.

It was pitch-dark outside and I'd think about our boys that Vera connected so well with. The risks they were taking. I remember hearing about the little ships coming from Dunkirk when I was still with the Fishers. Yes, and then suddenly there were far more men around. Some were billeted in the neighbouring farm, from the Second Battalion of the Staffordshire Regiment.

Having only ever met the same local lads with whom she had grown up, Edna's world suddenly felt full of new possibilities; she'd pedal past groups of soldiers in khaki and give them a wave, enjoying reciprocal wolf whistles. Even when the troops were posted to neighbouring Woolsthorpe, there was still a weekly dance to look forward to, and the novelty of a man in uniform to walk her home.

Mum would stand at the top of the path and shout, 'You coming in yet?' Ooh, it would be at least two in the morning.

No, they never got more than a kiss!

I couldn't dance very well, but I always helped with the refreshments.

I even met a boy from the empire; no it wasn't Canada, I can't remember what country he was from, but he was definitely from the empire.

With evidence of it all around, a formalised role in the war looked increasingly appealing, and by the end of 1941 it was also obligatory. That same year, Britain found itself alone and stretched, fighting in the Balkans, North Africa and the Atlantic; finally, the overwhelmingly male parliament conceded the war could not be won without the compulsory engagement of the fairer sex. In December 1941, despite considerable misgivings, for the first time in British history conscription for women was introduced. The use of firearms was prohibited (heaven forbid a girl might take a life that threatened her own), but from 1942 women were the official handmaidens of war. As a single 25-year-old without dependants, Edna anticipated the summons. 'Well, I knew I didn't want to work inside a munitions factory. My sister Kathleen did that and only lasted one day, she hurt her back. So I applied to go into the Women's Land Army.' It didn't occur to Edna to try for any of the three military services – her love of horticulture made farming the obvious next step. Together with her friend Phyllis, she walked to the neighbouring village and applied to sow and thresh, milk and gather, clip and harvest. Edna wanted to make her role in this dynamic, charged war official, and working in the Land Army had one additional perk. 'It came with a uniform you see, I wanted the uniform. I didn't want to have to use my own clothes.'

Breeches, a hat, stockings and sturdy shoes – for Edna, the idea of a free uniform was a boon and a badge, but for Ann it was quite the reverse. These two women came from opposite ends of the social hierarchy – the melting pot of war could not rub away poverty, expectation or experience. However, despite her enthusiasm, neither Edna (nor her friend Phyllis) were accepted into the Land Army – their work at home in Denton's kitchen garden was deemed too important. Edna didn't need a uniform after all – she was already growing more than enough produce for King and country. 'It was probably a good thing we didn't get in, as we might have got sent away somewhere. And I was still making meals for the Fishers and I worked with the Women's Institute. But the uniform would've been nice.'

JOYCE

'So far we haven't dealt at all (as far as I can remember) with my years of wartime work (very important in my view).' Today an honorary fellow at Newnham College, Cambridge, Joyce's letters enjoy a degree of infamy among colleagues and former students. Recently, she tartly let the university's Classics department know in writing what she thought of new shelving arrangements. She also attended a lecture on the Roman Empire's economy and fired off a letter containing 'feedback' to the lecturer in question. Therefore, my receipt of this note in her inimitable hand demanded attention. Beyond studying 'Greats' at Oxford, what exactly did Joyce do during the war? Despite protracted fire-watching duties, Somerville College's students achieved eight first-class degrees in 1941 and Joyce was among them. 'I was just within the group that was allowed to finish their degrees.' After four years of study, she graduated the same year that the government introduced female conscription. Like Ann, Joyce had clear ideas about what she did (and didn't) want to do.

'I could have put down the Land Army. I had in fact done the Land Army for six weeks over the summer and liked it, but I wouldn't have wanted to do that all the time.' Undergraduates were expected to take on war work in the summer vacation. Joyce, imbued with a long-held love of the countryside, had happily picked hops in Herefordshire. 'It was wonderful; the hops were for the soldiers' beer. I enjoyed it enormously. There were a lot of us from a whole series of different universities and colleges.' She describes a coming-of-age August, sleeping on pallets in a barn, outside and upright all day, picking zesty conical hops, enjoying casual chat with like-minded young people and eating hearty food cooked by Girl Guides. 'Yes, it is sunny when I think back. It was fun to meet people outside the Oxford circle.' But ever-assiduous about her life choices, Joyce was mindful not to blur one fun-filled summer with the tedium of long-term agricultural work. She was hoping for an altogether more substantial wartime challenge. In the autumn of 1941 Joyce, like Ann before her, began work as a temporary civil servant; but unlike

Ann, Joyce found her work at the Board of Trade 'very un-normal and fun'.

> We were supposed to assess how far essential goods other than food were being reasonably well distributed around the country. Pots, kettles, saucepans, teapots, mugs, kitchen utensils and that kind of thing. The aim was to make sure as far as you could that instead of suppliers sending their goods to the customer who had bought more things in peacetime, that they were fairly distributed.

With characteristic precision all these years on, Joyce describes a micro-example of Britain's wartime socialism. An effective system which (on the whole) enjoyed the goodwill of the worker and the acquiescence of business, this revolution in Britain's economic life operated by a means of 'direction and control' until the country was 'more fully socialist than anything achieved by the conscious planners of Soviet Russia'.[9] Joyce was an integral part of this levelling process.

> The country was divided up into areas and, in your area, you and your colleagues visited town after town. In my section, you visited all the ironmongers and you said what you were trying to do and they hoped you were going to make sure they got more supplies.

With her first-class brain, Joyce forensically examined the books of relevant shopkeepers. 'You discovered how many saucepans they'd had in the last six months and you added this up for all the iron-mongers in the town and then compared it with the population.' The numbers were crunched and the reports were duly sent off to the relevant production departments, which got in touch with the wholesalers and urged them to send more saucepans to one par-ticular town. Nothing, not even a saucepan, was left to chance in wartime Britain.

That Joyce sent me a letter flagging up the importance of her war work is indicative of its relevance in her life. The work suited her instinctive thoroughness – she was promoted from assistant to principal – and perhaps there was a smidgeon of filial pride that she'd followed in her father's footsteps. She concedes some aspects were repetitive but the experience proved greater than the sum of its parts. 'I got on well with the people in my department. I remember the boss, he was quite a well-known poet.' Joyce describes a man who thought 'he was a bit fancy'. She picks her words carefully.

> He had been brought up in a rather more luxurious world than I had and his life ran on lines that, er ... would have shocked my mother. In my mother's world if you had a girlfriend and you weren't married, that was terrible. Well he certainly had a girlfriend ...

Beyond the cloistered walls of an all girls' education, Joyce's ideas required some adjustment. She was working for a man who *lived in sin*.

If a maze of modern morality fanned out in front of her inquisitive mind, so too did treasured England. 'I learnt to drive during my war-time job, in one of their official vehicles. I drove all around England.' Out on the open road, Joyce had her first taste of real independence. 'The world has changed since those days but then there were very, very clear distinctions between different bits of the country. I found it exciting to see that.' Joyce's remit spanned the Midlands and the North (Scotland and Wales were assigned elsewhere); she revelled in the different dialects and frank attitudes and won't concede to J. B. Priestley's identification of three Englands: pastoral, industrial and modern.[9] 'I would put England at many more than three. You are bedevilling the meaning if you write of just three.'

Beyond the rich tapestry of accents and mindsets and landscape, Joyce was struck by an anti-London rhetoric. 'Ooh, yes! Some would say, "You are getting everything down there!" Of course things were being evenly distributed, but one couldn't say that.' Aware of the bubbling discontent in the 1930s, only during the war did Joyce come face to face with a pugnacious resistance to the south. She repeats slowly, 'They believed there was a pull to the South East.

They'd say, "You get all the things you want in London, why can't we have them?"' This doughty girl, who'd stumbled home on unlit trains and sat scared under a Morrison shelter in her parents' London dining room, was taken aback. 'The resentment was a revelation to me.' Bearing the brunt of the bombings, wartime London was no picnic, but Joyce was far too polite to say anything. And few bore a grudge long: 'If anything, they were nice to me because they thought I could get them more supplies. I could do that if they were bombed. Or if it became clear they seriously needed more kettles, yes, I could push for them . . . I had a wonderful time travelling around England.'

CHAPTER TEN

Love Bombs and War Boys

England! The perimeter of Joyce's war was England. But the conflict, especially the victory, will always be remembered as Britain's. In recent times, as our Celtic nations tug to redefine and strengthen their own ancient national identities, unionists fall back on a nostalgic idea of a precious *British* nation; they cherry-pick history to emphasise what the British Isles have achieved together and no reference point better exemplifies those collective efforts than our 'plucky' role in the Second World War. Unlike Britain's old empire and most recent wars, 1939–45 is devoid of squeamish overtones. Against the Nazi horror story, it surely was our 'finest hour'? Churchill predicted as much when the nation eyed the prospect of imminent German attack on 18 June 1940. He assured the country that men would hark back and say, 'This was their finest hour.' The quote from Britain's greatest wartime orator has spawned innumerable reiterations. But it is, as most quotes are, invariably taken out of context. Churchill was not referring to Britain alone; single-handed, our puny archipelago could not have crushed German might (nor did it). '*Their* finest hour', according to Churchill, belonged not just to Britain but to 'the British Empire and its Commonwealth'. Days earlier, in the wake of the Dunkirk retreat, the prime minister had made another sonorous promise to the nation. To fight 'on the beaches ... in the fields and in the streets'. But again, it was the empire that would save the day.

We shall never surrender, and even if, which I do not for a moment believe, this island ... were subjugated or starving, then our empire beyond the seas, armed and guarded by the British fleet, would carry on the struggle.

For the final time, the colonies and their Mother Country fought together. Britain was never alone in the Second World War.

PHYLLIS

The British viceroy announced India's entry into war without even consulting the leaders of the Indian National Congress. It was presented as a fait accompli – Britain needed India's army and that was that. Phyllis doesn't remember any portentous message or declaration. 'To begin with, we listened to the Empire Service and it had a great impact on the army, but not on me.' In fairness, she was tucked away doing a spot of private nursing for the mollycoddled son of an Indian raja (prince). The pay was good and the work minimal, but as a solitary white woman living in a cottage near the palace, Phyllis felt lonely and underwhelmed. 'All I did was take his temperature when I came on duty and a pill to sleep. He would then entertain his friends 'til midnight. There was really nothing wrong with him.' Bored, she soon swapped remote Indian opulence for a return to St George's Hospital in Bombay and there, all of a sudden, Phyllis found herself slap-bang in the centre of things. By 1940, India's biggest port daily facilitated an almighty exchange of manpower bound for a new theatre of war – the Middle East. Australian soldiers refuelling and the Indian army arriving, now more than ever Bombay was the throbbing epicentre of international soldiering. Young, uniformed men were everywhere. Even Phyllis, brought up in a cantonment and now living in another in Bombay's Colaba district, was struck by the charged atmosphere. 'I led a very social life, especially in the evenings!'

Her world remained a white one, only now the colonial social whirl swept her up like never before. Young women were at a premium: 'Troopships would arrive and officers had all the nice girls lined up, then we would entertain the soldiers on board and they came ashore.' With sufficiently pale skin, clean manners and an appropriate job, Phyllis was in demand. The tomboy had to ditch her pressed nurse's pinny and wriggle into compulsory evening dress. 'The top colonel's wife organised a group of us after being "vetted" as suitable to go to Green's Hotel in the evenings to meet and dance with the army or navy lads passing through.' Phyllis pauses, then almost laughs: 'No ladies were allowed out on their own without a male escort. There could be no private assignations. How times have changed!' Chaperones, gin and tonic, whirring fans, small talk and thin stockings. Phyllis waltzed through the beginning of her war.

In St George's Hospital, they'd cleared wards for the wounded but initially none came. She remembers empty beds and an air heavy with anticipation. In June 1940, the Italians had charged into the war, dreaming of a new Roman Empire; Britain responded by stopping the gaps in the Middle East and North Africa with Commonwealth troops – many from the Indian army, including Phyllis's brother. 'Terry joined the army at fourteen. He went off to Abyssinia during the war. Ach yes, he was in a different regiment from the Indian soldiers. No, I didn't worry, it wasn't in my nature.'[*1] Phyllis waited, a uniformed nurse guarding empty beds, thankful for the evenings, with their light relief.

The nursing duties she did have weren't taxing. There was one British merchant navy captain, called Hill – his tanker's arrival in Bombay provided the opportunity for a much-needed hernia operation. Phyllis delighted him with her firm, competent manner and, for her part, it was always nice to chat to someone British. Grasping at fleeting possibilities was standard wartime practice and Phyllis was soon introduced to one of Captain Hill's officers and asked to find appropriate girlfriends to show the crew a good time. It was Christmas after all. The boys in question weren't soldiers, they

---

* British soldiers in the Indian army were paid 75 rupees a month and Indians just 18 rupees. The pay discrepancy led to complaints, but most Indian soldiers fought loyally.

belonged to the merchant navy (more specifically British Petroleum, BP) and their vessel was *British Pride*. They spent the war dodging German destroyers and U-boats, delivering oil to Britain's global war machine.

Phyllis talks of rounding up a couple of nursing friends and her sister Molly. She anticipated yet another night out with anonymous men in uniform, but this time there was more freedom. The request had come directly to her from the captain – she could pick whom she liked, and she did. Even by her own standards the result was a 'busy social round', which began in a group. 'Then he asked me to marry him.' What? Who? 'It only took him a fortnight, then he asked me to marry him.' Having delivered her bombshell, Phyllis stands up from the lunch table and returns with a framed photograph. It's a his-and-hers picture – Jim and Phyllis, Mr and Mrs Ramsay, officer and wife. Jim's squinting slightly from beneath a peaked cap – he's shy behind his brass buttons and binoculars, but Phyllis isn't; flashing her cheeky teeth with a direct smile, she knows she's got her man and she's as pleased as punch. In the winter of 1940, under the baking Indian sun, it had taken her two weeks to meet, date, dance and formally commit to Scotsman Jim Ramsay, second mate on *British Pride*.

Phyllis isn't a great one for memorabilia, but her photos are abundant, with album after album of pictures carefully choreographed to show off the memories she wants to hold on to. That Christmas has its own page. *Bombay, 25 December 1940.* Phyllis is in a tea dress with her hair waved and clipped back, white heeled shoes dangle over the edge of the rock and Beach Candy's in the background. She has taken her beau down to the shoreline and together they're looking out across the Arabian Sea. Jim is in mufti, a checked tie and long legs in slacks. He can't believe his luck. There's a war on apparently, but it's Phyllis that's turned his life upside down. His hostess knew time was finite and she didn't waste a minute. 'As nurses, we were working from three till seven and then going out on the town. Jim found it hard going, not being used to that kind of life.' A conservative Presbyterian Scot who spent his life among men on deck was

suddenly exposed to the full gamut of colonial delights at the hands
of an unplaceable, wilful girl. There were numerous imperial hotels,
the ornate Mazagon Dock Club, cinema halls and the exclusive
Beach Candy swimming club.

> Oh, it was always ballroom dancing. We went to the big Mazagon
> Docks and if Jim wasn't first up, I was up dancing with someone
> else, so even though he didn't enjoy dancing he took me onto the
> floor straight away.
> He proposed to me at Beach Candy on the 28th of December
> and I accepted!
> I think we'd kissed, although I hadn't known him a fortnight,
> but I did get to the kissing stage by then. Oh no, not French kiss-
> ing, that came in after the war, it was just a peck. Morals were
> very high in our social class. Kissing was as far as you went and
> it was very polite kissing too.

Phyllis gambled her life on a man after a two-week acquaintance,
a peck on the cheek and couple of waltzes. 'Yes!' she would marry
Jim and 'Yes!' she would leave India and come to live in Scotland.
'Why not? I love an adventure.'

There was a war on, people made snap decisions all the time;
uncertainty intensifies feelings. There are numerous explanations for
Phyllis's whirlwind engagement, including Ann's belief that 'no one
thought about the future during the war'. Phyllis was simply living
in the moment. But she'd met (and danced) with dozens of men in
uniform – what made her so sure, so soon, that Jim Ramsay was Mr
Right? She laughs, it's hard to remember, the immediate attraction
blurred by forty years of marriage. 'Oh, I liked him well enough and
I thought it was good to have a boyfriend. Yes, I'd had two before.
There was an engineer of some kind and the other fella, he was in
the big textile factory, Tata's.' The latter had felt significant at the
time. 'I was very pally with him but it suddenly stopped. We were
very, very, very close.' The first man Phyllis felt strongly about left
her without explanation. The rejection stung, more so because it

felt unfair. 'It was the snobbery in India. Our family was below the army and the government. This man came out from Britain to run a big commercial firm, so if you like he was on the same social level as me.' But unlike Phyllis, he was unambiguously British.

> The young managers came out but they weren't allowed to marry a 'girl from there'. I was considered 'a girl from there' because I was born in India. You mustn't acquire a domiciled wife; yes, I think that is the reason he dropped back. The boss said something.

When Phyllis was a child, her parents had circumnavigated the snobbery that stifled interactions within Raj society, but as a young woman she had to negotiate them by herself and that could hurt. Colonial India was riddled with petty racial rules.

> We used to go to a big swimming pool but they wouldn't allow you in if you were dark-skinned. Two friends of ours, they were sisters, and their parents were Anglo-Indian but, you see, you can get a throwback so there was a very white one and the other one was dusky. They let the white one in but not the other sister.
>   Oh yes, I got in no problem.

No Hindus, no Muslims, no Jews and no (dark-skinned) Anglo-Indians – they were locked out of British Indian society and, by definition, the British were locked out of their India. This segregation explains why Phyllis shrugs when asked about the rise of Indian nationalism. The resistance movements and resentment were not part of her world. But the British Raj's snobbery very much was. Jim was the perfect antidote. Measured, good-looking and from a different world, he represented a clean break. And for him it was love at first sight. An unfussy Scot, miles from his Lothian home, he knew a good woman when he saw one – here was a girl who would travel well.

Phyllis's impulsive engagement, the passionate collision of two different worlds in human form, resonates with a common perception of wartime liaisons. Heady, euphoric and dangerous – Phyllis promised to cross enemy-infested seas to be with her man. Back in blitzed London, Graham Greene and his literary contemporaries found equal intensity in the bursting bombs that held one 'like a love charm'. From Homer's *Odyssey* onwards, fiction revels in the love-crossed wires of war, delivering a kaleidoscope of foreign romance, snatched intercourse, fleeting infidelity.[2] But the reality was more nuanced. Phyllis happened to be living and working in Bombay, a shipping port heaving with transient life. That it took her until December 1940 to find her beau is the surprising story. Elsewhere pickings were thinner.

Ann

The First World War mowed down the flower of a generation; nearly a million men never came home. In 1920s Britain, there was a surfeit of females and unhelpful headlines overstated the case – 'Problem of Surplus Women – Two Million Who Can Never Become Wives'.[3] Interwar women had grown accustomed to being the majority, with 'the spinster problem' a recurring lamentation. For the generation born during the Great War, maiden aunts and precious baby boys were the norm; nonetheless a second war so soon left a startling gap. By the end of 1939, 1.5 million young men had joined the British forces and thousands more were in the merchant navy. The war machine scattered them across the globe – very few were left in London office jobs. Joyce nods and, pushing her spectacles up her nose, stares across the table with a look that says, 'How could it have been otherwise?' Ann, also a wartime civil servant, is adamant, there were no (decent) men. Good friend Elizabeth 'was parted from her husband, our respective brothers were in the forces, as were all the young men, our pre-war friends'. She worked in an office full of 'nasty, resentful, middle-aged colleagues'. To emphasise this dearth, Ann recalls her flatmate Barbara's gallant efforts to find a suitor, a mission which occasionally involved bringing a man back to their apartment.

> He was mad. He was dressed in navy uniform but he always seemed to be on leave and he had a rolled-up scroll of paper and this was a plan for how to win the war in three weeks without a second front. While Barbara was in the bath, he would sit on the end of my bed and he would tell me why I ought to be grateful for Horatio Nelson. Quite literally mad!

Barbara's man-hunt did not tempt Ann. 'Anyway, one didn't feel like a social life.' She won't be budged by notions of a romantic London under siege.

> One was too numbed with exhaustion by the evening to do much, also money was scarce and in the winter it was perilous to go out in the pitch-dark.
>   Unlike many government offices, ours had no canteen which might have supplied a hot cheap meal a day, so we had to go out and see what we could buy in pubs or small restaurants. We were always hungry. One does not sleep well if hungry.[4]

Food has always mattered to Ann, but in wartime London edible pleasure came to a halt. The subject is sore even now. It leads to a second uncomfortable anecdote involving Barbara and another fellow. On this occasion, her suitor was David Kossoff (later a well-known religious broadcaster). For three weeks, she'd saved her meat ration; the result was a piece of beef no bigger than a pat of butter. 'If you served your guests meat, they knew that you had been depriving yourself.' Barbara duly roasted the beef one Sunday and served it with a feast of potatoes and vegetables. David wolfed it down and accepted more. Ann shakes her head. Not the done thing. A tiny piece of pink meat remained. Again it was offered to David. Again he accepted, this time accompanying his greed with an audacious disclaimer, 'Rather than see it go to waste, better to finish it up!' Beef 'go to waste' in the war! Ann is still indignant on her friend's behalf. David was ditched and the phrase 'rather than see it go to waste' became the girls' sardonic wartime catchphrase.

So, no man for Ann. She's sanguine about the matter, other things were happening. If, by the summer of 1944, the D-Day landings spelt the beginning of the end of the Nazi war machine, it didn't feel like that in London. Hitler had a secret weapon, one he promised his generals would turn the war. The first V1s, or flying bombs, fell across the capital in mid-June. Ann was having tea with an old lady from the War Damage Commission ('the only agreeable, interesting person I met there, even though she was older than my mother'). Very deaf, the old woman switched off her hearing aid when the throbbing engines became unbearably loud. 'We don't want to listen to that.' But Ann had no choice. It was decided that the bombs were too frequent for her to risk going home, so she spent the night curled up at the end of the woman's bed. They didn't sleep.

> At intervals in the night she jumped out of bed in her chiffon nightgown to put on another diamond ring, 'to have something to pay for treatment if they dig me out of the rubble alive'. At other times, she put the eiderdown over my face, 'You are young and pretty and I don't want your face cut to bits when the windows blow in!'[5]

They survived the night, as did Ann's complexion. A couple of months later Ann was lunching with a friend in a London pub, when again there was the ominous throb of a flying bomb and the hallmark pause before its worst. 'We got under the table and there was an enormous explosion. It had landed a few buildings away and broken glass poured down onto our lunch plates.' Another narrow escape for Ann. How she mourned the fleet-footed London she'd known in the 1930s. Hers was a long war.

PHYLLIS

Phyllis writes of 3 January 1941 (the day Jim Ramsay's ship left Bombay), 'life quietly went back to normal'. Except that wasn't quite true. She was biding her time, waiting for fiancé Jim to give word he'd arrived in Cape Town; only then was Phyllis to make arrangements for her voyage to Scotland. Within one month, she was on board *Orama*, a requisitioned cruise ship carrying army personnel and troops. 'The fare was my mother's wedding gift.' Never a woman for introspection, Phyllis turned her face seawards and looked west. She was leaving India, so be it. Had she not left every house she'd ever lived in? Every school she'd ever attended? And her father was long gone from the subcontinent. (Separated from Phyllis's mother in 1933, back in Burma he contracted malaria and returned to Britain three years later, where he bought a house in Hampshire.*) William Gargan had seen the writing on the wall. Over the next decade, British rule in India would be fatally undermined. What was there to stay for?

Phyllis is nonchalant. 'Yes, I suppose the journey was risky.' Her first stop, in Kenya's hot, dry Mombasa, brought little succour. 'We were waiting for a convoy to take us to Cape Town.' It didn't show up but the Italians did. 'There was an air raid but they missed the harbour. Hopeless shots!' Minus the protection of an armed fleet, Phyllis was given a tin hat and an 'emergency handbag' with money, a passport, chocolate and a miniature brandy. Questions about pre-nuptial anxiety feel unnecessary – the girl was living hand to mouth, day to day. Worry was futile, the best-made plans fell apart. After days of waiting in Cape Town and still minus a convoy, there was an outbreak of smallpox on board the ship. 'I remember some burials at sea and we were not permitted to return to port.' Fresh water was rationed to a pint a day. It was late April by the time *Orama* finally anchored in a chilly wind off the west coast of Scotland and Phyllis

---

* William Gargan never divorced Irene, but he married again in Britain and had one more son in 1940.

took a launch into Greenock Docks. 'Nope, none of it bothered me.' Phyllis had enjoyed the trip. 'I've always been a traveller! Itchy feet, that's me.'

~

In the 1930s, half a million people had returned 'home' to Britain from a fading empire; the imperial sun was beginning to set. Go back four generations in Phyllis's family tree, and there's evidence that in some ways she too was returning 'home'. 'My great-grandfather, George Drummond, came from Perth in Scotland. He was just fourteen when the East India Company put out a thing about enrolling people in their army. He joined up. There was nothing else in those days.' Young, obliging boys were needed for the Company's army which was, by the late eighteenth century, conquering the subcontinent by proxy in Britain's name. George took his chances and enlisted. It would be well over a hundred years before his direct descendant – Phyllis Gargan – returned to live in Scotland. Entering a new, cold, wartime reality among pale practical Scots, Phyllis stood out. 'They said I sounded a bit Welsh, a sort of up and down accent if you like.' Now overlaid with nearly eighty years of Scottish living, it's hard to imagine how she once spoke. Or how she looked, stepping onto the shore in dreich Greenock, sporting an unseasonal tan, dated elegant clothes and a spirited *joie de vivre*.

People must have noticed she was different? 'It didn't bother me! No, I didn't mind the cold, I'd been to school in the mountains.' But there were things that bothered Jim's family. While other women in this book occasionally succumb to dewy eyes, not Phyllis, she doesn't emote. However, adjustment to life in a tight-knit, Presbyterian, working-class family wasn't easy. That's apparent from the sparse entry in her memoir.

Jim met me at Glasgow and we proceeded to Edinburgh. I cannot say I was accepted with much warmth from his parents. I suppose they didn't know anything about me and my being a Catholic didn't go down well. Jim's father was very bigoted about Catholics. We just had to rub along, keeping our own space.[6]

From Protestant Scottish stock, Phyllis's mother Irene Drummond had married an Irish Catholic, William Gargan. Growing up, Phyllis had never paid much attention to church. 'Oh, we're lapsed Catholics, I suppose you would say.' It was a shock that Jim's family took issue with her religious identity. Jim hadn't anticipated a problem (he was too busy falling in love). But his father, a dour kirk-going Presbyterian originally from Northern Ireland, belonged to a generation within the Church of Scotland that was highly suspicious of Catholics. Mass immigration from Southern Ireland in the nineteenth century had fostered sectarian tensions. In 1923, the Church of Scotland produced an inflammatory report – *The Menace of the Irish Race to Our Scottish Nationality*. Catholics were accused of drunkenness, crime and wanton behaviour. By the 1940s, hostility was on the wane, but as the surprise recipient of a Catholic daughter-in-law (of Irish descent), Mr Ramsay's Christian resolve was sorely tested.

Phyllis is philosophical. 'When I was coming from India they didn't know whether I was black, brown or yellow and the fact that I was a Catholic ... ' She doesn't say more but miles from home, with no friends or family, it wasn't easy. Sharing a room with Jim's sixteen-year-old sister, Phyllis bided her time and (on the whole) kept quiet. The wedding plans were fractious. Shy Jim was out all day working for his Master's Ticket at Leith Nautical College. That left Phyllis to negotiate with her father-in-law over the wedding venue. 'You see, he wanted me to get married in his church. I said, "No, nothing doing."' Recalling the story, Phyllis's face is a picture of defiance, jaw set, eyes locked. For the first time in his life, Mr Ramsay had met his match.

A compromise was eventually found in Edinburgh's Morningside, at the simple Plaza Dance Hall. Apparently, a Church of Scotland minister made an appearance but Phyllis has chosen to forget. Her marriage was a happy one, but not the wedding. 'I didn't know anyone, just my mother-in-law and father-in-law, they were all Jim's relatives.' Phyllis quickly learnt that Mr Ramsay ruled the roost – the wedding venue was teetotal.

~

'Phyllis, do you mind if I come and interview you next week?'
'Okay.'
'Are you sure it's okay?
I've just told you it's okay!'

Phyllis is forthright and absolutely knows her own mind – both now and then. In 1941, she'd given up her old life and crossed several lethal seas to be with her Scottish man. Effort demanded return and Phyllis was very aware that Jim would soon go back to sea. Before they'd even got married, Phyllis spent hours padding Edinburgh's pavements in search of a house. 'I didn't think about India. No, I didn't miss home.' Pause. 'Not really. I wanted my own home.' As soon as they were married, Phyllis left the Ramsay's pebble-dash family terrace in Corstorphine and with husband Jim she rented a teeny-weeny maisonette on Roseburn Avenue near Edinburgh's Murrayfield. One of many interwar new homes, flanked by a wide street, a green park and a large ice rink, Roseburn Avenue represented proper, grown-up freedom.

The next three months fizzed with beginnings. Even at the peak of female mobilisation, the number of women in full-time war work (7,250,000) was fewer than the number who were full-time housewives. Briefly, in late 1941, Phyllis joined over 8 million British women in the home. 'I didn't have a clue!' Perhaps that's why it was all so exciting. Phyllis, accustomed to legions of Indian servants, could not cook (she'd hardly been in a kitchen) and now she was in charge of her own. A wedding gift from the butcher – a piece of roasting meat – presented a terrifying conundrum. As did the potatoes that accompanied it. The newlyweds tentatively prodded the hard vegetables with a fork, wondering if they would ever cook, and nearly ruined the meat by pulling it in and out of the oven. Eventually, a triumphant meal was served. Mother-in-law Mrs Ramsay was duly invited to sample the goods; tea and meat were happily consumed in the marital home.

Side by side in an album, there are two pictures taken from this time. Phyllis and Jim are photographed separately in their front room; the wallpaper has a mottled hue, the fireguard is black and on the mantelpiece beside the wooden clock, a framed wedding picture. Phyllis, with her prominent profile and dark features, stares directly at the camera, her hands folded in the lap of her floral dress. She looks touchingly young. In a different picture, but the same arm-chair, Jim sits with a cigarette in hand, his eye just failing to connect with the lens. He is blond and handsome but unmistakeably gauche. They are freshly married and in the pictures the shared anxiety is palpable. They are still discovering what it means to be man and wife.

> Sex was a different thing completely from what it is now. It wasn't a big thing. You grew up, you got engaged, you got married. That was it. Nobody knew what went on when the bedroom door closed. I mean, I never ever saw my mother and father have a cuddle or a kiss.

Phyllis was not unduly disturbed by the wedding night. 'No, it wasn't shocking, you are expecting that. You don't get married for nothing. You take what comes.' Just as she had with every other aspect of her life, Phyllis took marital sex in her stride. 'We rubbed along, I mean he knew more about it than me. We were brought up very, very narrow-minded. My mother never told us anything, never ever.'

In their first three married months together, the young couple set up home, learnt to cook meat and potatoes and consummated their union. By the time Jim returned to sea, Phyllis had mastered housewifery, started her own recipe book and fallen pregnant. That was the high point. Nine months later, a dead baby was the low point. 'It was born with spina bifida and things. I didn't want it to live, I'm not a martyr. They just let it slip away.' Phyllis won't indulge her emotions. She didn't then and she won't now. 'You had no option, Jim was at sea. You had to do it yourself, got to be tough, got to be tough.' It sounds like a mantra – perhaps it is. 'Out in India, you see so much death and destruction and everything.' She concedes to feeling some sadness but that too was an obstacle to be overcome.

> I suppose I was a bit tearful but you have to tole it. That's an old Scottish word. It means you've got to put up with it, because there is no option, and there was a war on, and I had nobody here that I knew. I had my in-laws, but they weren't fond of me.

Phyllis drew on a well-developed emotional armoury. In her short life, she had experienced loss – her baby brother, her father. She had experienced isolation – remote boarding schools, nursing assignments, 'foreign' Scotland. She had experienced fear. She was a survivor and that's exactly what Britain wanted. Her baby dead and her husband at sea, in 1942 Phyllis was summoned to Edinburgh's Labour Exchange.

> We were having a row! This seventeen-year-old was telling me that as a nurse I would be sent to a hospital. She couldn't say which hospital and she couldn't say if I would be allowed leave when my husband's ship came in.

Phyllis lost her temper. Even now it surprises her, but she's sure the sudden display of extraordinary self-assertion was a result of all she'd been through. Only twenty-five years old, but carried thousands of miles in the backwash of global war, Phyllis stood firmly on her own two feet. No pipsqueak was going to tell her what to do. She refused to accept a job that would prevent her from seeing Jim (whenever that might be.) 'I said, "You shouldn't be dealing with this. You're much younger than me!" Well, that got her back up! Then I said,

"Well, I'm not talking to you any more!"' There is a certain pleasure in imagining Phyllis venting her loss at some unimaginative, surly teenager behind a desk, her sing-song voice shouting in righteous, wifely indignation – surely a woman should be allowed to see her husband!

The upshot of the fiery exchange was a chat with the manager and a training placement to work in a munitions factory. Phyllis never nursed again. (And no, she didn't miss it.) 'I had wanted to go into the services but Jim wasn't keen. I think he worried about the other men and I didn't want to add to his burdens at sea.' Munitions work was notoriously tough, with long hours and low pay, but Phyllis made it her own. 'The main thing was I wasn't going to be pushed around.' Her first job in the Sciennes area of Edinburgh didn't last. In fact, it didn't begin. 'They were making six-inch guns, well the barrel was six inches, they were big things, ten-foot long.' She stretches out her arms. 'They took me to see where I would go and there was this woman by a big machine, knitting! And another one, she was reading!' Phyllis describes a five-minute cycle involving a ping, a pulley and lever, and much sitting before the next ping and pulley and lever. And more sitting. No way. That was not going to be Phyllis's war. 'I told them I couldn't knit for a start and I couldn't get in for six in the morning. The tram didn't run that early from Corstorphine.'

Phyllis's war would mean something! She would find her own job. And she did, but it took her outsider's pugnacity to go into Corstorphine's brass foundry (now the local PC World) and demand a job making ammunition. This coup she then presented to the Labour Exchange as a fait accompli.

They said to me, 'You can't do that sort of thing.' Well, I told them, I just had!

I enjoyed it at the brass foundry. There were a lot of young men and boys; they were called dummies cos they had speech impediments or were deaf. There were a lot of women as well, and some were bussed in from the countryside.

Being treated with a lack of respect bothered Phyllis, as did the prospect of mind-numbing boredom, but she was more than capable of extreme hard work. Twelve-hour days, on the lowest pay grade, working with sharp metal – screws for cartridges, casing for projectiles – she worked until her hands bled and then she worked some more. Phyllis's boss spotted her calibre.

Unable to cope with the often unforeseen consequences of suddenly employing women, he singled out this unusual former nurse and asked, 'Would you take on these women's welfare?' That meant more money, but as welfare officer diminutive Phyllis had been given a loaded task. The services (in particular the Wrens) fished girls from the classier end of society, leaving heavy-duty munitions factories with Hobson's choice. 'These girls were tough, the toughest. They had worked in rope factories and I couldn't stand their language for a starter, it was shocking.' Phyllis, from imperial India, could not tolerate cursing. But she had a job to do.

> It was obligatory to wear a cap and a hairnet. There'd been an accident with somebody catching their hair in a machine so the boss said we all had to wear them. Well, these women weren't having it, they had no respect for anyone and the foreman – Big Bob – he wasn't very assertive.

The order about headwear was issued and for two days the girls strode into the foundry swinging their loose locks and laughing at Bob. Phyllis winced. By day three, she'd taken matters into her own hands. 'Big Bob and I agreed we would have to catch them when they came in. I said, "They've had their warnings and they've paid no attention so that is it."' What came next has comedy edge – small, couthy Phyllis standing on an apple box in the half-open door, waiting, bold as brass, for the rebels.

> 'Get your hair tied up!'
> 'Who're you tae tell us whit tae dae?'

'Factory orders are you can't come in unless you have your hair in a snood.'

'Jings, yer na ginnae tell us whit tae dae!'

'Then go home! It's as simple as that.'

Laughing, the girls went home. The charade continued for three days. Big Bob started to waver, but Phyllis insisted he stood firm. 'I said to Bobby, it's all right they'll come in tomorrow with their hair up.' Sure enough, the next day the girls arrived in uncharacteristic silence, hair meekly tucked under snoods. Phyllis had won. 'I knew they would back down. You know when you deal with people like that, you have to stay calm. I knew they had no work anywhere else. They had to back down.'

From that day, Phyllis was the brass foundry's unofficial authority.

> The rough lot were from Leith. Half the time I couldn't understand them and they couldn't understand me. There were boys too, who would throw snowballs and shout and yell, but as soon as I walked past they would stop and wait until I passed and then start again.

Phyllis was untouchable. 'They wouldn't do anything to me. They didn't know what to make of me. I had something different. I was different. They didn't know what I was. I never bothered to tell them.'

Forged in a different world, from a different time, Phyllis fought her own war alone in Edinburgh and won. Her resilience paid off. When Jim was finally granted leave in 1943, she went to meet his ship. Nine months later, Jim Junior was born. For the rest of her long life, Phyllis never had another paid job.

Between the wars most women married in their mid-twenties (the average age rose slightly during the Depression). Phyllis recalls that at twenty-eight, girls were considered worryingly old if still single.

'At that age, they would send them out with the fishing fleet to India to see if they could find a man in the empire,' she giggles. However after an initial push down the aisle in 1940, marriage rates fell during the war, just when the women in this book reached plum marrying age. Ann didn't find a suitable man so there was no marriage, but she attended all five of her siblings' weddings.

Her elder sister Elizabeth married just before the conflict started, in 1938. The Sidgwicks were unenthusiastic about their daughter's low-class, communist fiancé and insisted that the ceremony took place in an Anglican church which was 'very, very much against' the couple's wishes. Ann shrugs – it worked out okay in the end; war made good a working man who was soon promoted to officer rank. Her eldest brother married a German girl – a period of heightened national suspicion ensured his foreign wife held back his wartime career and the relationship didn't last. 'He had at least two more wives.' A second brother married a local girl from Bath, where he was stationed in the navy. 'It was all very formal and in a church.' So much so that Ann recalls the efforts she took with her hat. 'I made it myself. I got some broad tape and made the crown and then I sewed this so that it was like a big ruff all the way around. I looked rather distinguished!' Rations prevented neither style nor celebration. 'My sister Mary married Bill Horsfall in a church in Putney with a Harrods cake that had false icing, inside which there was a cur-rant cake.' Bar one younger sister, Ann was the only Sidgwick still unmarried in 1945. 'No, I didn't feel wistful during these weddings, because it was their affair not mine.'

Joyce is equally matter-of-fact about her unmarried status. Overnight fire-watching in Westminster was an awful nuisance. 'I wanted to go home. When you were doing the kind of work I was doing it was refreshing to go home and read a Greek tragedy.' Men were not a priority. Contravening both her era and gender, for Joyce marriage was potentially more of a cul-de-sac than an opportunity. 'Educated girls went into jobs from which you were forced to resign if you got married. I thought, well marriage would be nice but if you had a career, you stuck to it. The civil service had a marriage bar until after the war.' In a society where dependence was still a core attribute of femininity, Joyce was ahead of her time. Along with thousands of others, her mother had given up her beloved teaching career when she got married. Joyce opined such a sacrifice would require a very special man. In wartime London, he failed to materialise.

HELENA

Unlike Ann and Joyce (and Edna, who never got further than the odd dance with a passing soldier), Welsh Helena met her future husband in 1938; Percy Jones came from a farming family in Elan Valley, but it was six long years before they eventually married. It wasn't war that got in the way, rather the needs of her own large family which forced Helena to delay her nuptials. And then delay them again. 'Well, I suppose Percy did really have the patience of an angel. My sister-in-law told me he worked himself up into quite a stew.' With a long, kind face and gangling limbs that saw him play badminton for Wales, Percy first met Helena when she came to teach in Elan Valley School. An unassuming man with bright blue eyes, it took Helena a little while to realise that she was falling in love. A nimble athlete in her own right, the two of them played badminton in the school hall. It was good clean fun and appropriately dark by the time they packed up.

> We were leaving one night and there was a great big long wall and I'd have walked straight into the wall, but Percy grabbed me. I suppose he put his arm around me really, and he said, 'Look out! Here, you nearly went into that wall!' 'Oh,' I said. 'Thank you, my glasses aren't so good!' That was the first time we ever made contact, if you know what I mean.

The incident gave them an excuse to take stock and chat for a minute or two. 'After that, he used to wait for me to go home. Then it got a bit more.' Helena remembers 'a very, very gentle man, a wonderful farmer and the best husband a woman could have'. Soon she was regularly spending time with Percy.

Sunday, 29 January 1939. Met Percy at night, had quite a pleasant evening.

Sunday, 5 February 1939. Percy at night. Had nice evening, I told him my ideals etc. Speculating as to result.

But it wasn't all plain sailing. Another girl had her eye on Percy at badminton, and Helena remained ambivalent.

Tuesday, 21 March 1939. Finished with Percy after [badminton]. Still friends but I feel blue about it. Couldn't sleep.

Wednesday, 22 March 1939. School. Still feel gloomy, music lesson at night then badminton. Missed Percy terribly.

They patched up their fledgling relationship but Helena's diary reveals competing struggles. Her mother, Ada, whose health had long been compromised, was seriously ill and spending bouts of time miles away in Cardiff Hospital. Back at the homestead near Brecon were Helena's younger siblings, with one brother not even school age. Term times were speckled with anxiety and frequent weekend trips to the hospital in Cardiff or remote Pengarn. By now, war, with its additional demands, ate further into her schedule. Back in Elan Valley, time alone with Percy was often snatched. 'The headmistress, Miss Thomas, didn't like living on her own so I had to sleep in her house. Well, yes, I was a woman in my twenties but that was that.' A controlling spinster, Miss Thomas insisted that Helena was back by 9pm. Any later and questions were asked. Percy and Helena couldn't dawdle when he escorted her on the four-minute walk from Stonehouse, where she ate dinner. Nor did Miss Thomas have much time for Helena's choice of man. 'She frowned at me when I was going with Percy. She said, "Oh, don't be so stupid, you can't marry

into that family. He's only a farmer and he's beneath you!"' That
her most talented teacher was dating a Jones rankled, but Helena
was unbowed.

The young couple spent more time together. Church, concerts,
conversation, card games, eisteddfods and walks; a war was on but
they were blessed. They kissed and cuddled and Percy, seven years
Helena's senior, tried for more. 'He didn't – well, I wouldn't say he
didn't put any pressure on me because he tried it out the same as
anybody else, if you know what I mean, but he knew me well enough.
He knew the line. We went around the edges but he knew ... ' The
romance was neither flash nor sexy, but it gradually dawned on
Helena that patient, kind Percy was the man for her. Yes, she would
marry him but, no, she couldn't say when exactly.

However, surely no one, least of all Percy, expected to wait
another four years.

Wednesday, 1 January 1941. I have once again decided to keep
a diary. Last year was satisfactory in some ways but losing dear
Mam caused a terrific wrench. Every time I go home, I feel a sense
of overwhelming loss. Impossible to buy a diary so am using an
ordinary notebook.

Ada Jones died slowly and painfully. It was a tumour on the brain
that shut down first her sight and then her body. For Helena, 1940
was blighted by the premature demise of her mother, the once stout,
fecund anchor of their family home. Mr Jones beseeched his eldest,
most reliable daughter to relinquish her new life in Elan Valley and
return to help him with the farm and younger children. Helena felt
compromised – despite her remarkable capacity for work, even she
couldn't be in two places at once. Social norms, especially those in
close-knit rural communities, demanded that she returned home.
Family responsibility remained a grey area fraught with confusion
and contradictions dating back to Elizabethan times. Official bodies
that might be expected to provide relief in difficult circumstances
exploited the ambiguous definition of family. Legalities aside, Helena

was still single and had always assumed the mantle of responsibility for the numerous children her parents brought into the world – regularly sending them a generous portion of her wages. Once her younger sister Glenys had married (mid-war, at eighteen), Helena felt obliged to forgo Elan Valley ('the best time of my life') and return to Pengarn. Percy would have to wait.

In the spring of 1942, she found a job in the local school, Trallong. She notes, '*I have 16 children – not too bright but very nice.*' Before and after school she committed herself to running the family homestead. Helena's diaries record endless lists of chores – papering walls, ironing hankies, patching trousers, walking three miles to school and three back, cleaning the grate, changing the beds, mothering her youngest brother, Eirvil. The day began before the sun and often she went to bed after 1am. Helena didn't sleep well, was obsessed by the weather and had the first sick day off in her working life. Time with Percy was relegated to high days and holidays. Helena concedes that by now his patience was wearing thin.

It was with great relief, then, that she received her father's surprise news in 1943.

> 'I don't know what you think about it, but I am considering getting married again. You don't mind, do you?'
> 'No, Dad! That's great because it means I can get married as well!'
> 'Oh no! You can't leave and get married yet, because Lottie doesn't know anything about little boys! I'll still need you here.'

Helena shakes her head. 'Now today I would've said, "Bugger you! I'm going!" I'd been home all these years but you see you didn't say things like that, did you? So I said, "Right, I'll stay for a year with that stepmother, yes, just a year.' She stops mid-story and looks up; perhaps she's thinking of Percy. 'Well, what was I to do?'

There was no love lost between Helena and her new stepmother, Lottie – whom she obligingly called Aunt.

She was a tidy woman, if you know what I mean. If you were
Welsh, you'd know what a tidy woman was. That's right, she was a
spinster who'd been brought up by her mother. She had no history
of being immoral, she didn't drink or anything. A tidy woman.

This puritanical stepmother, thickset with glasses, was jealous of
John Jones's eldest daughter. 'She wasn't nice to me. She'd use all
my rations.' There was also the matter of Helena's brown frock. 'I
thought that's funny, I was sure I hadn't left it in Elan Valley. Then
I saw she was wearing it beneath her overalls.' Helena challenged
Lottie in front of her father. A spat ensued, with John commanding
his new wife to go upstairs and remove the offending item.

Helena had had enough, and so had Percy. A wedding date was
finally set for August 1944. The successful D-Day landings lightened
the national mood and Percy's in particular – 'his brother Trevor was
a sailor and survived'. It was with a spring in her step that Helena
perused Brecon High Street for off-cuts and wedding trinkets.
Among her papers she still has the invoice from Brecon's Quarrell
and Sons – fruiterer and florists. One bridal and two bridesmaids'
bouquets, two Victorian posies and three gents' button holes came to
a modest £3.63. But for Helena the standout bargain was her shoes.

You couldn't buy shoes and frocks without coupons and there was
a shop in Brecon, Pullows on Ship Street, and I went there to have
a look and I couldn't believe it! They had a pair of high-heeled,
strapped silver shoes and there was a little brown mark on the
side and that meant I could have them without coupons. Oh, that
was wonderful! They were ideal for the wedding. I felt very lucky.

A squiggle of silver decadence sitting in the modest market town of
Brecon. What serendipity! Helena hid the brown smudge beneath
her blush pink wedding dress. 'I didn't wear a white dress. I suppose
I couldn't get one, and I thought that if I had a coloured frock and
it was very pale pink I could wear it again. And I did, you know. I
wore it a lot. And the bridesmaids too.'

The wedding photograph is a happy black and white snap of nonconformist 1940s Wales. Libanus Chapel frames the shot with handsome simplicity. From beyond its arched doorway and creamy walls, women in dark two-piece suits and sensible-brimmed hats flank the image. They outnumber the men more than three to one; uncles and brothers were missing. Helena was lucky and her smile, curling up between the family nose and chin, is unabashed. At last her day had come. Friends and family smile too. Good cheer is in abundance – beyond the jovial gathering there is something more profound at play. The end of the war within sniffing distance, surely rebirth was just around the corner?

Well, yes, it was a happy day. There were speeches back at Pengarn and it was very hard to get enough food for the reception, but I remember everybody gave me their butter and sugar rations and I did my own cooking. I had a nice cake somebody made.

Aged twenty-eight, Helena Jones finally became Mrs Percy Jones – it was a Welsh union that had already survived a test of time. The wait was over, the guests filtered away and Helena and Percy travelled forty miles to overnight at a friend's house in Cardiff. 'Oh heavens, yes, we had our own room.' She laughs, it was meant to be their night of discovery but years of anticipation took their toll. 'Do you know, I can't remember that I enjoyed my wedding night all that much.' Over seventy years on and Helena's tone is still one of surprise. She's reassured by the news most virgins don't enjoy their first foray with intercourse. 'Oh, that's all right then because I don't remember getting any joy out of the sex that night.' A perfectionist, it rankled that she was not immediately granted the opportunity to improve matters. August brought a commitment to an annual harvest camp to garner wartime produce. Helena was a regular participant – with Percy, she had agreed it would do as an alternative honeymoon. The sun shone, but single sex billets undermined any prospect of hanky-panky.

A week passed and the memory of that first night remained bothersome.

Then I can remember out on the hills, amongst all the heather, we were alone, Percy and I. We sat down or we lay down and that was the first time I sort of had what I call proper sex, I suppose, because it was more relaxed. There was all this heather around us, people couldn't see us, well, I hope they couldn't see us up on the hills! I always remember I thought, 'Ooh, that was nice!' I was looking forward then, you know . . .

Marital bliss in all its stunning simplicity beneath a wide Welsh sky had begun in earnest.

Ann Baer (née Sidgwick)

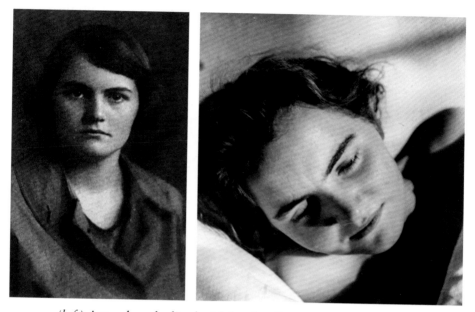

(*left*) Ann when she lived with her family in Kent aged thirteen.
(*right*) Ten years later as an art student in 1930s London.

Ann's engagement
photograph, taken in
Harrods, London, 1964.

Ann with her husband Bernhard and step children James and Susan in 1967, it was Susan's 21st birthday.

(*left*) Giving a speech at her 100th birthday party in the Ritz Hotel, London. Ann made her own dress and hat for the occasion. (*right*) Aged 103 at home in Richmond, 2017, looking up definitions of the word 'shag' in her dictionary.

Joyce Maire Reynolds

(*left*) Highams Park in the late 1920s, Joyce aged about ten, playing with her younger brother David in their back garden. (*right*) In sun specs at an Italian trattoria in 1950 sitting beside Margaret Ward-Perkins and her daughter Catherine. The man at the table is Anthony Blunt.

(*left*) Newnham's Senior Members in the College gardens, 1968. Joyce, aged forty-nine, is in the middle row, third from left. (*right*) Joyce's father, civil servant William Reynolds at his desk in Whitehall.

Somerville College matriculation photograph 1937. Joyce aged eighteen is in the second row, third from left.

Newnham College's Senior Common Room in 1953, Joyce is standing behind the sofa third from left.

Newnham College's Senior Common Room some thirty years later, on the occasion of Joyce's 'retirement'. She is mid-speech.

Joyce at home in Cambridge, just after the
EU referendum in 2016.

Enjoying some downtime in Tripoli's Copper Market, Libya, 2008.

Edna Cripps (née Johnson)

Edna, on the right, aged about nine in Denton village, with her younger sister Kathleen and brother Charles.

(*left*) Edna when she worked for Granny Parks in the 1930s. She croqueted the top herself. (*right*) Aged eighteen outside the family cottage – part of the Welby estate – in Lincolnshire's Denton.

(*left*) Ernest and Edna Cripps at home in Wroughton, Wiltshire, in the late 1960s. (*right*) Edna lace-making (competitively) in her seventies.

Aged 102 giving two 8-year-olds a 'huggle' – the author's daughter Mara Luca and her friend Charlotte Kitchen.

Helena Jones

(*left*) Helena aged 10, off to compete in a local eisteddfod. (*right*) Helena's parents, John and Ada Jones, who married in 1915.

(*left*) Avid reader, performer and trainee teacher – Helena aged eighteen. (*right*) She returned to the classroom once her daughters were school age. Helena is in the back row, first on the left, with her pupils in Trallong Primary School.

Helena's wedding photograph outside Libanus Chapel in August 1944.
The bride is wearing glasses and holds the biggest bunch of flowers, to her
immediate left is bridegroom Percy.

(*left*) Helena's two daughters, Elaine and Meryl, in the mid-1950s. (*right*) Going
to a friend's wedding in Brecon with husband Percy, 1970.

(*left*) Helena performing on stage at the 2016 Abergavenny National Eisteddfod just shy of her 100th birthday. (*right*) A year later at the Anglesey National Eisteddfod where she was honoured with the blue robes of the Gorsedd of the Bards for her numerous contributions to Welsh life.

August 2016, Helena revisiting Pengarn in the Brecon Beacons, the farm where she spent much of her young life.

Olive Mable Gordon (née Higgins)

Olive in front of the Guyana's Kaieteur Falls on a return trip to her homeland.

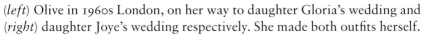

(*left*) Olive in 1960s London, on her way to daughter Gloria's wedding and (*right*) daughter Joye's wedding respectively. She made both outfits herself.

(*left*) Ray Gordon, Olive's second husband. (*right*) Aged thirty-seven in London, on the day of her wedding to Ray in early 1953.

(*left*) Wearing their Sunday best, Olive with her mother Rosalind in 1980s London. (*right*) Olive as a young woman in 1930s Guyana.

1945, Olive and her three children, Joye,
Gloria and Terence in Georgetown, Guyana.

Returning from the polling booth in Archway
North London on EU Referendum day, 23rd June
2016 with author Tessa Dunlop.

Phyllis Ramsay (née Gargan)

(*left*) William and Irene Gargan with their first four children in 1920s British India. Phyllis, their eldest child, is standing on the right. (*right*) The three oldest Gargan daughters, Phyllis, Barbara and Molly on their way to a fancy dress party in Rangoon, Burma.

(*left*) The Gargan family in London, 1933. It's Phyllis's sixteenth birthday, she is sitting on the right next to her mother, surrounded by three sisters and brother Terry. (*right*) Phyllis's engagement photograph, taken in 1941 aged twenty-three.

(*left*) Phyllis with her new sister-in-law Sadie on a holiday which doubled up as Phyllis's honeymoon in England's Framlingham, 1941. (*right*) 1942 was challenging year for Phyllis; her first baby died and Jim had returned to sea. Later that year she too would join the war effort.

Phyllis in Kensington Gardens in the summer of 1946 with her oldest son, Jim.

In 1951 on the top of Largo Law in Fife, Scotland with her two Jims – husband and son.

Phyllis's second son, Geoff, was born at the height of the baby boomer era. Here he is enjoying Christmas in 1950s consumer Britain.

(*left*) Phyllis continued to travel after Jim died, touring the Canadian Rockies on a bus in 1989. (*right*) Aged ninety-nine she visited Scotland's Western Isles, including Staffa.

CHAPTER ELEVEN

IT'S A LOVELY DAY TOMORROW

OLIVE

Olive is in her Sunday best – unsheathed from an ocelot fur coat trimmed in mink, she sits beneath a vivid purple hat with a dress to match – it's a Thursday in October 2016 and she's not in church. Olive is holding forth in a London primary school in the borough of Lambeth. It's Black History Month, an annual curriculum corrective to address the absence of a black narrative in the history Britain promotes as its own. Olive is their esteemed 101-year-old guest, and her audience is aged between four and eleven, among whom there is a large number of ethnic minority children. There is potential for a simple upbeat conversation on identity and migration, empire and modern Britain, but these south London pupils, like millions of others across the country, have been reared on the same set of textbooks. They stretch their hands skywards and persistently ask Olive about the Second World War – they understand she is old and surely must know about 'the war'.

'Miss, Miss! Was you scared in the war?'
'Did you know anyone who died in the war?'
'Was anything of yours hit by bombs from the Nazis?'
'Eh! All de questions about de war. I wasn't nothing to do with de war! I lived in Guyana, we didn't have a war in Guyana, just some soldiers, rations ... '

In fact, the whole of Britain's empire fought in the Second World War but British Guiana, a modest slice of land at the top of South America, remained a colonial backwater. In the global conflagration, it represented little more than a recruiting ground for fresh West Indian troops and a staging post for American GIs. 'Dat's right, I remember de American soldiers.' Back in Wales on 8 May 1944, Helena's diary notes '*lots of black men on the hill*'. Their novelty in white Britain made black soldiers worthy of a mention. The face of the Western world was about to change for ever, but neither Olive nor Helena could have known that.

Olive's right, for its six-year duration she was not directly affected by the war; Germans were not camped across the sea, nor were they bombing her home town. By the time war broke out, Olive was already married with two children and an established sewing career; although in her prime between 1939–45, the conflict neither punctuated nor framed her most memorable experiences. The fighting took place in other parts of the world; she prayed to God that the Mother Country would be victorious and continued to focus on her growing family. Her prayers were duly answered and Guyana's young soldiers returned with tales of wealth and wet weather and white girls and a whole new world – in comparison, their homeland felt small and poor. That the long-term convulsions stemming from this giant conflict – economic hardship, labour shortages and mass migration – would include thousands of West Indians (Olive among them) travelling back across the Atlantic was a point too subtle for a south London primary school.

'Has anyone got any questions for Olive that aren't to do with the war?'

ANN

In the spring of 1945, the last ghastly spasms of the German army ceased; Hitler shot himself in a bunker and the Russian army arrived in Berlin. By early May, the darkest horrors of the Second World War were not yet common knowledge and vicious fighting in the Pacific continued, but in London there was light. The wireless announced that the German forces in north-western Europe had surrendered to General Montgomery. It was the end of the war on the Continent. Churchill intoned: 'The evildoers ... are now prostrate before us ... We may allow ourselves a brief period of rejoicing, but let us not forget for a moment the toil and efforts that lie ahead ... Advance, Britannia! Long live the cause of freedom! God save the King!' Although the Allies' victory had been predicted for some time, Ann was stunned.

> All during the 1930s, when I was so aware that a world war was approaching, I never imagined that I would survive it ... but that I had survived it, that I suddenly found I had a future, was a very great shock.*[1]

The 8th of May was declared a public holiday. Ann's old employers, the Ministry of Food, guaranteed sufficient beer supplies in the capital and blue, red and white bunting was purchased coupon-free. Ticker tape, bonfires and blancmange prevailed. Never one for crowds, Ann relented to the idea of a party, but she didn't join the mobs in central London, where balcony appearances from Churchill and the King and Queen unleashed delirium. Together with her friend Elizabeth, a plan emerged to attend a gathering on the grassy expanse of Lincoln's Inn Fields, the capital's biggest, most sumptuous public square. Naturally, Ann's victory parade involved an artistic detour.

'We first walked across Hampstead Heath to the Lawn Road Flats; this was architectural survival from the 1930s, which one knew about.' Not entirely coincidentally (he'd lived around the corner before bombs started dropping), sculptor Henry Moore and his wife were there and an unofficial victory party was already under way. During the war, Moore had produced drawings that

---

* During the Second World War, 130,000 civilian adults were killed or seriously wounded; 48 per cent (63,000) were women.

established his international reputation – pictures of Londoners in the Underground awaiting the siren during the Blitz, but long before that he'd made an impression on Ann. There was a memorable first encounter in 1930 with one of his sculptures – a reclining woman – in an Oxford don's home; then by the mid-1930s, Moore was the stand-out teacher at Chelsea School of Art (so much so that Ann wrote him and his passion for football into the script of her end-of-term play) and in 1939, as a teacher's assistant at Chelsea's design department, she occasionally walked to lunch in the same group, remembering 'his admiring the shapes of the many pigeons which were pecking about on the pavement'.[2] And now here he was, enjoying a knees-up in a stylish corner of north London – there could have been no more fitting totem for the richer times that lay ahead. Ann was glad she'd braved the crowds.

The girls, buoyed up by the atmosphere, walked on to Lincoln's Inn Fields:

> There we danced all night. We had a fun, rather exhausting time. Then, no matter how late, we had to walk home and as there were crowds of people all over the place and with nobody going home, people would go and pee in front gardens. Did I hitch up my skirts? Yes, I think so! Haha!

The tedium of Ann's war had finally been broken with a night to remember (for ever).

PHYLLIS, JOYCE

Victory in Europe Day was a snapshot in time preserved up and down the country in blurred Brownie box photographs, patriotic keepsakes and exuberant diary entries. Street parties and good cheer were nationwide but London – majestic nerve centre of war, primary target of Nazi fury and capital of Britain and the empire beyond – was the place to be. Edinburgh-based Phyllis, with her 'itchy feet', needed no persuading. She'd criss-crossed Britain whenever her Jim's ship came into port. 'Sometimes it was London, sometimes Falmouth in Cornwall and sometimes Newcastle.' And by 1945, there was additional cargo.

> I took baby Jimmy with me. The trains were so busy, you know, you just had to sit and feed him. It was full of soldiers and everything else. My younger sister Pat, by then she'd come over from India, she used to say, 'Phyl, you can't do that here!' I said, 'Ach, I just get on with it!'

Phyllis had no time for faux modesty. 'You're got to feed the baby! I was done, there were so many people going to London for the victory parade. Yes, that's where I was heading too.' By 1945, Phyllis's mother, Irene, was in the capital staying with her sister. Briefly Phyllis had a base in London and (crucially) she also had a babysitter. 'We went early in the morning, I fed the baby at about five o'clock and dumped him with Mother, she got very angry!' There's glee in Phyllis's voice. Footloose at last, the two sisters made their way to Green Park. 'We went and stood behind the troops all lining the avenue.' There the two girls spotted a young soldier, boyish with pink cheeks and neatly pressed khaki. 'He told us he'd been there since six o'clock and by this time it was eight o'clock, he was just a young fella so we gave him some chocolate. He put his hand out behind his back and we'd pop a piece into his palm.' More giggles. 'Yes, we felt very hopeful!' The rest of the day unspooled amidst the hordes; down the Mall they went on the big walk towards Buckingham Palace, where the King and his doughty Queen made eight appearances. The 50,000-strong crowd roared. Churchill gave an impromptu speech. The pugnacious war leader leaned over the balcony and shouted, 'This is your victory!' 'No!' came the reply, 'It is yours!'

And the victory was Churchill's, on that day at least. But within a fortnight, he'd disbanded his coalition government and a general election was called for 5 July. The future belonged elsewhere, Phyllis shakes her head. 'Jim and I voted Conservative back then.' Steeped in the history of empire, Phyllis was a natural Churchill supporter – he believed in a bigger British picture and fought for it. With war ongoing in the Far East and much of Phyllis's emotional capital invested outside Scotland, the Conservative Party was an obvious choice. But in 1945, closer to home, people were exhausted, housewives included. Britain had mobilised women during the Second World War like no other belligerent; 8 million were directly involved with the war effort and even those who stayed in the home did their bit as air-raid wardens, fundraisers and food producers, bearing the brunt of shortages, queues, rations and bombs. Above all else, women wanted austerity to end and some even dared hope things could be different. Led by the quiet, unassuming Clement Attlee, Churchill's competent coalition deputy since 1940, the Labour Party took on the world's greatest war hero with an optimistic manifesto: *Let Us Face the Future*. Audacious in its ambition for change, the party promised to tackle the multiple problems of peace with a Dunkirk spirit and a socialist agenda.

This bold mission had particular appeal among the young. Four years after Joyce's departure from Somerville College, Oxford, Margaret Roberts, one of the college's then chemistry undergraduates dismissively conceded that, yes, in 1945 voting Labour was indeed very *fashionable*. However, *she* was entering politics with an eye on the long term. Young Thatcher, with her china-doll smile and pale curls, proved as good as her word; one contemporary recalled that even then she 'was not "playing" at politics. She meant to get into Parliament and there was more chance of being noticed in the Conservative Club just because some of the members were a bit stodgy.'[3] Joyce sighs at the mention of Margaret Thatcher. 'Well, I never approved of her thinking, but she was a clever woman.' Unlike her fellow Somervillian, Joyce wasn't a political animal, but memories of July 1945 still impinge over seventy years later. 'It was maddening! At the time, I was still working for the civil service but I was based in Bristol at this stage, and because I had not been able to register there I didn't have an ordinary vote, only a university one.' A liberal by instinct, Joyce concedes that in 1945 she would've voted

Labour. In a wartime job, where she was tasked with distributing 'fair shares for all' and had been exposed to pockets of extreme poverty, this decision wasn't surprising. Many others reached the same conclusion. However, the nation (Joyce included) anticipated Churchill's return to office. His personal ratings had rarely fallen below 80 per cent in four years of war and he'd just pulled off a staggering feat of arms. On election day, even the *Manchester Guardian* cautioned:

> The chances (or danger) of a clear Labour majority able to carry out a Socialist programme are slender, almost remote. But if the votes are cast wisely there is at least a chance of a Liberal–Labour majority, the most fruitful kind of Coalition in these times.[4]

In order to give absent servicemen and -women the opportunity to vote, the result was delayed by three weeks, but Joyce was privy to an early (and accurate) prediction. 'One of the members of our Bristol office had been a paid employee of the local Conservative Party. On election day, she and I were driving to a job on the south coast.' The solemn girls puttered through the green glades of Dorset and Somerset – traditional Conservative heartlands. The weather was mute and wet and Joyce's travelling companion would keep peering out of the window at passing towns and villages, staring at the polling stations and their attendant straggle of voters.

> After a bit, she turned to me and said, 'The Conservatives are going to lose.' And you know, she was quite right. She had been able to tell from the look of the voters and from the numbers queuing in towns where the Conservatives expected, and had always had, a high turnout. She could tell, I couldn't. It was extremely interesting.

The Tories didn't just lose, they were thumped by a Labour Party which claimed a staggering 393 seats and a majority of 183. The nation was stunned – overnight, their outstanding wartime leader had been plunged into a political abyss. Churchill's military success had left him both redundant and exposed. Rubbing the tips of her fingers together, Joyce remembers her own reaction to the prime minister's humiliating defeat.

> I would not have voted Conservative but I couldn't help feeling a bit double-edged. After all, Churchill had been rather important in our winning the war. There was a certain conflict. Before the war, he was not a politician I would have related to but one felt that his leadership had been something really important.

Joyce sums up what many people felt beneath the bravado of shiny new socialism – a small worm of discomfort. But successful, well-timed endings are often elusive. Alive for nearly one hundred years, Joyce knows that. 'It's a pity Churchill came back as a dinosaur leader in 1951, a dignified withdrawal at the end of the war would've been altogether better.'

Jobs and healthcare and homes – expectations ran high in the wake of Labour's victory. Despite seismic social change as the welfare state was ushered in, disappointment was inevitable. Britain had bankrolled its war on America's dollar; in 1945, the country owed £4 billion – money was scarce. Rations persisted, with cabbage the watery staple, three quarters of a million people were missing and damaged houses gaped in streets like snapped teeth; nurseries and canteens were closed and men came home broken, lost or not at all. The country was down at heel and national morale, no longer buoyed by an external enemy, soon bumped along the bottom. But, if not optimistic, large swathes of the population could at least hope for better times, and irksome inconveniences were dumped. Joyce never romanticised the war – in many respects she was glad to be shot of it. Working in London she'd disliked making her way home after dark and all-night fire-watching put her off trousers for life. Ever since, she's stubbornly refused to wear them despite the practical demands of negotiating ancient sites as a classicist (and later her nonagenarian exercise classes). 'No, I don't ever wear trousers! They remind me of the war.' One knows better than to argue.

However, Joyce had relished her wartime work at the Board of Trade. With thousands of other women she'd been employed as a temporary civil servant and by 1945 looked forward to converting that status into a permanent position. But it didn't happen – 'I failed the examination.' Joyce is a top scholar. Failed the civil service examination? It's hard to believe. Seventy years on, perusing her record in Newnham College archive, the news that Honorary Fellow Joyce Reynolds failed the civil service exam is met with disbelief. The archivist shakes her head and the college historian wonders aloud if Joyce's poor exam result was a by-product of returning soldiers in need of work. Back in her solid Edwardian home, Joyce acknowledges that failure hit hard; telltale pink points on her cheeks suggest she can still feel the pain of disappointment. 'It was depressing.' Joyce was not used to failing exams.

Characteristically, she's not content to explain away her failure with the surmise that men had indeed been demobbed and needed jobs. But overnight a sea change in attitudes towards employing women had taken place, with the Attlee government encouraging girls to leave the workplace, embrace domesticity and 'the vital work' of 'ensuring the adequate continuance of the British race'.[5] Under the Control of Employment Act 1945, demobilised women at the Labour Exchanges were secondary to men.[6] Although the civil service had a long tradition of employing women in administrative roles, after the war, the selection and promotion of men was a priority. To combat this flagrant sexism, Joyce needed to perform exceptionally in the examination.

'In fact, it was an intelligence test and I had never done an intelligence test.' Surrounded by hundreds of eager young men whose public schooling and army careers often included performing well in timed tests ('they trained a particular muscle in the brain'), Joyce tackled an examination which demanded speed above all else.

'I took my time over each question, but in fact you have to go like the clappers. Nobody told me this, so I was giving each answer due consideration and I ran out of time.' Failure was the result.

'I suppose I could have taken the exam again but I decided not to.' Ambitious, thwarted Joyce was a pioneer struggling in a man's world well before the righteous indignation of second wave feminism – protest and anger were the tools of the next generation. In contrast, she swallowed her disappointment and decided on a change of direction, promptly writing to her old Oxford college, Somerville. A classical scholarship to the British School at Rome was soon forthcoming. Destined for Italy, an escapee from male-dominated post-war Britain, aged twenty-seven Joyce was finally on track for the fulsome career she deserved.

CHAPTER TWELVE

PLACES, LOVED ONES

PHYLLIS

The famous Beveridge Report of 1942, upon which the Labour
Party had boldly staked much of their 1945 manifesto, was a comprehensive plan for universal social security. Much of its idealism
was drawn from the pre-war period, with the abolition of abject
poverty and mass unemployment primary targets for a new post-war
progressive society. Significantly, the agenda was focused on redistri-
bution not equality; it clearly stated: 'The attitude of the housewife
to gainful employment outside the home is not and should not be
the same as the single woman.'[1] In the new National Health Service
Act, married women were categorised as their husbands' dependants
and elsewhere wives were told explicitly they had no right to deprive
a man of a job. Within a year of VE Day, the number of working
women had fallen by 2 million, with the *Daily Mail* reminding readers, 'there is not room for them all, especially women'.[2] Phyllis nods.
'We didn't want to go to work. What for? We wanted our freedom
to do what we wanted.' Cooped up in a munitions factory, ripping
her hands on metal shards and ticking off unruly girls, it was little
wonder that Phyllis cherished her subsequent free time. She wasn't
alone. During the war, most women's work was low grade and
poorly paid; when it came to an end, few felt inclined to storm the
professional barricades. Unlike 1918 with its Enfranchisement Act,

1945 provided no great feminist watershed. 'What for?' Phyllis had her man (before he went back to sea) and her son Jimmy, '9lb 9oz, he was a beautiful placid baby'. Any changes to ease a woman's lot were modest. Eleanor Rathbone's years of persistent campaigning bore fruit and a Family Allowance of 5 shillings or 25 pence was paid directly to mothers from 1946, but even then Phyllis had to wait.* The first child was exempt. 'We had no money but it didn't matter. I lived on four pounds a week.'

Her photographs testify to happy times: in one picture, baby Jimmy is grinning in a wicker basket and in another he's plump and curious from the lofty heights of his perambulator. Phyllis's generous grin and bright eyes are always cheerful, and there are plenty of young friends grouped together smiling. Just one thing was missing – her little family didn't have a home. The owners of their rented cottage had returned at the end of the war and, like thousands of other couples, Phyllis had to make do at the in-laws. In early 1945, a Coalition White Paper had estimated that in order for every family to have a place of their own, 750,000 new houses would have to be built. To stop the gap, prefabs mushroomed across the country and waiting lists soared. Jim returned to his BP tanker and for once Phyllis and her Presbyterian father-in-law agreed – their domestic set-up couldn't continue.

Mr Ramsay was a Woodbine cigarette salesman; as he touted his wares, he asked about accomodation for his daughter-in-law and baby, and one day returned home with the news Phyllis had been longing for. Yes, a lady customer knew of a house – well, it wasn't exactly a house but it would do. And, no, it wasn't in Edinburgh but beggars couldn't be choosers. Phyllis had soon moved into two rooms at the top of a house on the Temple in Lower Largo, an ancient east coast fishing village in Fife. Big skies, cold winds and an expanse of sea appealed to her outdoor spirit, but the dour locals required a bit more work. 'I was always considered an incomer.'

---

* In fact, the Family Allowance paid to women in 1946 was less than the amount Rathbone had initially pushed for in 1917.

Phyllis sniffs. She had handled India and Edinburgh – she could handle a Scottish village. At least she had broken away from her in-laws, 'that's the thing, in the war a lot of girls worked for the first time and that emancipated them in some way. We were used to being independent.' There was one room to live and cook in – 'I had a tiny gas stove and fed an electric meter with a shilling.' In the second room she slept with her son, and together they climbed the stairs to a communal bathroom.

> Jim only came home once a year, unless his ship was getting a refit. BP would send a cheque from London and I would cash it in at the local bank. I had an allowance but there was always a bit extra in the kitty. The main thing was you couldn't be in debt. When Jim came back, he'd shoot rabbits for the pot because there was still a meat shortage.

Alone in an insular community, Phyllis found a friend – Jean, married to a Pole who'd been stationed in Largo during the war. The outsiders understood each other and their toddlers were the same age. Phyllis relied on this friendship, it was the difference between isolation and kinship. Jean's little girl Marysia was soon her goddaughter and the two children 'practically lived together'. In every photograph, they are on the beach crabbing, shell-seeking, running and laughing, dawn 'til dusk. Thousands of miles from India, there is a touching similarity between her son's outlandish beach life and pictures of Phyllis's own childhood swimming in the Hooghly river and larking in the jungle. There are differences too. No large family surrounded Phyllis, her husband was absent most of the time and Jimmy remained an only child until he was ten. She concedes, 'That was deliberate.' The post-war era of new houses, free healthcare and 'happy' marriages ushered in record birth rates – families of three and four children presided over by a full-time mother were the norm by the 1950s. But bringing up a child alone in austerity Britain without any Indian servants was hard, lonely work and Phyllis relished her own time.

I looked forward to going to meet Jim's ship when it came into the docks. I didn't wear make-up but I made sure I looked nice. Baby Jimmy would sleep in a drawer in the cabin. Perhaps the time apart kept our marriage fresh, we sent each other photos. Yes, that's Jim, he's posing on deck there.

Still only in her mid-twenties, Phyllis had an eye on the future; once Jimmy was at school, she could accompany her handsome husband, already promoted to first mate, at sea. Unlike many women of her generation, Phyllis knew there was a whole world out there.

HELENA

Just as Phyllis's had, Helena's married life began in cramped conditions with her parents-in-law. Their farmhouse was not an ideal location to capitalise on the sexual awakening she'd enjoyed in the heather. A neat contemporary of Barbara Pym's *Excellent Women*, Helena frames the problem more tactfully. 'It wasn't much fun living with the in-laws. They were good to me, but you'd think, "I'll go and have a bath now and you'd get up and discover somebody else would be in it."' Percy had three brothers – two of whom drifted back from war – and a sister. Helena was itching to escape, the couple had already done years of waiting. 'Eventually we moved into this little farm, the Perthy.' She claps her hands together and smiles. 'It was lovely being there. I had done a lot of living with other people, finally we had our own place.'

It was a small farm near Elan Valley – too small really to make money, just a handful of livestock and a few fields rented from the big Lloyds estate. The homestead was simple – 'more of an old dairy really'. In an era when electricity and running water were almost commonplace, Helena still had to do without. 'You'd carry paraffin for your lamps and I went to fetch the water in a pail. No, I didn't have a bathroom. I'd never been somewhere with a bathroom.' But in the Perthy, Helena only saw what she had. 'I remember making it my own, I loved that. There was a little shelf above the door and I put my books up there. And in the living room there was a big fireplace on the floor and on each side of it I stacked the logs to dry.' She experienced a subtle yet exhilarating emotional shift when carrying out her daily chores. Briefly, the humdrum became spectacular; for the first time in her life she was working towards her own home for her own husband and that resonated somewhere deep in her core.

Helena continued teaching once married. 'Was I paid less than male teachers? I didn't know that.'* The couple couldn't live off forty acres of farmland and Helena missed the classroom (it's hard to imagine her sitting, waiting at home, warming Percy's slippers). She did all the housework and taught during the day. 'Yes, I suppose I did work harder than Percy in a way.' She pauses, perhaps this thought has only just occurred to her – after all, women were meant to run the home, post-war society was very clear about that. By the 1950s, 22 per cent of married women had paid employment but few worked full time. Helena was an exception. 'No, we didn't have children straight away.' With seven younger siblings, she knew as well as anyone what a baby involved. She had every intention of fulfilling Beveridge's vision that 'in the next thirty years, housewives as mothers have vital work to do in ensuring the adequate continuance of the British race', but only when she was ready. Bent up now in an old frame, peeking out from beneath round glasses, is a woman who was well before her time. In the 1950s, nascent movements to support women in work hadn't reached Elan Valley – Helena didn't need them. She did things her own way.

Contraception? Oh, it was up to Percy to be careful. What do you call it when a man . . .? Yes, that's right. I can remember Trevor, his brother, coming home and giving him French letters once. He was a sailor, we wouldn't have known where to get them in Rhayader. So he said, 'Let's try these.'

---

* A Royal Commission in 1946 tentatively concluded that women in teaching and certain areas of the civil service might benefit from equal pay, but teachers had to wait until 1961 for wage parity to become a reality.

She looks up and smiles, it matters much less now, nothing's so important that it can't be shared. Their first daughter, Elaine, eventually arrived in 1949.

> When I was pregnant, I was very sick. I can't tell you, I used to cycle to school three miles each day and can't tell you how sick I felt. I did wonder very often how I would get through the day, but then it only lasted three or four months. I managed.

Helena's timing was impeccable. The National Health Service was optimistically launched in 1948, and its main beneficiaries were women and children. Shored up by a midwife on a motorbike, Helena's mother had given birth to all eight of her babies at home, but in 1949 Helena had her first child in hospital and enjoyed a luxurious ten-day confinement. 'I had high blood pressure or something. My husband took me to the hospital in Builth, but then he sugared off. Labour! Oh God it was terrible, I will never forget it. No, I didn't have any pain relief.' Nonetheless, Helena was looked after, for free, by the state. Percy came by that same evening with a bunch of wild flowers: 'Oh, he thought she was very cute.' Rosehip syrup, clean sheets and a tightly swaddled pink baby. Helena was grinning from ear to ear.

After years of caring for her siblings, Helena could do the motherhood gig standing on her head; she knew about babies – how to nurture them, love them, feed them, wash them. Unfazed, she went back to work when Elaine was six months old. How old? 'Yes, that's right, six months, I used to take her to my parents-in-law's home. They had a housekeeper and she'd look after all their children. I paid her 10 shillings a week to look after mine.' Nearly seventy years ago, Helena coolly disregarded post-war thinking on childcare. The fecund wife at home with a string of bonny babies and a plentiful larder had become the symbolic repository for British optimism; after the horrors and dislocation of war, public thinkers and politicians invested heavily in this soothing domestic idyll. In 1951, child psychologist John Bowlby's pioneering attachment theory argued that 'the infant and young child should experience a warm, intimate and continuous relationship with his mother (or permanent mother substitute) in which both find satisfaction and enjoyment' and his work was hugely influential.[3] In the 1950s, a 'good' mother did not leave a child under three with anyone else, except perhaps granny for a few days' holiday. Helena laughs. In rural Wales, newfangled thinking on child-rearing wasn't top of her reading list but a thrusting maternal culture was pervasive. 'Well, yes, sometimes people did comment. But you know, if anything had gone wrong, Percy, her father, was there working on the farm.' But it wasn't about the father, in the 1950s, it was all about the mother. Helena knows that. 'Well, I suppose my sister-in-law was a bit envious. I mean, yes, it could absolutely be boring staying at home all day with a baby, especially when you've been doing other things.' Out it pops, what millions of women have thought down the ages but feared to say – that looking after a baby full time is boring. It would be more than ten years before Betty Friedan's book, *The Feminine Mystique*, exploded the myth of the happy housewife on the other side of the Atlantic in 1963. Helena (once again) was a pioneer.

'I'd pick up the baby by half past three and be home by four o'clock. I'd spend the rest of the day with her and all the holidays, you see.' In 1950, Helena was fine-tuning the juggling act that would consume many working women in the late twentieth century and she did it without electricity, running water, fast food, a car or a hands-on husband.

Well, I suppose I have always had a lot of energy, that's true. And I felt so lucky. I wouldn't have wanted to have been a man if I'd had the choice because to be a mother, I think, is very special, isn't it? I remember bringing my first baby home from hospital and putting it in the corner and I was nearly in tears, I felt so emotional. It was lovely.

Motherhood was the most important thing in Helena's life, but it wasn't the only thing.

EDNA

Edna is waving a long, bony arm, the visit has been a success – two eight-year-old girls adorned her with daisy chains, skipped on the grass and festooned her with *huggles*. 'They, my dear, are a cross between hugs and cuddles.' Edna loves a huggle, especially from children. She still teaches lace-making at the local Wroughton Primary School on Tuesday afternoons and her most prestigious one hundredth birthday card was the handmade one she received from her young charges. She is a deeply maternal woman, her tiny bungalow heaves with the dolls and knitted teddies she's made or accrued at local rummage sales, and on the walls there are contemporary photographs of children – great-nephews and nieces and the progeny of a family she once looked after. With characteristic equanimity, Edna accepted she wasn't going to have any children of her own and made the best of it. 'If you weren't married, dear, you didn't have them and at that time I wasn't married.' She looks faintly surprised at the suggestion not having a husband or children might have been a challenge in the baby-boomer 1950s. 'You couldn't worry about what you didn't have in life. Nowadays, people expect to have what they want, not what they need.' But there is some pain there. She pauses. 'In a way, well, I suppose they were my family – up there.' Edna nods at a bright picture of smiling faces across several generations. 'Their dad, Mr Huggins, was the headmaster of The King's School in Grantham and I went to work for them in 1947.' The post–war era was credited with the demise of domestic service – a shortage of labour finally gave women more choice and few opted for live-in skivvying. But change didn't come overnight, and in 1947 32-year-old Edna, relinquished from Denton's kitchen gardens, needed a job.

What I didn't realise when I accepted it was that the couple were in the process of splitting up. The children were being sent off to boarding school so my first job was sewing in name tapes. The youngest, Pat, was only seven and a half and her dad said to me afterwards, 'Edna, if only I had known that you were coming to live with us I would never have sent her away to school.'

The couple's separation was acrimonious. The wife and children moved to Sutton on Sea, and Edna went with them. She enjoyed the flat Lincolnshire coast and occasionally took the bus to Skegness for a day trip. Her employers' marriage continued to deteriorate; Edna recalls a turbulent visit from the husband ('he was a lovely man, very distinguished, but he had a roving eye'). The attempted reconciliation ended in a milk jug sailing across the room. 'The place was a terrible mess, she did have a temper.' Edna mopped the milk and Mrs Huggins's tears and said no more about it. It was important she stayed above the fray for the children, especially for the children.

I did everything, I did the cleaning and the cooking, but best of all I liked looking after the kids. The job was better, I suppose, because of the children. The mother was ... well ... they had more to do with me than they did with her. They had their meals with me ... everything.

Edna was the family's mainstay. In the shadows of their decaying marriage she picked up the pieces, prepared comforting food and made everyone feel that bit better. She needed no manual to tell her how to embrace and love children – it was instinctive. Like so many spinsters, her own independence was subjugated to the service of someone else's family. In contrast to footloose bachelors, society rarely identified single women with freedom and choice. Mr and Mrs Huggins were given plenty of space to be dysfunctional, secure in the knowledge that Edna was theirs. Edna, meanwhile, took comfort in her relationship with the children. Testimony to its strength, they still travel to visit her in Wroughton seventy years on, there are birthday cards, Christmas cards, photographs and memories. When Edna left the family after five years' service, 'they all came to the station to see me off, including the mother of one of their friends who came down from London'.

The heyday of the nuclear family reached its peak in the 1950s, when the average marrying age for women fell to twenty-two and family sizes grew. This conservative society had little sympathy for maiden aunts – it would be another four decades before John Major sentimentally alluded to spinsters cycling to evensong across a village green.* According to Barbara Cartland, in the 1950s, 'however much women believe in emancipation, however much they talk of careers and professions, they all of them know that unless they can capture a husband and have a child they have failed – as a woman'.[4] It's ironic that during this same period, a crucial prop for the family unit was the single woman. Invisible and unrecognised, Edna and thousands like her provided the heft of childcare for numerous middle-class families across the country. Elsewhere, spinster aunts, single friends and siblings stepped in to fill the breach.

JOYCE

Joyce's stimulating career as a classical historian unfurled in the 1950s, when she was granted a research award at the British School at Rome. She worked under the acclaimed John Ward-Perkins, who identified her emerging talent as an epigraphist. But his children remember her differently. Bryan, now a professor of history himself, then a lively schoolboy, recalls a very kind woman, 'with an excellent sense of humour. When I think of Joyce, I always think of her careful, soft-spoken voice and the twinkle in her eye.' His mother's contemporary, Joyce, aged thirty and still single, invested time and effort in the Ward-Perkins children. Bryan remains enraptured with these memories. 'It is a pleasure to be able to think about Joyce.' She was nicknamed Ajax by the family,

> for reasons that have no logical explanation and involved a donkey
> in a Donald Duck cartoon book – wholly inappropriate if one

---

* Prime Minister John Major made this reference in his 'Back to Basics' address at the 1993 Conservative Party Conference.

thinks of Homer's hero that went tragically mad; but we liked it and so did Joyce ... There were a few regulars at the British School who played an honorary aunt/uncle role in our lives – Joyce was one of these.

Back in England, Joyce was a sterling aunt to her brother's three boys. Bernard, diagnosed with schizophrenia as a young man, has lived with Joyce for the last twenty years; in her dotage their relationship has become one of touching co-dependency. He answers the door in a faded jacket and fusses in the kitchen for Joyce and her many guests. Bernard remembers a young aunt – compelling and pretty with lively eyes, a woman who enchanted him with Greek myths and encouraged the three brothers to play conkers in the university gardens. It is perhaps not surprising that when life became difficult for Bernard, he turned to Aunt Joyce for succour and support and has been with her ever since.

Edna

'I wasn't single all my life.' Edna laughs, and points to a black-and-white picture of a middle-aged couple sitting in homely comfort. 'That's my Ern, I met him when I was on holiday visiting my brother. Charles had stayed on in Wroughton after the war and married a local girl. Ern was her brother.' She clasps her palms together. 'I knew he was the one for me.' A shy woman in her early thirties, Edna was drawn to this modest, working-class man. At first just friends, they'd walk in the grounds of Wroughton's church, where Ernest was the clerk of works and Edna would enjoy the hollyhocks he grew in his parents' garden.

It was a very innocent courtship to begin with. We used to write each other letters. I remember in Sutton on Sea, Pat saying, 'Look, you've got a letter from Ern!' We just clicked. It was the feeling that both of us had. I really looked forward to going to Wroughton; I dreamt about it.

The story is infused with a hesitant correctness. 'It wasn't physical, not then. We wanted to get married but his parents intervened and he stayed back. We were kissing, shall we put it that way, when they intervened.'

Ernest and Edna first met in 1946, but it was another sixteen years before they got married. The stumbling block was Ernest's mother and father.

> You see, he was the eldest living brother, cos Ted died in his late twenties of heart problems. It meant Ern took over as head of the family, his parents were his responsibility and they didn't want him to get married cos he looked after them. It was normal back then.

Sweet, meek Edna was no match for Mrs Cripps (nor did she try to be). A working-class woman, born in the previous century, she'd spent her whole life scrimping and hiding money from a husband who preferred to drink it in the Fox & Hounds. In old age, Mrs Cripps's son Ernest was both her carer and her keeper. 'Without Ern's money, she didn't have enough to live on. She'd not have let him go.'

Incomer Edna recalls a galleon of a woman, squeezed into an uncomfortable corset. 'She'd sit like this with her arms folded after we'd had something to eat. She'd sit like that for ages and tell me all about people who lived in Wroughton, all about the secrets that were hidden in their cupboards.' Edna visited once or twice a year, travelling from Denton or Sutton on Sea, waiting patiently as she had done throughout most of her adult life, nodding, agreeing, appeasing, helping. 'I did think it would be nice to have children, but there was nothing I could do.' Filial duty trumped all; only at death did mother and son part.

> I was on holiday in Wroughton and Ern's mum had just passed on. It meant that Ern had all the cooking to do for his dad and I just looked at him and I said, 'Well, it's your own fault now, you know. There's no need for it!'

Ern and Edna were married six weeks later at eight-thirty in the morning in St John the Baptist and St Helen Church, October 1962. 'I was forty-seven by then. Three times, they called out, "Does anyone object to this marriage?" No one said a word. I loved being Mrs Cripps, I felt very, very lucky.'

CHAPTER THIRTEEN

A BRAVE NEW WORLD

In 1953, coronation year, the writer and social reformer Violet Markham mused on BBC Radio that 'with the end of the war ... a great weariness has fallen on our nation'. She longed to 'have done with unworthy murmurs that we, with our great past and great traditions are now a second-class power'.[1] Thrown into the suffocating embrace of emerging giant America, Great Britain's overseas ambitions were much diminished post-war. Huffing, the delegate and economist John Maynard Keynes complained that the States was trying to 'pick out the eyes of the British Empire'.[2] With their elbow jogged in Palestine and a rushed departure from the Indian subcontinent in 1947, imperial Britain didn't get off to an auspicious start. This retreat gave way to a folksy enthusiasm for the restyling of a 'new' empire. The foreign secretary, Ernest Bevin, cooked up numerous fanciful projects to manage (and profit from) the remaining colonies.

At home, a more benign 'people's empire' was an easy sell. Colonial support in the war had been impossible to miss. 'I remember the first black man I ever met was at the RAF in Spittlegate; he was a West Indian gentleman in a uniform. And you know, he had a white wife! She was lodging with my aunt and uncle. They could bring over their wives sometimes.' Edna was fascinated – here was living proof of colonial love for the Mother Country (the big pull-down pink map in Denton elementary school wasn't forgotten). Post-war Britain capitalised on this feel-good factor. The airwaves brimmed with rich anecdotes of far-flung places, there was colourful pageantry at the Victory Parade in '45, the royal wedding in '47 and the coronation in '53, as well as a rash of films which reinforced the idea of an adventuresome togetherness. Beyond the country's bruised interior existed a fuzzy, nostalgic idea of Britishness in the remnants of higgledy-piggledy empire. A sunny escape route was sorely tempting – between 1945 and 1948, 100,000 working people left Britain, the vast majority of whom headed for Commonwealth countries. Phyllis's family were a case in point, her sisters and mother stayed in the shabby Mother Country for just a couple of years before they opted for the space and warmth of Australia.

OLIVE

Olive sighs in the half-light of her London living room. People certainly weren't arriving in British Guiana. It was the white dominions – Canada, Australia, New Zealand – that attracted newcomers, not West Indian and African backwaters. Investment in innumerable swanky-sounding colonial schemes rang hollow. There was no money to back up Britain's enthusiasm; in Guyana, trade unions proliferated, unemployment soared and a new political class banged the drum of independence. Olive's eldest daughter, Joye, fills in the blanks from the kitchen, explaining how as a teenager she became a member of the People's Progressive Party and attended political rallies – she namedrops meeting Cheddi Jagan and Forbes Burnham* and briefly breaks into song.

> Oh comrades here,
> Oh comrades there,
> Oh comrades everywhere!
> Our cause is just and win we must,
> We'll grind oppression in the dust . . .

---

* Jagan later became president of independent Guyana, and Burnham was the country's first prime minister and later president.

Olive is silent, she wasn't interested. She belonged to the older generation; choosing to believe the Mother Country was sacrosanct and thousands of miles away over there, while she got on with her life in the here and now, sewing and mothering. Yes, it was gratifying to 'hear dem stories of de war and dat. De soldiers come back and tell us all about de tings over der'. How in Britain the wages were high and the high life was heady and 'so on'. But to begin with they were just stories, that was all. Olive had no intention of leaving Guyana.

~

'Let me ask you someting. You know, I been thinking all de time and I was wrong about de serpent.' With no warning, Olive suddenly joins our conversation. Abruptly changing its direction, we leapfrog from post-war Guyana to God. She's riffing through the Old Testament – Adam, Eve, the Garden of Eden, the serpent forced on his undignified belly, the woman forced to bear children in pain, Cain killing Abel and God's harsh judgement. She delivers a torrent of knowledge and supposition, then she stops and wheels around, accusatory, 'You don't believe in God like me! Well, you know why not? Because you are not bruised, so you don't have to say, "Oh God help me!" Your water runnin' straight, but de day your head get under water . . . you get no help from nobody, from nobody!'

Olive's parable has reached crescendo, then we are back where we began, somewhere after the war, but one big piece in her Guyana puzzle is missing. Her husband is dead (the first one, the father of her children, the meat and sanitary inspector that she doesn't want to talk about). He has died – it might have been 1949 or maybe 1948; anyway he died suddenly, a heart attack. Olive's ordered world – sewing for the good and great, running a household, a proud mother – overnight, it was imperilled. 'You know in my country, you don't get no help, my faith stronger when my husband died. I had to look for succour. I only come to Britain cos my husband die.' Buttressed into one small sentence, there it is, Olive's personal story squeezed into a mammoth slice of demographic history. One of the first black women to reverse the colonial equation and leave Guyana, Olive did so because she felt she had no other option.

She leans forward, eyeing me, cupping her hands.

I held der future right here. I came over here because my children's future was at stake. Because if I couldn't keep dem ... imagine you having children and going to a private school and suddenly you've got to take dem out. I am a proud woman, yes. I stooped to conquer.

In Olive was the distilled Victorian conviction that education conquered all. Her children's attendance at the British Guiana Education Trust was non-negotiable. 'In Guyana, you didn't get free education, well you could, but you couldn't get certified. My children had to go to a private school.' For Olive, it was inconceivable that she might have to relinquish their education on the basis she could not afford it. Shame, failure, denigration were out of the question. Olive shakes her head, no matter that her husband was dead, his salary gone, the perks of a public post lost.

A noble-looking woman, wide set eyes, dainty nose, immaculate style, back then in her mid-thirties Olive still cut it. But no man wanted a woman with incumbent children, not permanently anyway. 'From de time Sigismund died to de time I came here, dat was de worst time of my life. I got tossed about.' A young widow, exposed and outside marriage, men came at Olive – sergeant majors and schoolteachers, government employees. 'Dey is rude to me, dey want me, you pucker for a goodnight kiss and de next ting dey go to touch your breast!' She rarely let them in her home and quickly rejected her only lover out of wedlock (the sergeant major). He wouldn't marry her, and Olive was no one's mistress. 'Like dat I can't go to communion, I can't go to church.' It was all so undignified and in Guyana dignity mattered, and so did money. 'Der were three children at de school, I was runnin' out of money. I started selling tings.' Olive was trapped in a vicious cycle, her piecemeal dressmaking was insufficient and a knight in shining armour had not materialised. She needed a plan.

I never thought of leaving for Britain but I had a broder-in-law over der. He wrote tellin' me about England and how apparently it was paved with gold and how de girls going on de train in de morning, and you get eight pounds a week and how I can sew.

A kernel of hope, a solution even and a story of trans-Atlantic familial support that soon would become commonplace right across the West Indies. That talisman of later immigration, *Windrush* – a refitted Nazi troopship full of young Jamaican men – had in 1948 taken the British government by surprise. But its arrival was in the spirit of the times. In keeping with a renewed enthusiasm for empire, that same year the Nationality Act expansively gave all imperial subjects the right of free entry into Britain. There were some mutterings of Borneo headhunters replacing Lords on their red seats but on the whole the sentiment was clear. 'We are proud that we impose no colour bar restriction.'[3] Britain's empire was proof, was it not, of the nation's cosmopolitan core? The bill was a grand gesture, but little thought was given to its implications. No one really believed the empire would start coming home (and government ministers fervently hoped it wouldn't).

Back in Guyana, Olive calculated that eight British pounds a week would just cover her children's school fees. Her mind made up, she moved quickly. 'I had a sister so I ask her to keep my children. To get my fare, I sold my tings in de house. What I could get. I had expensive furniture and I sold everyting!' Olive won't concede to emotion: she had made her decision, the Mother Country would save her, God told her this was the right path and anyway the move was only temporary, just until her children had finished school. 'I did it for my children, I tell you.' For the first time in their lives, they wouldn't be together, Olive and the almost teenage offspring she would leave behind – Joye, Terence and Gloria. It hurt, yes, okay, it did, she nods – 'Dey were my children.'

The night before she left, her steel trunk packed and locked, the pedal-powered sewing machine labelled as cargo, she walked along Georgetown's quayside, taking in the air, the smell of salt and fish, and warm evening light. Her sister's husband, Joseph, the esteemed governor of Georgetown jail, walked with her.

'Olive, what about de children?'
'What you mean?'
'Dey are not babies. What about der food?'

Olive didn't need telling twice. She returned home, collected her Raleigh bike and wheeled it through the streets. 'I paid hundred dollars for dat bike and I pawning it for seventeen. I gave my broder-in-law de ticket.' Ask Olive today about leaving her homeland and she always returns to the demeaning act of trading in her beloved Raleigh. Olive had gambled everything on a good salary in the Mother Country; that night, on her knees in supplication, she begged God to make sure London's streets really were paved with gold.

'I had to go down to de bottom of de earth and come up to educate my children. You hear me! My children was my life and my all.'

JOYCE

The 1950s have been derided as the housewife's decade; the lull before the feminist storm. Wives expected more companionable relationships with their husbands, while retaining their status as domestic handmaidens, there to facilitate spousal success with the execution of a full and functioning family life. Meanwhile single women, an unprotected minority, had to fend for themselves. During her twenty-one-day crossing, first to Surinam, then on to England's Southampton, Olive planned to do exactly that. She had her sewing skills and the Mother Country had money. Olive was an economic migrant (and a British citizen). Joyce migrated for work too. Bumped out of the civil service by incoming blokes, she had few qualms about moving to Rome. In fact, it was 'frightfully exciting. A mixture of pleasure, pride, excitement and, to an extent, fear.' Anticipation mounted during three long days by train, travelling back to the one-time heart of the Roman Empire, secure in the knowledge that she had secured a research studentship in the prestigious British School at Rome. Beneath her characteristic quietude, Joyce was sufficiently self-assured to enjoy the hustle of post-war Italy. 'In 1946, they had a roughly free election and I went mid-election season. There was very little paper about, so in order to advertise their political views people scrawled on walls – I've never seen so much graffiti.' Charming people, an excited ferment, good coffee, colour, noise and fruit. After Britain's drab fare, Joyce marvelled at the glistening strawberries and oranges, the pastas and cheeses, and the overflowing cheap market stalls. Europe was recovering and the Italians led the way.*

It was amidst this contemporary hubbub that Joyce established her academic career. 'I was hoping to produce a piece of work that would persuade a university in England to appoint me to a lecture-ship.' Initially granted a two-year research scholarship, she began examining a strand of imperial Rome's administrative system. Joyce's capacity for work is legendary, so when, after weeks and months of effort, an academic in France delivered 'a good thesis' on the same subject, 'it felt like a disaster, like a bomb going off'. Joyce, a single woman dedicated to her research and dependent on the dint of her own hard work, was devastated. She need not have been. What came next – the Director of the British School, John Ward-Perkins identifying Joyce as the person to help in the exacting task of reading and translating ancient inscriptions – was to propel her into a fresh academic landscape. John Ward-Perkins had been stationed in North Africa during the war; there, he'd collected, and begun commenting on inscriptions from the stonework of Tripolitania's ancient sites. But other commitments had delayed the preparation for an anticipated volume. He said to Joyce:

---

* Italy's First Republic was established in 1948 and during the twenty years between 1950 and 1970, per capita income in Italy grew more rapidly than in any other European country.

'You know something about inscriptions, here are my papers, why don't you have a go at these?' And I found I liked doing this enormously. I began with some sort of puzzle. Faced with lots of photographs, on each my job was to read the letters and, if one was damaged, to work out what it was and what groups of letters made words and what the groups of words can have meant. And when I'd done my best with reading the ancient text, I had a his-torical document.

Seventy years later, Joyce will say that epigraphy – the study of inscriptions, and clarification and classification of their meanings – is so embedded as to almost feel part of her DNA, that she can call up walls of ancient words in her mind's eye and toy with them. She sits among her papers and jottings still; her work is never done, the relationship is symbiotic, each looks after the other. She was to become Britain's leading epigraphist, a highly specialised career that not only nurtured her mind but took her into new worlds.

'It's much better to read the inscriptions off the stones. So John said, "You'll come with us on our next archaeological expedition to Tripolitania and start looking at the texts themselves."' And she did. 'Flying was terribly exciting; we went from Naples to Tripoli. I can remember sitting in the aeroplane and feeling very frightened. It was a small one and it shook. We landed in a field in a desert.' She laughs – Tripoli airport is now a gleaming, strip-lit slice of modern Libya, and 'the enchanting country road through desert and patches of vivid green' a major thoroughfare. Back then, Joyce entered a region in transition – shops and taverns still run by Italians, and a fledgling independent country temporarily overseen by the British military. There were whitewashed hotels and a dinky single-track railway that took her to Sabratha, one of the three ancient cities of the one-time Roman province. It was here, under African skies, against the azure of the Mediterranean, amidst startling marble ruins, basilicas, baths and amphitheatres, that she began hunting for the inscriptions of an ancient people.

Joyce loved working on site, and thrived in challenging foreign communities. A lecturer in Newcastle upon Tyne* from 1949 and at Cambridge University from 1951, her research took her across the ancient world – Turkey, Syria, Romania, Libya. Often, she was the only woman with an uncovered head. She spoke to men as their equal and they respected her. 'I knew things they didn't, I would tell them things, show them things, I would educate them in a way.'

Today Joyce commands respect (awe, even) – she is a very old, highly esteemed Cambridge academic. It feels almost impudent to enquire after her emotional fulfilment during this period of professional epiphany in the late 1940s. Pictures of her firmly ensconced in the bosom of the Ward-Perkins family – enjoying hot Italian vistas with a hanky on her head, eating a picnic in the surrounds of monumental marble columns or smiling beneath sun specs in a trattoria opposite Anthony Blunt – suggest a happy time. But Joyce was only in her early thirties, and like other young women she had feelings and desires. 'Yes, I would have liked to have got married, as I was very much in love with somebody when I was a graduate student in Rome.' She recalls a man not much older than her, but admits, 'I would have quite a lot of trouble to dredge up his name,' nor is she able to describe his appearance, beyond 'moderately short and British'. For Joyce, his physique was not where the attraction lay.

> He was very, very intelligent and that was hugely appealing. He was very knowledgeable. His research subject was interesting and he talked interestingly about it. And he was, as I recall, very intelligent about everything else, current news and so forth.

Joyce looked forward to seeing him at conferences, in common rooms and the dining hall at the British School at Rome. Her feelings towards him grew, they were deep and sincere – 'love' is how she describes them. It was therefore a bitter blow when she discovered he 'was much in love with somebody else. One of those silly situations.'

---

* As King's College, it was part of the University of Durham until 1963, when it became the University of Newcastle upon Tyne.

She concedes that, no, perhaps he never knew of her strength of feeling for him – academic circles in the 1940s and early 1950s did not provide the space for such an expression of sentiment (especially from a woman), nor has Joyce ever been inclined towards emotional indiscretion. But the realisation it wasn't to be hurt. 'It was painful, yes, yes, but you know, one does get over these things.'

Her unconventional mother tried to help: contrary to the times, 'she endeavoured to make it clear that there wasn't much in marriage. I think Mother would have liked me to get married and have children, but it wasn't an overriding feeling. She was very enthusiastic about my academic career.' Nellie Reynolds had lost her own teaching career when she married, and once her children left home she felt unfulfilled. In contrast, Joyce could take refuge in the ancient world, explaining in a letter, *When I have had troubles, I have always found that it helped to get back to work – starting with an hour a day and building up to eight or, eventually, ten.'* Her feelings towards this man gradually faded, he remained a friend and Joyce recovered and triumphed. *The Inscriptions of Roman Tripolitania* was published in 1952; although begun by John Ward-Perkins, because Joyce had done the brunt of the work he insisted she was named first on the book's cover. 'Edited by J. M. Reynolds and J. B. Ward-Perkins' is a testimony to her expansive intellectual capacity and the excitement she derived from academic discovery.[4]

ANN

In October 1955, on the crest of a glossy wave, *Women's Own* insisted that marriage was 'the ultimate goal of every rational female who seeks happiness'. According to social historian Virginia Nicholson, in post-war Britain 'every film, advertisement and shilling romance aimed at women sent the same message – that to be a wife was to be complete'.[5] By the end of the 1940s, Ann Sidgwick was surrounded by plenty of men: John Roberts and Michael Hodson, managers at the *New Statesman*, E. C. Gregory of the art publishing house Lund Humphries, and Ronnie Sterck from the Allied Control

Commission in Germany to name four. None were her husband. 'Good heavens, no', but all were gathered together for a fascinating meeting at her workplace in the attic office of the *New Statesman*. As she walked through London's statuesque Holborn that evening she reflected on her 'good fortune to be working with people who had such marvellous ideas'. Needless to say, Ann didn't read *Women's Own*. Her focus was on the establishment of Ganymed, a pioneering printing firm and gallery which would produce facsimiles (high quality copies) of famous art works. That it was men who led discussions on a possible London equivalent to the pre-war, Berlin-based collotype printers Ganymed Graphische Anstalt is not surprising. Post-war, the higher echelons of the workplace remained a male affair. Ann was simply grateful to be within earshot.

Persistence (and a fine publishing pedigree) had already paid off. After the war, Ann left the dull War Damage Commission without permission and landed a job in the *New Statesman*'s offices, working for their experimental publishing house, Turnstile Press. Once there, she finally got a chance to show off the artistic know-how she'd accrued over a lifetime. On one occasion, her boss, John Roberts, enthusiastically summoned Ann into his office. On his desk was a Ganymed copy of a Renoir pastel.

> It was of a naked girl drying her feet; well this was the most familiar piece of art in the world to me, as a copy from the exact same facsimile had hung behind our head teacher when she did the roll call every day at Hayes Court School. I said, 'Oh, that old thing, I know all about that.' I was very blasé.

A woman with exceptional artistic knowledge collided with a broad-minded employer. 'I didn't realise at the time but John Roberts became convinced I knew about these things.' Ann was duly tasked with organising the launch of Ganymed in London. A beautiful Georgian house in Bedford Square hosted all the distinguished artistic and literary names; they supped champagne beneath an ornate Adam ceiling, and on the walls original artwork hung next to perfect facsimile reproductions. The next day, the gallery opened in a quirky one-time Tudor alley, Great Turnstile, with Ann in charge. Alongside a couple of directors, she ran this highly specialised artistic venture. 'The reproductions were exhibited in the shop. There was a desk in the corner, where I or my assistant sat, and an office at the back.' Ann won't acknowledge that her success just five years after the war was unusual for a woman, but does concede, 'when you are in the middle of change, you don't notice it, it's just life'.

Managing Ganymed, and all that came with it, consumed Ann's life. The shooting star of socialism had fizzled out – by 1951, old Churchill was back in power and the economy in recovery. Rationing was almost over and most people chose shopping over social angst. A car on hire purchase and a first television set pre-occupied the majority, but Ann soon discovered there were plenty of intellectuals keen to spend money on a high-quality print of a painter they couldn't otherwise afford. 'We were a business.' Modern art was finding its feet and Ganymed traded with the greats. Henry Moore and Graham Sutherland, former Chelsea School of Art teachers, were already famous and over the years Ann had dealings with them both. In the 1950s, Sutherland was commissioned to paint Churchill on the occasion of his eightieth birthday. She laughs. 'He started the picture too low down and cut off his feet. Someone said, "The portrait looked uncertain, as if Churchill was sitting on a lavatory seat and didn't know where the loo paper was!" You know Mrs Churchill destroyed it.' Her recall is pitch-perfect: the ageing prime minister wanted no reminder of his shaky grip on power, least of all from a modern artist. Needless to say, Ann has kept her own Sutherland – the painting, an original of bees, was a gift from the artist. 'It's in the family still,' she says with a wry smile.

Nor was Ann's work confined to modern art. 'I was always searching for original paintings – Old Masters, even kitsch popular stuff – anything that we could borrow from the owner which would enhance the reputation of Ganymed.' She spent numerous week-ends wandering around exhibitions and festivals, eyeing potential paintings for reproduction. Single, with a mews flat in Knightsbridge and a stylish wardrobe, Ann was financially dependent upon the company's success – acquiring the next picture was a vital part of her job. 'Oh yes, if there was a collection of Renoir or Degas in somewhere like Edinburgh, I'd go and look at it.' Almost accidentally ('one just goes on from where one is, it was a fluke that I was in the *New Statesman*'s offices at the right time'), Ann was a frontrunner among London's emerging career women; an invariably single breed that ran counter to the domestic drumbeat carefully orchestrated by conservative commentators. Ann shrugs, 'I didn't bother with these things. Yes, I suppose I was a spinster, but it didn't bother me.' I stop her – she's 103, pertinence fades with time. 'Well I was sorry and so on, I occasionally met men and thought, "He would have been rather nice," but you know ... ' In her late thirties, Ann discovered that most men were already married. 'Sometimes there were people one met in business who seemed to be ready for a bit of flirtation, but I didn't want that.' Impropriety was of no interest to Ann: 'I didn't want that sort of life. Lots of my girlfriends had affairs but the feeling if you get involved with someone who's involved with someone else, it complicates life intolerably, and you can't quite trust them ever.' Ann's analysis chimed with the times. Princess Margaret's love for divorcee Peter Townsend wracked the governing classes; in 1950s Britain, the pretence that blemish-free marriage was the only model for a fulfilling and loving relationship persisted. Townsend was relocated to Belgium, Margaret never fully recovered and Ann wisely stayed single. Yes, she wondered about sex, and yes, 'I did feel I was missing out. More and more as I got older.' But society remained coy (and judgemental). There was only one major British sex survey during the 1950s and the title made clear the parameters: 'The Sexual, Marital and Family Relationships of the English Woman, 1956'.[6] Officially, at least, physical intimacy was still out of bounds for single women.

All of Ann's brothers and sisters had children – one sister had four, another six. Ann is an assiduous aunt (and great-aunt and great-great-aunt), but she's adamant she didn't envy her siblings. 'I never regretted not having children. Motherhood then was a full-time affair. Nappies had to be soaked and washed and dried. I let them get on with it.' She was more protective of her best friend, Elizabeth, who left their communal flat to be with her husband after the war. 'When she had a baby, I paid for a nappy service. Someone would come and take the dirty nappies away in a bag and deliver a new set.'

At Ann's great age, life has had numerous beginnings and endings – she would eventually marry – but in the 1950s there were painful, lonely moments. The dignified retort, 'they were my own private concern', gives a clue as to her staggering survival. Mastering stray emotions, coping with isolation and making the best of her lot has stood Ann in good stead. Timing too proved fortuitous, attitudes were beginning to change and the world was shrinking. 'Going on holiday on one's own, it needed a good deal of courage. I would set my own itinerary. I can remember going to Holland. Looking at paintings was always one of my major preoccupations. It was my passion.' Her engagement with the art world filled the gaps in her personal life and fuelled Ganymed's success; never destined to be ordinary, Ann's freedom post-war ensured that she, like Joyce, was exceptional.

Ann, Olive

Ann pauses to think. She can't remember when it was exactly, perhaps it was 1956, but she can recall seeing West Indian immigrants at Waterloo.

Unfortunate women coming over in March in flimsy, brilliantly coloured dresses and brilliantly coloured hats. I thought how ill-informed these poor women were. You know, that time of year in England you need warm, waterproof clothes and a good pair of boots. I thought it was sad that this interesting collection of people who had clearly put a lot of thought into their preparation were not better advised.

Practical Ann, she was worried for London's newcomers. Having endured long wartime winters, stuffing paper between window panes and blowing on chapped hands, she felt their pain. And perhaps she saw a deeper vulnerability, their skimpy Caribbean clothes a metaphor for the frailty of their position – alone and black in 1950s England.

Olive looks at me; still defiant at 102, she's propped herself up against the kitchen counter and is making cassava bread, bits of dough stretching between her ringed fingers.

> I arrive in de night at Southampton. I travel with de boat and de man on de boat gave all a cigarette. I said, 'I don't smoke,' and he said, 'When you go there you got to do it, everybody smokes in England.' So I put de cigarette in my mouth. He said, 'You going to have to work with gloves on your hands', so all de girls put on de gloves.

The ship purser's essential advice: gloves and cigarettes for an October arrival in Britain.* Olive stared out at the black sea: 'Just water, water is all I see.' The steam liner docked in Southampton at nine o'clock in the evening, and a few hundred West Indians, jaded and apprehensive, walked down the gangplank into dark autumnal England in 1952. A trickle came to Britain in the years immediately after *Windrush* and the vast majority were men – the women Ann saw at Waterloo arrived later.† Olive was a trailblazer.

Dank, sour London late at night and alone. The train from Southampton had deposited its passengers, but still waiting was one small black woman in a neat suit standing on the concourse. A man approached, accepted a parcel and left. Olive stayed standing, waiting some more. Her brother-in-law had not come. With one pound in her pocket, she hailed a taxi from the station and headed north

---

* In 1928 the Imperial Economic Committee announced the British smoked more cigarettes than any other country.

† 1955 was the first year a sizeable number of women arrived, with one third of the newcomers consisting of women and children.

to an address off Holloway Road. 'London, it look all closed up. I thought, "Where are de people?"' The Mother Country was not twinkling; there were bright spots and billboards but post-war recovery was patchy. Olive, from a land of colour and light, blinked out at dark shapes and shadows. 'All my thoughts were on my children, dat's it, just my children.' She hardly noticed the man who greeted her on the steps of her new home. 'Welcome to Enger-land, you must be Olive. I'm Ray Gordon.' A Trinidadian, tall(ish) and present, he jammed a kiss on her jaw, adding, 'I told your broder-in-law you'd be here tonight.' With a photograph of Olive gripped firmly in one hand, he took her case with the other. She was bustled into a small living area, and there Olive drank her first cup of milky tea in front of this man, Ray.

'How was d'trip?'
   'Good.'
'How were your friends?'
   'I met these girls on de boat and we slept in a cabin.'
'Girls?'
'Yes.'
'Who you left behind?'
'My children.'
'What about your better half?'
'What better half?'
'Your boyfriend?'
'I ain't got no boyfriend.'

Mr Ray Gordon stopped briefly to consider this new information. He looked at the woman across the room, blazing beneath one bare bulb, a gloved hand curled around the mug of tea.

'What about on de ship? You haven't got a boyfriend on de ship?'
   'No. Look, Mr Gordon, I travel all de time, I'm tired, der is no need for questioning me. What do ya want?'

The door opened and her brother-in-law, just back from work in High Wycombe, walked in. Ray withdrew. Olive was shown her room, and presented with a coat and boots and a bill. She could pay it when she started work, which began at 1pm off Shaftesbury Avenue the following day, once she'd sorted her papers in the morning. Okay? Ray would look after her because he (her brother-in-law) was working. Okay? Olive was already asleep.

~

As usual Olive's story doesn't emerge as a linear narrative. She jumps to her first weekend when 'Ray took me to St Paul's Cathedral. He brought a car, me and my broder-in-law go.' In particular, she wants to talk about her visit to the Whispering Gallery, 259 steps up, six days into her new life in England, an excursion with Ray at the wheel and a chance to touch a marvel of the Mother Country. 'I was excited, it was lovely.'

The visit was to prove much more than a sightseeing anecdote in a letter home. 'I heard, "Olive! Olive!" I said, "Who callin' here?"' The voice was indiscreet, almost a shout among the whispers – she did not need to press her ear against cold stone to hear it. '"Ray! It's Ray!" He said, "Forgive me, forgive me, but I have to tell you I'm terribly in love with you."' Olive chuckles, picking her little finger up in her other hand, she motions his small movement, the way he tugged her pinkie. 'I pull it away and he put his arm around my back. I said, "In love with me? I don't want a man. I'm going home after five years to be with my children."'

And that Sunday she still hadn't forgiven him, not yet anyway. Now Olive lowers her voice, there's a tension in her throat and her eyes are fixed. 'De Monday I come to England, de Tuesday Ray take me to do my papers and passport. Yes, I start my job.' No, she doesn't want to talk about sewing – she shrugs, sewing distracts – 'On de Tuesday evening he sit down.' We are back in the boarding house, an all-male affair bar an Irish landlady and Olive. It was Ray who was sitting down in her narrow room, hunched over the edge of her bed. It had been a long day. Olive was still fatigued after three weeks at sea and she'd just completed her first shift as a sample cutter, a black woman in the white girl's world. 'Dey call me "ducks" and "darlin".' She waves her hand, this is off the point. 'I said to him, "Mr Gordon, I am very tired, you excuse me, I can't talk much." Cos he drilled me, you know, askin' me questions. And I said, "Please push de door shut for me."' Wrapped in her dressing gown, Olive lay down on the bed, murmuring her prayers, washed face turned to the wall to hide hot tears. 'Naturally I was cryin', I was far from home, missing my children. I dropped, I dropped to sleep, I tell you.' Not accused but already indignant, Olive needs it to be known she was asleep. Then, suddenly 'Ray was behind me! I thought, "Oh God!"' He was there, against her back, she felt him in her dreams. There was sleep-filled panic and groggy protest. 'Oh Good Lord.' Olive's voice cracks. '"Mr Gordon!"' She shakes her head. 'I don't know how cos I had on my dressing gown. I could die. I was so ashamed of dis thing. A private thing like dat!' Mr Gordon finally spoke. 'I am here six months and I had no woman in dat time. I kept myself for you.'

In December 1952, thick fingers of airborne filth clotted London's streets. Ann was at Hyde Park Corner coming home from work, it was a Saturday afternoon and the fog had just begun to settle, wrapping itself around walkers and between street lamps. In front of her, a French couple stood enraptured. 'They looked around in great delight, here was the famous London fog, *"Oui, oui! Le brouillard!"*' Ann was somewhat less enthusiastic. 'A fog was not all that unusual at the time. There were others during the war, it was disgusting, horrible, dangerous! Every house had its own little coal fire, every room if you were rich.' Ann lived in a flat with windows adjacent to chimney pots, dirt regularly filtered in, but that December the smog was exceptional. Windless cold weather had trapped London's pollutants and increased traffic fumes added to the problem; the metropole's inhabitants were swaddled in their own filth. Four thousand people died immediately, and many more were bedridden. It was a fatal event, the worst in London's history, and within six years three Acts to clean up the air had been passed. That was of little consolation to Olive, whose bulbous morning egg stared back at her in the pokey dining room. She felt awful – sick and tired. She'd had no idea the Mother Country was this squalid, nor the food so bad. She'd only been in London six weeks and already she was feeling unwell.

It was Ray who filled Olive's plate every morning, he'd noted her paltry appetite and sickly pallor. Worried, he recommended a doctor. 'He took me to Dr Pitt – you know, Dr David Pitt? He was a friend of Ray's from home.' In the 1950s, David Pitt was the only Afro-Caribbean doctor available in London. Originally from Grenada, educated at Edinburgh University and with first-hand experience of Caribbean politics, Dr Pitt was constantly in demand from growing numbers of West Indian migrants. Later an iconic figure in British race relations, by 1975 he was created a life peer as Baron Pitt of Hampstead.[7] 'Eh, see!? I told you Dr Pitt was somebody.' Olive is triumphant. 'I not forget nothing!' In December 1952, it was Ray who took Olive to Dr Pitt's North Gower Street surgery. A bright, sympathetic man, the doctor delivered, and expected, high standards. Anything less would let the black community down.

Olive had her tongue pressed with a spatula, lights were shone in her eyes and her heartbeat was monitored with his finger. Dr Pitt sighed. She dutifully provided a urine sample and sat and waited.

'How long did you travel?'

'Twenty-one days. Four days in Surinam and seventeen days on de ship.'

'Did you have a nice time?'

Olive was surprised by the doctor's tone, and his question.

'Yes, Doctor.'

'Who were your friends on the ship?'

'Three girls, Doctor.'

'Girls! Hahaha. Then who did you leave at home?'

'Sorry, Doctor?'

'You're playing Cinderella or what? No man came on to you? You're pregnant!'

He snapped his head around to address Ray.

'Be careful of this woman, Mr Gordon, she travelled twenty-one days and she had nobody and she's pregnant!'

'NO, NO, NO, NO!'

Olive rushed from the room, stumbling out across the threshold, onto the foggy pavement, gasping for air. 'Oh, my good Lord. Pregnant.'

'By de time I get to de bus, I been sick.' Olive retched over the entrance step, she'd no space to feel shame, her head was spinning, and a mantra clogged her brain: 'You have three children, you got your moder, you got school fees, and den you is pregnant! So what is going to happen to you?' She crept to the back seat, Ray dared not follow, only stepping forward to ask how she was when they got off the bus. He risked feeble reassurance. 'Um, don't worry. Do you know why I come to dis country?' Olive spat back, 'I don't know nothing about you and I don't know what de world think about me!' Ray persisted, and tried to tell her about the Chinese woman in Trinidad who was pregnant with his child (that is, until she gave birth to a white baby with Chinese features). Appalled, he'd done a runner, worked on a ship and skipped the same ship for mighty London. Now he'd met Olive, so it was the right thing, that is what he tried to say. How he'd seen her photograph and fallen instantly in love, how he couldn't help himself. But Olive wasn't listening. 'You know how I look at it; I got three children's life to bring up. Three children to educate! I have to be careful, if I slip, dey fall.'

Ray turned to face Olive. Holding her by the shoulders, his gaze was direct, willing her to focus on him. 'I do love you, Olive. I'm going to marry you. We'll get married.' Olive tutted, she didn't want to get married, she didn't want a husband, she didn't want a baby. Ray's promises came thick and fast. He would give up studying engineering, he would make better money, he would learn to paint and decorate, he would improve himself and, 'I love you, I'll take care of you.' It was back at the boarding house, damp and cramped, that Ray bent down and proffered Olive his entire life savings. 'One hundred pound. He gave me dat hundred pound. Was de money he earned on de ship. He said, "Send it home to your moder for her to pay de fee for your children's fees until we can do better."' And that was that. Silently, Olive accepted the money. She was now complicit in his plan, his baby was in her belly, they would get married. It wasn't mentioned again. Not for a few weeks anyway.

Olive caught an electric bus to work in Shaftesbury Avenue, where she bought milk and cakes in a little bar and climbed the steps to her workroom, above the machinists. Home was the same route, trundling back to sullen north London. Then one morning the tram threw her over, or perhaps she pulled the cord – the pain was excruciating, really terrible, 'pain pain pain'. Olive crawled to work, the pain continued, cramping and sickness too. She crawled home. 'I have nobody 'til night.' Bleeding, sobbing, Olive was alone when the first baby came. There were two, the other came between screams in Whittington Hospital. Ray had found her, administered Lamictal for seizures and took her to hospital, where they smashed a needle into her thigh and waited for contractions. Two tiny dead babies and lots of blood. In clumsy earshot, one nurse said to another, 'She may be black, but I do feel sorry for her.' Olive woke to find Ray on her bed, sobbing. 'He save my life, and every night he come to de hospital and see me. He not eat nothing, he sit on my bed to see me. I was sick one month.'

Olive looks up, 'I was his illustrious wife, but at de time I didn't want to get married, Ray marry me!' She laughs, a big chortle, and shows me their wedding photograph. One month after the miscarriage, Olive is grumpy in tailored white and long white gloves with hand-sewn buttons. Ray is a young pup, five years her junior and pleased as punch. '"Yes, yes, yes," he scream when dey ask if he want to marry dis woman! "Yes!"' Ray got his way. Mr and Mrs Gordon were joined in a story of redemption and forgiveness. Devout Olive now had her own saga of biblical proportions, with a complex hero at its heart. 'Yes 'twas a very unusual relationship. Ray was my protector, you know. He was my all.'

CHAPTER FOURTEEN

ELIZABETHAN BRITAIN

Joyce is the youngest woman in this book – born in 1918, she is yet to receive her hundredth birthday card from the Queen, the arrival of which is not a priority. A liberal academic, the British Royal Family didn't matter much when she grew up, and they still don't. Joyce laughs. During her stay in Rome, an Italian fruit trader exposed her ignorance. 'I was buying oranges and the nice lady who was selling them to me said, "How, my dear, is your lovely Queen?" I had no idea so I had to make it up. She would've been disappointed if I said I didn't know.' The Italian fruit seller spoke for many. The shadows of a masculine war, drab austerity and a tense stand-off between East and West guaranteed a certain thirst for the ascension of beautiful, blameless Elizabeth II that transcended borders.[1] A young woman was about to be prematurely catapulted onto the world's most famous throne. Midway through a Commonwealth tour and grief-stricken at her father's death, in 1952 Elizabeth returned to Britain and assumed her responsibilities as head of state. She quickly became a feminine icon in blighted times and Britain, keen to shore up a wobbly empire, jumped on her benign appeal. The coronation would be the BBC's first live television broadcast – Queen Elizabeth's regal elevation was beamed around the world.

Olive left Guyana in 1952 a staunch royalist and by 1953 she lived in the same city as her queen, and yet she has no memory of the coronation. In a golden carriage, under a downpour, wearing a puffy dress, Elizabeth II wowed the London crowds but Olive wasn't watching. She shrugs. 'When I get to Southampton, there ain't no queen der to meet me.' The empire's tinsel-covered version of Britannia – inclusive and majestic under the magical rule of the royals – proved a sham on arrival in the Mother Country. The personal invariably transcends the public. Olive had just got out of her own white dress, she had no time to look at someone else's charade. 'Eh, de Queen, she eleven years younger dan me! And my daughter and granddaughter been to one of her tea parties.' Subsequent black generations would (begin to) break into the rarefied circles of the British ruling classes, including Olive's own family, but in 1953, stuck in a mean boarding house minus a television, the arrival of a white queen on the British throne was an irrelevance. 'It didn't bother me, I just workin' for my children.'

Another child of the empire, Phyllis also began life as a committed royalist. 'I had that feeling that even if you lived in India the King was always there, and always on the King's birthday there was an army parade to show off British might.' Unlike Olive, June 1953 was a high point for Phyllis's monarchical convictions. 'I've still got coronation plates, and the ones for the Queen's eightieth birthday too.' The coronation, amidst all its pomp and ceremony, saw Phyllis tap back into a nostalgic seam of colour, open carriages and fancy dress from the vantage point of a family home in Edinburgh. She enjoyed access to a novel television set in her sister-in-law's living room. 'We watched it nearly all day, eleven in the morning until well into the evening. We ate sandwiches and were very excited.' Despite an exotic childhood thousands of miles away from the Mother Country, Phyllis visibly belonged among the Queen's British subjects. She was white.

In London, Olive's colleagues had not yet given her the benefit of the doubt. It was at Jaeger that one girl approached her as she worked.

'We were told that we are better than you.'

'Better?'

Olive didn't miss a beat.

> What way you better? You don't go to de toilet? You don't bathe
> in de morning? Even de Queen of England, she has de children and
> she hire a maid and de maid get de children. In what way better?
> De only difference with you is because you are a different colour
> but inside of you is de same.

Olive, the physical embodiment of empire, sitting in a superior
sewing job in London. How dare she. 'I was sewing one day, de
machine prick my finger and de girl said, "Your blood red!" Olive's
reply – 'What you think, it black?' Curiosity curdled with ignorance.
Olive let it wash over her. 'Ray take more of de problems, he was my
shield.' But that sacred imperial infrastructure implanted at birth had
been bruised. Was Elizabeth II really her queen?

'Of course, she wasn't going to be queen initially. I remember when Elizabeth was born. It was 1926, I think.' Ann has a
knack of felling lofty sentiment – the Queen will always be her
junior. 'Her longevity is nothing to mine!' Well, quite. Suitably
detached, Ann's account of the coronation is sentiment-free.
'There were street parties all over the place and radios out in the
street playing 'God Save the Queen' all the time, and my little
nephew said, "What's the matter with the Queen that God has
to keep saving her?"' The anecdote pleased Ann, so she shared
it with Her Majesty. 'I wrote a letter to her Lady-in-Waiting and
got one back saying the Queen was very amused.' Hierarchy was
no barrier, all Ann's life Elizabeth II has never been more than a
first among equals.

'In poorer areas, the streets are thick with bunting and there is
much enthusiasm for street parties.'[2] Among the working classes
were those who really believed in Elizabethan mystique and celebrated accordingly. Edna was working for a couple in Grantham;
her mother was invited along and they all watched the television
together. 'It was a lovely time. Her coronation dress was beautiful;
when you think of the history that was there in that dress. I was

reading about it the other day.' At 102, Edna rattles off the gown's key credentials: the dress was made by a British man, the silk was locally produced; there were gold beads, diamanté and pearls. And then she smiles. Edna is living proof as to why the 'coronation dress is regarded as one of the most important examples of twentieth-century design'.[3] As for the Queen herself, Edna was in awe. 'She was very young, wasn't she, and she wasn't really born into it. But I always thought it was the best thing that ever happened, Elizabeth becoming our queen.' A young, vulnerable Defender of the Faith, Elizabeth was in her rightful place, doing her duty just as Edna did hers. For better or for worse, everything was as it should be. Forcefully, Edna prayed for the new queen that night.

HELENA, PHYLLIS

Helena shakes her head. 'It's no good, I haven't got a clear picture – I can remember these men taking her up the steps, yes, I can remember that and putting her on the throne. I wonder whose telly it was? I think the children had a holiday from school.' Helena is Welsh and nonconformist and, if she's honest, not terribly interested in British royalty, but her hazy recollection of a coronation that some historians claim 'was for women the defining event of the decade'[4] says more about her extraordinarily full life. 'I suppose I did like to be busy. Percy was always worried I was overdoing it.' But Percy always got his breakfast, lunch, tea and supper on time. By 1953, Helena was also the mother of two small daughters. The little family had grown out of their Elan Valley croft and bought a farm, Lower Cwmwysg, just outside Sennybridge, a Welsh village nine miles from Brecon. Helena enjoys the memory of their new, stout house.

There was water, running water in the house, in a tap. Hot water too, so I had my first bathroom at Cwmwysg. And electricity! I bought a vacuum cleaner and an electric iron, which made such a difference because before I used to heat the irons in the fire and

very often you'd have the dirt come off onto a white collar or
something.

Helena's face shines; the delicious novelty of each domestic marvel
was not wasted at Lower Cwmwysg. If, at the beginning of the
1950s, 'most women in Britain were still cleaning their houses with
the same basic equipment and materials' in use 300 years earlier,[5]
in less than ten years that was no longer the case. Just three months
before he became Conservative prime minister in 1957, Harold
Macmillan, the master of the middle way, reminded voters they had
never had it so good. 'Go around the country, go to the industrial
towns, go to the farms and you will see a state of prosperity such as
we have never had in my lifetime.'[6] Mass unemployment and poverty
marches were confined to history; consumerism and shopping would
define the decades to come.

~

In 1953, Jim Ramsay was given his first command at sea. The fruits
of this promotion were enjoyed in Scotland. Phyllis and her husband
borrowed £1,500 and upgraded from their rented flat to a cottage
in Upper Largo. A large, second-hand MG sports car was a new
addition to the family, so too a second baby – Geoff (the result of
a long-awaited sea trip with her sailor husband). Baby Geoff had
every mod con. 'When I came home from hospital, Jim had to go
back to sea but he left a little television set that he'd bought for
me and a tiny washing machine, about a foot square with a little
ringer.' With a bonny blond baby bouncing in the corner, by 1955
Phyllis's house was the place to be. 'None of my friends had TVs,
so we all used to collect in my living room and watch *Quatermass*
every Wednesday. It was a very scary science fiction series. There'd
be about five or six of us.' Christmas 1957, and Phyllis added a new
camera to her list of acquisitions; toddler Geoff is the centrepiece of
every picture – surrounded by a sea of toys and teddies, flamboyant
wallpaper, patterned curtains and a table-top model television set.

Phyllis eagerly embraced the perks of modernity. Time-saving designs gradually infiltrated every aspect of life; supermarkets, tea bags, sliced bread and washing machines helped free her up to indulge in the things she loved – gardening, tennis, baking, voluntary work, friendship and trips at sea with Captain Jim.

∽

In Helena's household, hot water and electricity were transformative, but the footprint of consumer Britain was held in check. Old habits die hard. Wedded to the land, weaned on hard work and a make-do-and-mend mentality, Helena still churned her own butter and baked her own bread. Supper in the summer was simple but unbeatable – homegrown new potatoes with farm butter. Christmas was especially chaotic, but Helena approached it with executive zeal. Together with Percy, she would pluck and dress a dozen ducks and eight geese in the back kitchen, ready for Brecon's seasonal market. No matter how hard Helena tried, an errant feather would always escape. The priority was getting the fresh birds sold before Christmas Day. It became increasingly important that the poultry 'looked better than those in the supermarkets, so they had to be plucked to perfection with giblets and trimmings'. For her younger daughter, Meryl, still the smell of burning wax is reminiscent of the candle used to singe off the down. Born in 1951, Meryl has conflicting emotions about her bystander role during those hectic Christmases. Guts and gizzards left their own distinct smells and messes. 'It did sort of spoil things for us children.' The memories are also encumbered with a retrospective sadness. 'I often think how terrible it is that in one generation all those skills were lost. All the things Mum could do – catch and kill a chicken and cook it, make butter, bottle fruit, all of those things that they did every week, it has gone.'

Meryl is a well-educated, good-looking woman in her sixties; an accomplished athlete, teacher and ballroom dancer, she has been a source of great pride to her mother. But unlike Helena, she grew up in an era when cock-a-leekie soup was available in a packet, ditto butter and bacon. Piano and ballet lessons, drama and eisteddfod performances occupied a childhood minus the graft that defined her mother's. Helena and Percy were keen that their girls should have a better life than them, 'Whatever that means,' adds Meryl. Helena continued to slice her own bacon, paper her own walls, clear out the Rayburn and polish the copper kettle, but there was no need for her daughter to do the same. Meryl sighs. 'The skill set was taken away from us. Unconsciously, we were being subjected to what was happening. The supermarket crept in, local markets closed and our dependence on the supermarket tightened. Only now is local produce appreciated again.' Progress came at a cost in Mid Wales.

Farm duties and two young children amidst the obligatory spit-and-polish domestic routines that consumed the 1950s home would have been more than enough for most women. But Helena was not most women. With the birth of Meryl and the move to Sennybridge, she briefly stopped teaching, but the break merely reinforced her desire to return to the classroom, a move that farm debts made imperative. When the girls were both school age, Helena went back to work. Meryl laughs. 'She was at a different school and she used to cycle home before us so I never knew Mum worked. She didn't tell us she was teaching, I always thought she was at home.' A complex pretence that exhausted its executor sounds preposterous, but in fact it was just a sign of the times. Children (and the culture surrounding them) expected mothers to be at home, even when they weren't. To imagine anything less would have been a betrayal. 'My husband was there if they'd had a fall at school, but I didn't want them to worry that I wasn't at home, so I didn't tell them for a long time.' By 1960, one third of wives were working, but rarely were their jobs full time and most didn't have school-age children. Helena was an exception.

'Well, I suppose I was a good teacher.' She hesitates, uncertain quite how to continue. It's easier for her daughter Meryl to explain. Years later, by now an adult working for the Brecon Tourist Board, Meryl was staggered by the numbers who sought her out and said,

'"Now, you're Helena Jones's daughter, aren't you?" Because they wanted to tell me all the things she had done for them.'

One woman, she was an ordinary, mousy person, down at heel almost and she said, 'I had two children, a boy and a girl, and my daughter is now a doctor and that is because your mother taught her. They were very quiet children, but your mother saw something in my daughter. My son was just as bright but nobody could see anything in him. He didn't have Helena as a teacher.'

Almost all her life, Helena has touched and changed the lives of others, and that vocational compassion burns within her still. ('Anything I can do to help you with your book, just you ask me.') Only last week, a man called Ernie paid her a visit unannounced. 'He was with his sister, and they were driving from Bristol. They had my name and asked the locals where I lived.' Out tumbles a story from long ago, a brother and a sister ('poor kids, you know the sort, without a father') whose mother went to hospital, the prospect of a children's home loomed and young Helena the teacher was called on to help. 'I was asked if I would look out for some clothes for them.' She did more than that. Helena took the pair back home to live with her own family, and there they stayed until their mother had recovered. 'At breakfast, they'd never had milk on their cereal, only tea. And I do remember washing them.' It was before she had a bathroom, they were scrubbed in the old zinc tub, and doused in clean water administered from a saucepan. 'Ernie went to school the next day and the headmistress asked if he'd been good. "Oh yes," he said, "Miss washed my head in a saucepan!"' Helena even took them to an eisteddfod, where they won a prize bag and a medal. That same pair, some seventy years later, had tracked her down to tell her what she meant to them. 'Ernie was seventeen stone! They still have the medal, you know, and she was hugging me, the woman, almost crying. I felt it was so nice of them to come and see me.' Helena pauses. 'The sad thing is, you wouldn't be allowed to do what I did today.'

ANN

'*Cool*, did you say? To me, cool means the opposite of hot.' Ann, still without a television in 2017, is occasionally stumped by modern terminology. (*Landline?* 'As in, not a mobile, Ann.' *Flaky?* 'No, not a pastry, someone who's unreliable.')

'*Gay*, well I suppose it has fewer syllables, but I always use the term homosexual.'

'So, are you cool with homosexuality?'

We've come full circle. For more than half of Ann's adult life, homosexuality in Britain was illegal. Her face settles in quiet disapproval. How ridiculous. How could the law have been so out of step with (her) society for so long? As early as the 1930s, a young single woman operating in the art world, Ann occasionally discovered men she found 'interesting' were either 'already married or homosexuals'. 'One didn't talk about it with them, but it was a common undercurrent, everybody knew and kept quiet about it. If one liked a homosexual, it just became apparent you were barking up the wrong tree.' Among her circle, a number of personal friends were gay.

'From early Cambridge days, many of the Stracheys were homosexual, certainly Christopher was. He was the one we knew best.' She moves on to other matters. Ann is discreet (she was born in an era that demanded discretion), but perhaps she feels our conversation of honest yet coded restraint demands a conclusion. In her handsome hand, a letter arrives two days later.

> I remembered a little story which may be relevant to what we were speaking of, that is, attitudes to homosexuality in the 1930s.

The story centres around a literary competition run weekly in the *New Statesman*, for which her father was occasionally a judge.

> The answers came to our home. One day the competition setter revived the old quotation, 'I am firm, you are obstinate, he is pig-headed' . . . and invited subscribers to invent more examples.

One of the winners was our Cambridge friend, Christopher Strachey ... his contribution was, 'I like boys, you are a Scout Master, he is in prison', which amused us much at the time. It was printed in the *New Statesman*.

Decades before change came, Ann was ahead of the progressive curve, part of the set that laughed quietly and publicly at nonsensical law. To underscore the prevalent madness, she concluded her letter with a list of Christopher Strachey's achievements. 'He was in future years ... a great contributor to the decoding machines at Bletchley Park, a great mathematician, a most amusing person and a great piano player.' In fact a pioneer in programming language design, in 1965 he eventually became Oxford University's first Professor of Computer Science. And unlike his colleague, contemporary and fellow homosexual Alan Turing, Christopher Strachey survived.

If, in the disreputable 1930s, surreptitious titters presupposed eventual sexual liberalisation, twenty years later there was no sign of legal change. Publicly, attitudes hardened in the uncompromising 1950s. Where once Britain's bright young things had flirted with communism, by 1951 the Cold War had heated up and the much-publicised flight to Russia of Guy Burgess and Donald Maclean (both homosexuals) rattled the Establishment. The new Tory home secretary prioritised the persecution of gay men. Comparative figures for 1938 and 1952 show cases of sodomy and bestiality up from 134 to 670 and attempts to commit 'unnatural offences' rose from 822 to 3,087.[7] Alan Turing was caught in the witch-hunt and sentenced to a course of organotherapy treatment that left him impotent with swollen breasts. He committed suicide. 'It really was absolutely terrible.'

By now a seasoned adult, Ann's reach extended to those in public office, namely the Labour MP Kenneth Robinson, husband of her best friend and former flatmate, Elizabeth Edwards. Initially stuck on the opposition backbenches, this liberal progressive pushed for change in areas considered a no-go for ambitious politicians. He tackled mental health, suicide, abortion and homosexuality head-on. Very close to both husband and wife, Ann remembers long discussions in their north London home as Kenneth tried to tease a way forward amidst a sea of cautious politicians beholden to their illiberal constituents. Against a backdrop of routine lobotomies and padded cells, he introduced the first debate in twenty years on mental health (a new act was passed in 1959), and worked on a bill which stopped suicide being a common-law crime. ('Thank goodness,' adds Ann, 'before that it was absolutely awful, if you failed to kill yourself you were in prison, if you didn't fail, you were dead.')

However, legalising homosexuality was fraught with social complexities and stymied by public revulsion. In an ominously entitled 'Evil Men' series, the *Sunday Pictorial* ranted: 'Most people know there are such things as "pansies" – mincing effeminate young men who call themselves "queers". But simple decent folk regard them as freaks and rarities ... There will be no joking about this situation when people realise the true situation.'[8] Tensions rose and, worried about the high number of prosecutions, in 1954 the Conservatives reluctantly commissioned the Wolfenden Report, tasked with finding an acceptable moral framework for the post-war world. Its publication three years later caused a furore: male homosexuality in private, for consenting adults, should be partially decriminalised, while penalties for public offences should increase. The latter recommendation became law, but gay sex remained illegal. Kenneth Robinson, still in opposition, introduced the first full parliamentary debate on the Wolfenden Report in 1960. 'I had conversations with him about this bill, it was just quite obvious what should be done. I suppose we were avant-garde, but I didn't feel ahead of my time, because everybody else I knew thought like me.' Cocooned in London, Ann was shocked when Kenneth's mission failed – the overwhelming majority of MPs voted against the legalisation of homosexual acts between consenting adults. 'They were frightened of their constituents.' That Kenneth persuaded ninety-two MPs to vote with him was considered progress. Ann sighs. 'We were extremely disappointed.' Fifty-seven years later, sitting upright in a cornflower-blue tunic beneath a Cézanne print, she is living proof that the liberal metropolitan elite has always been out of step with the provinces. It was another seven years, with the 1960s in full swing and Kenneth Robinson health minister in a Labour government, before gay men could enjoy a legal shag.

'A what? Oh, how cool.'

OLIVE

'Dey ask me where my tail was, I tell em I cut it off! Hahaha.' Olive laughs, she will not be bowed by old memories but holds them firmly in her palm, specimens to play with and examine. Back then, nothing could touch her, only Ray. 'Ray, he take most of de flak. He faced everyting.' Thrumming away on her sewing machine, amenable, pretty and, crucially, female, Olive experienced minimal overspill from white England's crystallising hostility. Working as a sample cutter, a nursemaid to dowdy 1950s fashion, Olive twinkled at the naïve white girls in their overalls, their ridiculous questions even amused her. A more flagrant discrimination was preserved for West Indian men, whose masculine presence was deemed fearful, even sexually threatening. No homosexuals and preferably no blacks – 1950s England didn't like risk, change or difference. Olive's new husband, Ray, did the shopping and negotiated the rent, he absorbed the prejudice and, if his wife was involved, he even fought back.

When I work, I put de children's money in de chest of drawers and on de Friday morning I look at it and on de Saturday when I get up to go to post it – no money! Well Ray, he call de landlord and he said, 'Dis girl was putting her money here for de children and she was lookin' at it every day and now it gone!'

The summoned landlord looked at the empty drawer and laughed. Livid, Ray grabbed him by the shirt and held him down. 'He tossed him around.' Olive smiles triumphantly. 'And he said, "Put de money back!" The money duly reappeared the following day. White landlords were no match for Mr and Mrs Gordon. They were a team, and both knew the rules – Ray had spelt them out on the wedding night.

'I do not accept infidelity. I do not like divorce.'

'If it happen, what you do?'

'If you find yourself another lover, I break your hip.'

'Well, for dat you will go to jail.'

'Yes. When I got to jail I serve my time and when I come out, you look on my back and see if you see prison. But you, you would walk with a broken hip until you die.'

Olive guffaws. She enjoyed their marital sparring. She misses it still and particularly likes this story (even sharing it with a surprised head teacher during her visit to a Lambeth Primary School). 'In-fi-del-i-ty.' She curls her tongue around each syllable. Olive didn't think much of infidelity either. 'I was a loyal wife.' Ray postured, proud of his male status, but Olive was not a subjugated woman nor a submissive one. Ray had wronged her yet loved her deeply. Initially, she didn't reciprocate that love; Olive was privileged with the emotional upper hand. 'Did I tell you dat Ray said I was his illustrious wife, a beauty, a cutie?'

Olive cannot pinpoint when exactly she fell in love with Ray, it began as a question of survival, a contract that shored her up – two are better than one, 'de children's future was in my hand I tell you. Dat is what it was.' Violation, dependence, survival, a *modus vivendi* that bloomed into love. And what of London, that great city that housed their affection, straining under the 1950s, chasing down a more colourful future? Pah. Neon lights flickered, the streets burst with blaring traffic, chic re-emerged with patent leather and flouncy skirts, but Olive believes she did not notice, held her gaze straight ahead instead. She worked on Shaftesbury Avenue, right in the heart of Theatreland and it was a new boom time for showbiz, big bands and bigger chorus lines. The Hippodrome always had another show. So what? Olive had her children to think about. She earned eight pounds a week, and that was more than half of British families. Not bad for a black woman. She laughs. Olive, always stylish, wore plenty of colour, rose-gold jewellery, well-cut suits, and hats, yes, of course hats. 'Sometime de people look but I not botherin'.' Olive wasn't interested in soaking up the sights or returning the stares. 'I had a job to do and dat was dat.'

On arrival in London, West Indians generally stuck with their own. Clusters of new hope: Jamaicans to Lambeth, Trinidadians and Barbadians to Notting Hill, and Guyanese, like Olive, to the north of the city, but the new disappointing reality they met soon saw lines blur. West Indian immigrant had to support West Indian immigrant. Olive and Ray brought two lands – Trinidad and Guyana – together under the roof of marriage. Accommodation was hard to come by, and financial leverage even harder. Olive and Ray acquired theirs not from a bank but Jamaican friends they met in a boarding house. Initially, they'd scuttled past each other in the corridor, but months later the same couple lent them the money to buy their first home. Their daughter became Olive's goddaughter – one of many new connections. Across London in selected pockets new communities emerged, with their own fruits and flavours and patois. White neighbours bridled and health secretary Enoch Powell took a trip to Barbados to tempt new nurses over – there was plenty of work, too much even. A community, a house, a job, good friends, a husband – Olive's original five-year plan wilted in the face of her success. She would not return to Guyana. No, like so many newcomers, the unforgiving city clawed her in, forced her to work harder for longer, made her dig deeper and then, after all that, it taunted her to stay. Guyana wasn't stable, money and opportunities were limited, an independent future was possible but even more precarious. The answer was obvious, her children must come here, to London.

Olive's eldest daughter, Joye, was sixteen when she was summoned to England in 1955. She travelled in familiar company, as it was the first year that a third of the West Indian newcomers were women and children; people who former colonial secretary Creech Jones had observed 'won't last one winter in England' had begun to lay down roots.[9] Joye arrived 'fully certified'; having passed her exams in Guyana with flying colours, she had high hopes for her time in London. Not quite yet homeowners, Ray stood on the threshold of a Finsbury Park boarding house to meet his new stepdaughter.

'Welcome aboard, how you travel?' Olive observed her proud daughter kiss him on the jaw and survey her new surroundings.

The mean accommodation dismayed Joye, the shared bathroom appalled her. The transition between two worlds wasn't easy. Joye is adamant – it was much harder for her to establish a new life in London as a teenager than it ever had been for her mother. Thirty-seven-year-old Olive arrived with one brief – to survive and provide for her family. Sixteen-year-old Joye had been brought up with higher expectations; a politically engaged, well-connected young woman, she was coming to Britain to finish off her education. 'We had different outlooks, that's certainly true, my mother was prepared to put up with indignities.' London was a rude shock; white women scrubbing doorsteps took the time to tut and study her; a Labour Exchange where the young girls had left school at fifteen and thought only of a future husband. 'I felt sorry for them, I knew more about Britain than they did.' And she felt sorry for herself, because in Britain she was too poor to study full time. Duped and undervalued, with race a restrictive common denominator, 'all the black people were lumped together as one'. Joye was angry. 'My goodness me, there was a lot of anger, if I am quite honest, a lot of anger, but there was nobody to share this anger with. I didn't feel I could share it with Mother.'

Instead, Joye channelled her frustrations into defying the odds and getting a first acceptable job. Olive butts in, she enjoys this bit of her daughter's story. 'Joye had shorthand and typing, and so she got de job at Drivers & Norris, at de corner of Holloway Road. An estate agent. She was front of house! I made sure all my children were fully certified.' Olive had succeeded, her daughter was employable. But really the success was Joye's – there she was, young and black and brainy, stalling people's expectations as they entered the office and saw her sitting there behind a state-of-the-art typewriter. She'd wowed the men in the interview, and trounced the opposition with her typing. Failure was never an option. Joye's subsequent teaching career bore all the hallmarks of a woman well equipped and sufficiently determined to resist rejection and discrimination. She would become an acclaimed head teacher, sought after by London's challenging secondary schools. Just in case there's any doubt as to her eventual status, Olive adds, 'She's had tea with de Queen.'

Her daughter smiles, the story has a happy ending. But for white Britain, the journey from angry teenager to leading educator disguises an uncomfortable truth: Joye's success was despite the Mother Country, not because of it.

~

After the war, Britain's governing classes tried to make good what was left of empire. Only when the Americans called a halt to their occupation of the Suez Canal in 1956 did Westminster concede the imperial game was up. Four years later, in a seminal speech, Prime Minister Macmillan referred to the 'wind of change' in Africa – cue an undignified scramble to offload complex colonial problems as quickly as possible. Britain could no longer even pretend to be a great power. Joyce was not surprised. 'I thought it was inevitable we would lose the empire.' She had been studying the relationship between Ancient Rome and its provinces most of her life – imperial fortunes rise and fall. Displaced peoples and population shifts track geopolitical change. Britain had put white men all over the world, they had shifted Africans and Indians to the Americas, and Indians to Africa in a giant human jumble. A small archipelago in northwestern Europe had distorted the face of the world and now that global face dared showed itself at home. Joyce expected nothing less. 'It seemed very natural when people started arriving from our empire. And interesting.' By 1949, Joyce was already a lecturer in a northern university at a time when only 1.5 per cent of women went to university. She knew about difference – she belonged to a minority – but concedes that her understanding of immigration 'in academic circles was different from other people's experiences'.

Ann echoes Joyce's interested but detached attitude. 'Well, the most famous black person I came across was Prince Monolulu. "I've gotta 'orse! I've gotta 'orse!" he used to shout at Hyde Park Corner; he had red ostrich feathers in his hair.' Elizabeth and Kenneth's daughter, aged five, was entranced by him. 'He was a bit mad I think.' Prince Monolulu, an eccentric of hazy origins, who made his name as a racing tipster, was a mainstay of British culture long before the war. One flamboyant black man was exotic (even his demise was fantastical – he choked to death on a strawberry cream), but the arrival of thousands of racially different people was another matter. Educated Ann and Joyce sat above the fray, but on London's streets hackles began to rise. Teddy boys released from national service kicked their heels, post-war construction schemes ran out of steam and Great Britain shrank. Efforts to change direction and join the European Economic Area were rebuffed. The question *'What's Wrong with Britain?'* preoccupied commentators and intellectuals alike.* Meanwhile, Olive's teenage daughter Joye wrote to her brother, Terence. 'I said to him, "You've got a job. If I were you, I wouldn't come over here."' Regardless, Terence arrived in 1958, one year after his sister Gloria, and a year before his grandmother, Rosalind. Commonwealth immigrants still only numbered 250,000 but they were concentrated in specific urban areas and visibly stood out. The atmosphere curdled, gang culture soon stalked the streets, threats of 'black-burying' and 'n*r-hunting' stopped men going out at night. Riots erupted in Nottingham, Notting Hill and Brixton, an Antiguan carpenter, Kelso Cochrane, was stabbed to death and 1,000 West Indians lined his funeral route. For Joye and Terence, it felt personal. Was this their future? The politicians panicked. From 1962, there were a succession of immigration Acts that restricted access to Britain; within a decade, what was implicit had become explicit, that only people from the white Commonwealth countries were welcome.

It was the arrival of Kenyan Asians in 1968 that saw shadow defence secretary Enoch Powell verbally froth that Britain must be 'mad, literally mad' to permit such an unhealthy influx.[10] Ann listened in horror as he used his classical education to draw dramatic

---

* This was the title of a series of Penguin books that explored this question in the run-up to the 1964 election.

parallels. 'Like the Romans ... I see the Tiber flowing with much blood.' The libertarian in her was incensed. 'It was appalling, absolutely appalling. Like the Nazis all over again.' But Ann was the exception, not the rule – the majority of Britons agreed with (sacked) Powell. The genie was out of the bottle, and in a matter of decades Gloria Britannica, whose identity had been formed across seven continents, was reduced to defining its nationality against the politics of immigration. It wasn't about overpopulation – throughout the 1960s, Britain was a net exporter of people*[11] – the nub of the issue centred around a perceived threat to white British culture. Edna, a product of timeless England, who had swapped one green heartland for another – Lincolnshire for Wiltshire – is vague about her thoughts back then. Her husband

Ern did watch the telly and say things, but I don't know what. I didn't know any black people then, you see, they weren't in the countryside, but I really like the woman who empties my bins, she always hugs me and tells me that she loves me and she's as black as the ace of spades.

Although the debate was framed as a British problem, immigration was mainly an English reality. New arrivals in Wales and Scotland were few and far between. Helena shakes her head: 'We've got different people now, mind you; one helps me in the mornings sometimes but not then, no.' Phyllis was equally removed in Scotland. 'We heard about people coming into Manchester and London. We never thought anything of it. It just happened somewhere else. You rarely saw a dark person in Edinburgh.' Nonetheless in the 1960s, the arrival of East Indians and Pakistanis piqued her interest; she visited her brother in Manchester and marvelled at the emerging Curry Mile. 'It was a whole street of curry restaurants, and that was the

* Around 20,000 to 60,000 more people left than arrived in Britain throughout the 1960s, with the flow of immigrants arriving from the New Commonwealth running at about 70,000 a year during the 'bulge' period of 1965–70.

only place I got real Indian sweets. I would ask the waiter where he was from. He'd say, "Madam, a small place in India," but I always knew it.' She occasionally dug up a couple of words of Hindustani. Phyllis enjoyed her exchanges in brash red and gold neo-raj-style curry houses, and the mish-mash of Anglo-Asian food designed for the ignorant British palate amused her. She understood the hybrid world these Indian men inhabited – it reminded her of home, a place that otherwise existed only in her head.

As for Olive, she remains defiant fifty years on. Her children were ruffled but Enoch Powell's speech did not surprise her, nor did it worry her. Powell is still 'dat man. Dat man could say what he like. But what he gonna do? Eh? I had two passports, one for Guyana, one for Britain, if he want me to go to Guyana he pay my ticket. Ha!' Unlike the second-generation immigrants who came next, Olive had options; she had chosen to come to the UK, she could always change her mind, although she had no intention of doing so. God had shown her the right path – she had pulled her family around her, they owned their own Victorian home and Ray had begun to make proper money. 'He learnt papering off de English men. You know wallpapering. Then he progressed and he learnt roofing and moved onto renovating whole houses. Soon he was employing men and teaching dem. He was an entrepreneur.' Olive laughs. Flash Ray, with his townhouse and property deals and new car every three years, proudly and consistently voted Conservative, because 'dat was de party for businessmen'. He wanted his wife to do the same. 'But I ignore him and vote Labour with de factory girls.' British citizen Olive Gordon did it her way.

CHAPTER FIFTEEN

THE TIMES THEY
ARE A-CHANGIN'

JOYCE

Perhaps being your own person, retaining an element of individuality, is a key to extreme longevity. But Joyce has no time for such generalisations. 'Careful,' she admonishes if I try to extrapolate likeness between her life and that of her centenarian contemporaries. So it's Joyce on her own. By 1949, on the strength of her references ('I was still in Rome. Good heavens, no, they didn't fly you over for an interview in those days!'), King's College in Newcastle upon Tyne appointed her assistant lecturer in the Classics department. Quiet, southern, scholastic Joyce, wearing spectacles and a sensible skirt, cut her teeth in front of an audience of young, northern, occasionally boisterous men. (Undergraduate women were a minority.) There were testing moments; Joyce was always an exceptional teacher but, reserved by nature, it took longer to find her feet as a lecturer.

I remember a large group of students doing a general degree and one rather obstinate and stupid boy kept insisting that although the Greeks had a word for beard, the only bearded people in the Greek world were foreigners – Greeks didn't wear beards. Yes, he was talking absolute nonsense!

The male student had sized up his prey – a novice, bluestocking woman – and launched a disruptive volley of ridiculous questions. The hall held its breath.

> He occupied the class quite a lot with this issue. Then my lectures were moved to the museum, where we were suddenly surrounded by numerous casts of Greek men standing on plinths. I said to him, 'Just turn around and look at these statues and tell me Greek men don't have beards.'

Touché. 'The rest of the class were frightfully enthusiastic; they didn't quite clap but they almost did.' Joyce had triumphed over a maverick and won the affection of the year group. She was soon promoted from her assistant role.

The great expansion of tertiary education remained in the future; in 1949, Butler's Education Act had not yet sent the first grammar school children into the university system. Nonetheless, Joyce taught a mixed bag. Previously cloistered among the elites of St Paul's and Oxford, she was now exposed to ordinary academic attainment. 'There were the first-year Classics students, but you couldn't bank on them having read the key texts. Sometimes you couldn't bank on them knowing anything. Things I reckoned I knew when I was ten, they didn't.' But Joyce rarely stood in judgement of ignorance or lack of opportunity (particularly prevalent among female students).

> A lot of the girls came from low-grade or medium-grade schools, and often one could get them very keen with very little effort if one talked to them in the right sort of way. Sometimes for the first time they were being taken seriously and their reactions were indeed exciting.

Two years later, in 1951, Joyce travelled down to Cambridge University for an interview at Newnham College. She insists that concern for her ageing southern-based parents was her primary motivation but concedes, 'I knew the teaching at Oxford and Cambridge was different and in some ways more stimulating. You could be fairly sure your students would be highly trained.' Once there, she impressed the appointments committee, accepted a pay cut ('it was an all-girls college – there was less money'), and duly took up her position as the college's Classics lecturer and director of studies. Ever matter-of-fact, she sees nothing romantic or predestined about this appointment (Joyce is an Oxford graduate, and Somervillians are very loyal). But find Newnham College today amidst Cambridge's golden stone, with its pungent herbaceous borders, feminine architectural harmony and all-girls ethos and agree that surely there was no better home for this shy, accomplished career woman.

In the Newnham archive, there's a photograph taken in the coronation year; Joyce is standing laughing, her head crowned with a muzzy perm, her comely figure fashionably tucked into a voluminous skirt and bold striped shirt. The eye is drawn to a silken bow attached to her cleavage, and a cashmere cardigan holds the look in check. Newnham's teaching staff have assembled in their common room after formal dinner. An entirely female occasion, the fashions are conservative and the smiles decorous; Joyce looks fresh-faced at thirty-five amidst a prestigious line of female achievement. For decades, women ('and some Sidgwick men!' adds Ann when talking through the Newnham connections in her own family tree) had supported and nurtured fellow women to preserve and grow their precious place in the foothills of academia. Dressed in black, imposing beneath dark brows and owlish specs and seated in front of Joyce, is Professor Jocelyn Toynbee.* The two women first met in Rome, where Joyce concedes that her eager uptake of Jocelyn's site visits and museum trips saw the pair become friendly. 'Yes, I suppose she was significant to me.' Perhaps there is no such thing as luck, just opportunity and preparation. Certainly, Joyce was more than prepared when Jocelyn was appointed as Laurence Professor

---

* Jocelyn Toynbee's brother was the renowned historian Arnold J. Toynbee and Jocelyn was *Guardian* journalist Polly Toynbee's great-aunt.

of Classical Archaeology in 1951 (only the second woman to hold a Cambridge University professorship). It was this appointment that left the vacancy in Newnham's Classics department. Joyce got the job.

Initially installed in Peile Hall, a red brick residence for seventy-two undergraduate girls, during term times Miss Joyce Reynolds was surrounded by the familiar buzz and worry of young women. Coal fires, mid-calf skirts, freezing rooms, burnt teacakes and Brown Windsor soup loomed large. Within the college, sightings of boys were rare and strictly forbidden after ten o'clock; Joan Bakewell (née Rowlands) – a study of cool – was an exception in black trouser ensembles, audaciously allowing gentlemen to slip in through her ground-floor sash window. Outnumbered nine to one with their college only just granted university status, it wasn't easy being a female student in the 1950s.[1] Miss Reynolds, always generously clad in 'Reynolds blue', retreating into her study, was a figure to be revered, even feared.

In 1952, Pat Easterling (née Fairfax) was bookish and northern and only just eighteen; Lancashire was home and Barbara Castle her local MP. 'I was terribly earnest, I was the first person in my family to go to university, and I was dead keen on study.' She was also the first girl that Joyce ever interviewed. Now eighty-three years old, Pat is enjoying hot pudding and custard in Newnham's capacious Champney dining hall. Her kind face belies a phenomenal academic force. In 1994, she was appointed Regius Professor of Greek at Cambridge University. A chair that dates back to Henry VIII, Pat was the first woman to hold the prestigious post. Over forty years earlier, Joyce had spotted Pat's ability and knew Newnham was the right place for her academic development. 'Cambridge offered me a scholarship, Oxford only an exhibition, so I chose Cambridge.'

Today, Joyce still casually refers to octogenarian Prof Easterling as one of her pupils. It's disconcerting but accurate. Pat insists.

I can attribute a great deal of my achievements to Joyce. She always gave very careful thought to the supervisors she sent one to. She sent me to a later Professor of Greek, Hugh Lloyd Jones, who was very high-handed and someone who set very high standards. I remember him saying to students, 'Most of you ought to be drinking coffee on King's Parade, not coming to this lecture on Aeschylus.'

Today there is a litany of pupils-cum-professors who remain devoted and indebted to, even delighted by, Joyce. Sixty-eight-year-old MM (Mary Margaret) McCabe is now Emeritus Professor of Ancient Philosophy at King's College London, but fifty years ago at Newnham College she was one of Joyce's students.

> Joyce was mind-bogglingly brilliant. I loved the way she taught ancient history. Her supervisions were so clear and precise. She'd set us against each other, she was an acute judge of character – out of five girls in the tutorial, she'd know who didn't like each other and she'd get hold of the girl I didn't like and make us take opposing views. I've never worked so hard in my life!

As an undergraduate, MM admits to being 'cool and sexy. Trivial-minded. I liked clothes and boyfriends.' All the things Joyce wasn't, but the power of Miss Reynolds was the defining force in MM's undergraduate life. 'I generally shook in my shoes waiting outside her flat to be told how my term had gone. I recall the devastation when it was complete rubbish.' Pat, by this time Joyce's colleague, recalls, 'She could be very frightening as a director of studies to people who hadn't done or read all they promised to read in the vacation. People got very scared about this.' Over fifty years later, MM still finds herself standing up when talking to her former tutor on the telephone.

By the 1970s, a social revolution was buffeting through Britain's universities, playing topsy-turvy with preordained ideas of womanhood and sexuality. Joyce, meanwhile, remained her timeless indomitable self. It was early December, the season for feted Oxbridge interviews, and a bright girl (according to the application form, 'an only child of elderly parents') with an impressive written entrance exam under her belt entered Joyce's hallowed space for further questioning.

> I went into this room, the like of which I hadn't seen. It was covered with books and papers, just the same as it is now. Well, obviously, one is very anxious. The telephone went in the middle of the interview and it was clearly about what name was to be put on some article and Joyce boomed, 'I do have a middle name, you know.'

Joyce Maire Reynolds (JMR for short) reprimanded her colleague in front of the silently seated interviewee. Teenage Mary Beard was suitably impressed. 'It came across with real punch to pack.'

Professor Mary Beard (OBE), famous for being an 'old', outspoken, female television historian, is, at sixty-two, one of Joyce's younger students. Today, they live around the corner from one another in Cambridge and enjoy an enduring friendship. A shared sense of place and purpose has long united them; both are thoroughbred classicists, Newnham Fellows and academic women, even their hallmark long grey hair suggests a shared defiance. (Joyce contains hers with kirby grips. Nearly forty years her junior, Mary's flies untamed.) Although housed within the confines of a girls' college, Mary claims her undergraduate years at Cambridge 'were the first time I realised there was sexism in the world. I had lived a protected life.' Often defined in the press as a maverick feminist, Mary has publicly recalled a memorable day during her first year at Newnham, when a male friend picked up an essay lying on her desk and read the tutor's comment 'This is very good; I think it would get a first.' 'You!' he spluttered, 'Get a first?' Women's liberation still had a lot of work to do. In the mid-'70s, there were 'lots of men who thought that women were destined only to get 2:1s'. This was especially the case in Classics, typically an elitist male discipline, and according to Mary run by 'curmudgeonly old sods'.[2] It was lucky then that her director of studies was a woman who'd already defied the odds.

Joyce didn't get caught up in the modern jangle of feminist

debate, she had been treading her own path before it even existed. Labels were extraneous for a woman who had always focused on maximising girls' academic potential. Upon arrival at Newnham, Mary and her first-year peers were given an introductory meeting with Joyce. She made little accommodation for their green-horn state, explaining, 'You are being paid for by the taxpayer to do this degree, and that means you have to think of it at the level of a job, and you should be doing eight hours a day, five and a half days a week, forty-eight weeks of the year.' The introduction of maintenance grants in 1962 was a privilege Joyce was determined shouldn't be squandered. Mary adds ruefully, 'You can't say that to a student today because the taxpayer isn't paying for them. But I try. I say that when I was an undergraduate, this is what was said to me.' Joyce's ethos reverberates down the decades, long after the money's dried up.

'You can't work in Cambridge for as long as I have without being aware that, as a woman, the dice are loaded against you.' Mary is talking about today. It was much worse when she was an undergraduate in the 1970s. This analysis provides context for Joyce's achievements twenty years earlier, in the 1950s. Within a year of arriving at Newnham, she was invited to teach first-year students ancient history at Trinity College (then all-male). Joyce dismisses this opportunity as 'an agreement between two friends. I knew the supervisor in question. He knew I would be quite a stimulating teacher.' She was eventually promoted to university assistant lecturer and received a pay rise that came, essentially, with teaching (men) at university level. No Equal Pay Act propped Joyce up, and the first Sex Discrimination Act was two decades away; women who occupied lectureships and professorships were still a rare breed and yet she had quietly progressed thanks to a meticulous and acute approach to study and work.* Her gift to the next generation of women was to

---

* Joyce insists that 'some credit should be given to the Classical Faculty at Cambridge University, which was more appreciative of its women. I was their first woman secretary.'

demand the same, and help them achieve it. No one, not even Mary Beard, is an accidental genius.

> Joyce had terribly high expectations, but she gave a huge amount back. When you went for a supervision for your essay in that same old messy room, she went on as long as it took. So you might have been there for two hours, but she didn't stop your supervision until all the points had been covered. It was very moving in a way and it was only gradually that I realised, even for that time, it was extraordinary.

HELENA

'I think we got a television when I was about nine. As a teenager, I watched *Top of the Pops*. How my father used to laugh. I liked the Small Faces and Herman's Hermits!' Helena's daughter, Meryl, giggles. First aired in 1964, *Top of the Pops* was appointment viewing in Mid Wales for young teenage girls. The cultural face of Britain was changing – by the end of the 1960s, nearly 90 per cent of homes had a television and more people were fixed in front of their sets than anywhere else in Europe, with the average Briton clocking up twenty hours' viewing a week.[3] Not Helena though. Meryl shakes her head. 'No, Mum really hardly had time for television. She went at breakneck speed; perhaps when she came in from running the youth club she would watch the nine o'clock news with Dad, but that was about it.' As with Joyce, it is not enough to contain Helena's achievements within a simple job title or description. Helena always went outside the lines of her teaching and domestic duties. Young Farmers' drama club, biweekly youth club, Sunday school, the Women's Institute (particularly their drama festivals) and eisteddfods, both local and national – while the majority of parochial Britain spent more and more time behind a barrage of home entertainment, Helena stepped up her external engagement with Breconshire's communities.

Meryl watched her mother's fraught efforts to get a driving

licence. 'It took a long time for Mum to learn to drive. At least four times she took her test.' Helena eventually triumphed – with local bus services cut, her presence at the Talgarth Youth Club was at stake. 'I got paid for that work, you know; the club was for disadvantaged children.' But there was a lot that Helena didn't get paid for. 'I suppose I'm most proud of what I did with the Young Farmers'. Producing plays at the highest levels and winning competitions.' Helena would select one-act dramas from the local Brecon Library, reading half a dozen to find the right one. 'I always used Welsh writers if possible – T. C. Thomas, I loved his, they were very funny, and Frank Vickery's.'

Farming had become increasingly mechanised, men and boys worked alone, and the introduction of the breathalyser in 1965 curbed pub gatherings in the evenings. Even the Welsh chapels struggled in the modern era (there was no one left to take Meryl's confirmation class). It was against this shrinking social scene that Helena plied her trade. She changed lives. Meryl nods. 'I don't know what we'd have done without Mum. I remember her staying up all night making costumes. She'd clear the decks and focus. My cousin always says, "There would've been nothing to do without Aunt Helena."' And back at the farm, patiently (proudly) waiting for her was Percy. Helena acknowledges their union was profound and enduring.

> He was extremely gentle and very kind, the best husband you could ever have. Wasn't I lucky? I was always very proud of him. He had a best suit and he'd only wear it for good occasions. I'd go into a hall with him and people would be talking and I would pick him out and, I would think, 'Oh!' He was quite good-looking, you know.

Lean, tawny Percy, with a thick riff of white hair, was Helena's mainstay. Meryl acknowledges her parents' relationship was special. 'He was her rock, he gave her the space she needed. She had someone to come home to and run things by.' Helena darned Percy's socks and daily left his lunch to be heated in a saucepan on the Rayburn but, by the standards of the 1960s, the man of the Jones's household was before his time. Theirs was a marriage based on companionship and mutual respect. Looking back, there's almost nothing Helena would change. 'But. Well, I was always so busy. I wonder if I might have prioritised ... you know.' She pauses. Physical intimacy between long-term married couples was rarely discussed in the 1960s. Now, surrounded by the contemporary din of a sexualised society, widowed Helena is left wondering. But the past is a foreign land, and never more so than matters concering a woman's sexuality. Her modest reflection suggests that the Jones's marital relations were considerably more enlightened than those of some of their contemporaries. For many wives, night-time rituals were never something to enjoy, sex was just another chore.

The 1960s have long been branded the permissive decade, a period when the legislative framework regulating sexual behaviour was finally overhauled. But if legal abortion and the arrival of oral contraception made 'free love' instantly viable, uptake proved elusive. Moral conservatism persisted across all classes, and even among married women the use of the pill was slow. Permissiveness took time to feed into behaviours. Helena will always be a girl of the 1920s and 1930s, she came from an era when adults rarely spoke about their bodies, and never in relation to sex. Only Olive will admit to an orgasm. 'One night I got dat feeling, dis thing is from my foot to my head!' It was a profound experience but one that happened after several years of marriage and a visit to the doctor on her husband's insistence. The sixties saw much more public discourse about sexual relations but most, especially the older generation, either disapproved or felt out of their depth. In 1968, *New Society* ran a survey which confirmed what many were thinking. 'Too much publicity was given to sex.'[4]

Meryl is candid. 'Mum, you never taught us about the birds and the bees! No, you didn't warn me about menstruation.' But Meryl did receive thunderous warnings about behaving herself, while any talk concerning contraceptive options in the late sixties was strictly off limits. 'I wouldn't have discussed it with my mother and she wouldn't have discussed it with me.' Helena nods. 'There was the morning-after pill I remember. I suppose I used to think if it happens they will know about it.' If, like her mother before her, conversations about sex were strictly off limits, horizons had shifted and Meryl could access information and help in the public arena. 'But still, I always knew that my parents had very strict views.' The sixties rocked, but parents silently hoped the refrain 'No sex please, we're British!' applied to their children.

ANN

Ann, aged 103, has arrived for dinner, stepping out of an Uber in a stylish black mohair cardigan (hand-lined with silk to preserve its shape), proffering a small pot of homemade gooseberry and nutmeg jam. She eats (and drinks) heartily and gets on well with the literary agent, Robert Kirby, to her left (he is familiar with her father's publishing firm, Sidgwick & Jackson). Keen on nostalgia, Robert enquires about the 'roaring' sixties. Ann replies pointedly: 'I was in my fifties in the '60s.' Her corrective is important. The general tendency is to live each decade through the lens of our own generation. In Ann's sixties, there was no 'roaring' nor psychedelic flower power (save the occasional piece of 'modern' art). However, it was to prove perhaps the most significant decade in her long life. When it began, she was a stylish career woman co-running Ganymed, the art gallery and printing house. It was a satisfying job, made all the more so with the 'mutual aims and work' she shared with her colleague, Bernhard Baer. A German Jewish refugee who'd arrived in London before the war, Ann first remembers seeing Bernhard on the opening night of the gallery in 1949, when all and sundry were clinking glasses and chit-chatting in the auspicious surrounds of No.1 Bedford Square. All, that is, except Bernhard.

Bernhard went around the room looking at the facsimiles where they were hanging next to the original paintings. I thought, who is this strange man pushing up his glasses and looking at such a short distance from the pictures, when everybody else was looking inwards and ignoring the display. What a peculiar man!

Shortly afterwards, they became work colleagues and proved the perfect double act; Anglo-Saxon Ann's artistic knowhow complemented Bernhard's technical expertise in colour and printing acquired in pre-war Germany. He was a (reluctant) lawyer when, in 1933, the Nazis outlawed 'Jewish activity' in the legal professions. Bernhard was forced to focus on his passion. 'He had been experimenting in colour photography privately in his own flat, and that gave him the entrée into a firm of printers in Berlin.'

Life became increasingly untenable for German Jews; by the mid-1930s, Bernhard acquired an advanced one-shot colour camera and clinched a job in London, off Charing Cross Road. Initially, he lived in penury in Hampstead, where he met his musical German wife, Ruth. After the war they had two children – Susan and, nine years later, James – and moved to Richmond upon Thames. A very good cook and highly companionable, Ann would invite Bernhard and Ruth over for dinner; they reciprocated, with Ann a regular visitor at their Richmond home. 'I got to know their daughter, Susan, but James was usually in bed.' Susan recalls that Ann was like 'a lot of other people who knew my father. Clever and knowledgeable.' What she didn't anticipate was that by 1964 Ann would also be her stepmother.

Suddenly, shockingly, Ruth had a heart attack aged fifty in 1963. The Baer family were on holiday in Italy, an ambulance was called, but it was too late, she died on the way to hospital. Susan and James lost their mother and woke up to a widowed father. Ann recalls, 'It was terrible; she had been an active, busy woman until then.' With characteristic tact and care, she wrote teenage Susan a letter of condolence. 'Mothers, especially good mothers, are very important at this time of your life.' Bernhard, a stringent intellectual, found himself alone and grappling with the practicalities of running a home, raising two children and directing Ganymed. Susan, a gauche, grieving adolescent, was tasked with looking after the house. 'I remember once Father came home from work and lost his temper. "Why isn't there any cheese?" I panicked. "I don't know why there isn't any cheese!" I couldn't even boil an egg.'

A man with children in the 1960s needed a wife. And Bernhard wanted one. Within eight months, he had proposed to and married his colleague and friend, Ann Sidgwick. 'I know it was very sudden and quick. Yes, I am sure that lots of people who knew both of us assumed that we'd been having an affair for years, whereas there was never any hint of that. Absolutely nothing. No impropriety. Nothing.' Ann wrote another letter to Susan, 'saying how glad she was to have been asked to be Bernhard's wife'. Susan admits she also took the trouble to make 'the embarrassing confession that nothing had ever happened before my mother died. I didn't think it had.'

Ann is certain that before their marriage she had never viewed Bernhard as anything other than a colleague. 'But, you know, we came to the conclusion we rather depended on each other and then when he said, "I think we'd better get married," there didn't seem to be any point not to.' But surely there was a romantic undercurrent? She laughs. 'He gave me an amethyst ring, and at New Year, when Ruth had been dead several months, he gave me an amethyst bracelet. I thought, "Dear me, this is serious."' And it was. Ann had her engagement photograph taken in Harrods – the woman in the picture is effortlessly stylish; contemporary glass beads complement a scoop-necked silk top. She is young for her fifty years, with a creamy complexion and curled brown hair. Bernhard had found a model wife and Ann finally succumbed to marriage. 'I wasn't bullied into it. I didn't miss my freedom, this is what I'd chosen to do.' Born into Establishment England in 1914, talking about her emotions doesn't come easily, but it's very apparent Ann's was a happy marriage. The newlyweds honeymooned in late April 1964. Their Venetian hotel was on the edge of the Grand Canal, where the bells of Santa Maria della Salute filled the air and spring blossom and the shouts of boatmen on passing gondolas graced their balcony. 'It was absolutely lovely.'

The wedding was low-key and non-religious, Ann wore a dark-green silk dress and only invited a couple of witnesses, including her mother (reluctantly) and a next-door neighbour. 'I had given an engagement party in my Knightsbridge flat shortly beforehand, for my brothers and sisters and Susan and James. I made myself a coral pink dress. I think Bernhard seemed quite pleased with all these strange new in-laws.' It was a more daunting experience for his state-educated daughter. Standing, accepting finger food amidst the hubbub of England's upper classes, Susan felt uncomfortable. 'All the Sidgwick nephews and nieces were tall and alien to me; it was like going to a foreign country. There were so many of them.' Susan had grown up in a Hampstead flat surrounded by displaced German Jews, the London she was born into was a different country.

In the middle of those 'roaring' sixties, fifty-year-old Ann became a wife and (step)mother for the first time, a new life she juggled alongside her previous one as a Ganymed director. 'She was immensely patient with us, although she must've found us both ghastly. I was a difficult, obsessed teenager and James was a very physical little boy.' In fact, James seemed to be delighted with his new stepmother. He met the news with: 'Thank goodness we'll get some decent food!' and looked forward to the arrival of a vacuum cleaner. 'Is she bringing that sucking monster?' For Ann, the adjustment was more challenging. She had to compact her working day to be home for James by four o'clock. 'And the school holidays were always a nightmare. How to find someone to look after and entertain and educate James.' Ann's situation pre-empted the existential and practical worries that working mothers would experience in future decades, but minus decent childcare. James's sister, Susan, observed that her young brother 'soon thought of Ann as a mother'.

After a stint in Italy, Susan left home to study history of art at the Courtauld Institute. An old-school liberal in the new permissive era, Ann boldly broached the subject of sex with her stepdaughter. The latter remembers 'a rather stilted conversation about contraception when it became obvious that I was "sleeping" with my "boyfriend".' Ann was a responsible woman, never a judgemental one – Susan needed to know the options available in a brave new world. A conversation about skirt lengths was less excruciating. Ann asked Susan how short was fashionably short in the age of the miniskirt. Perhaps she was more contemporary than she realised. But some matters remain private. In keeping with her generation, Ann won't talk about marital intimacy.

'No! I can't remember our first kiss and, even if I could, I wouldn't tell you!'

JOYCE

MM McCabe was a naughty girl when at Cambridge in the sixties. If provincial Britain was slow to embrace social change, universities were the fault lines along which the new generation pushed the envelope of tolerance and freedom. 'I hid a lot of *that* from Joyce.' MM is talking about extracurricular activities and boyfriends and 'stuff'. After all, Joyce was an academic spinster and her director of studies, hardly suitable material for sharing undergraduate antics with. 'But then I had a real boyfriend problem. I dumped him and he wouldn't go away. There was a bust-up.' In her third year, MM was in genuine distress; despite her reservations that Joyce 'was not going to care, because all she cares about is tripos',* MM decided to talk to her. 'And I was glad I did. I remember her helping, listening. I thought, "You don't tell Joyce about boyfriends," but she understands things that you don't think she is going to understand and she is terribly, terribly kind.'

After MM McCabe came equally wild Mary Beard, who still enjoys regaling the press with her sexy antics as an undergraduate in the 1970s – a virgin she wasn't. In the Newnham archive, historian Gill Sutherland laughs. 'Joyce is friends with Mary, not much can shock her!' Joyce herself points out that when Germaine Greer held a lectureship at Newnham College in the 1990s, she had found the controversial feminist to be 'respectful, charming even. She got many people's backs up but not mine. Has she been banned from some university campuses? That sounds quite wrong.' Around long enough to see Greer outlawed as a reactionary for her thoughts on transgender issues in the 2010s, Joyce was in late middle age when

---

* The final honours examination for a BA degree at Cambridge University.

the Australian polemicist began radically deconstructing womanhood and femininity in the 1960s and 70s. That era belonged to her
students, who entered a world that barely existed when Joyce had
grown up; she travelled with MM and Mary by association alone.

'When I was an undergraduate we didn't talk about sex.' To
underline the point Joyce recalls the furore during her first year at
Oxford in 1937 – a Somerville girl had been caught spending the
evening with her boyfriend. 'His landlady must have reported them.'
The female student was sent down (expelled) from the college, and a
vigorous protest debate was held by Somerville's students, who were
especially outraged because the boyfriend in question had only been
rusticated (suspended).

> What I hope you will find funny is that the whole discussion took
> place in terms which never actually described precisely what had
> happened, and a rather innocent friend of mine couldn't under-
> stand what it was about. 'Just sending her down because she had
> been out late!' The discussion was totally euphemistic; there was
> no mention of sex out of wedlock.

Eighteen-year-old Joyce, caught between the parental path ('My
mother would have sent her down') and the feeling that 'freedom of
decision was something one ought to have', abstained from voting.

Within that story are the parameters which helped define Joyce's
own personal life. Her generation was brought up believing sex
should only occur after marriage. But marriage was a serious business which normally precluded high professional attainment if you
were a woman. (There isn't one married woman in the photograph of
Somerville's teaching staff from 1934.[5]) She loved a fellow academic
as a graduate student but her feelings weren't reciprocated.

> I half fell in love again but never quite as deeply. I mean, I was
> very fond of this or that or the other. I suppose there were one or
> two I would like to have married but I didn't feel strongly or as
> strongly as about the first one.

Her colleagues confirm that Joyce enjoys men's company and in later years she travelled to ancient sites with male companions. 'On one occasion with somebody I respected and admired as a scholar and liked, but I didn't want to marry him. We went for several holidays together, visiting ancient sites in the 1970s I think. I wouldn't have wanted to wander all over Italy's islands on my own.' By this time in her fifties, Joyce and a man ten years her senior ('No, I can't remember a name') enjoyed time together discussing antiquity's problems. Both were knowledgeable and clever and both were single.

> He wanted to marry me, yes, but I didn't want to marry him. He wanted more than a companion, he wanted somebody to go to bed with. To get married to him I would've had to have liked him in a different way.   ·
> Certainly we had separate hotel rooms!

There's a stoicism developed in solitude and a virtue in abstinence; Joyce had form when it came to being single, and she wasn't going to compromise. She laughs when asked if there was ever a Mills & Boon moment with anyone. 'No, no nothing of that sort. I think I wished something had come of the first man in Rome.' In her ninety-nine years, there has never been a marriage and therefore no physical relationship with a man. In the same cluttered bookish space, Joyce sitting at her writing table, we are no longer discussing epigraphy or Cambridge students, we are talking about sex (or rather the lack of it), but with her usual quiet dignity she applies to each question the same careful consideration. Does she ever feel she missed out? 'Yes, I think I did. But I don't know what I would mean by missed out. I just felt ... I suppose I would say, "That would have been terribly nice."'

~

Change for women came incrementally. In 1963, Pat Easterling, married and working alongside Joyce at Newnham College, was one of the first members of staff who 'risked' having a child. 'I had the feeling that it would be quite a good idea if I could have my baby in the vacation. Heehee.' But mother nature proved less predictable. 'My son was a bit early so my husband and Joyce mopped up my supervisions for the rest of the term and the next. Oh yes, Joyce was very supportive of me having a child, she laid down no rules.' In the 1960s and '70s, second wave feminism was noisily challenging the well-established idea that the role of professional women versus those of wives and mothers was mutually exclusive. Beyond the hype, at an individual level, women relied on other women to help them push the boundaries of what was possible. Joyce was an integral part of Pat's groundbreaking story.

MM McCabe, a wilful teenager in the sixties, is adamant that 'as a woman, Joyce was absolutely essential' to her progression in the field of classical philosophy. 'I wouldn't have articulated this at the time, but when I was young I thought, "Look, here is somebody, no matter what her sacrifices, who is doing it."' But she also concedes that 'I wasn't willing not to get married and have children and all of that.' A new breed of women was emerging who expected to have a career and a family. A professor, a wife (twice) and a mother, MM McCabe realised her dream, as did Professor Mary Beard after her.

It is testimony to Joyce's generosity of spirit that she never looked back at what might have been, and she carries no retrojected animosity over her single, childless status. She concedes, 'Oh surely,' it is very different for the generations of academic women that came after her, but disagrees it's somehow 'easier' for them. 'No, I think it is more difficult. Because one has responsibilities in both camps and perhaps those responsibilities clash or are compromised in some way.' The example Joyce gives is a dramatic one. 'I only twice had this, a student who was liable to commit suicide, and if you've got a sick child at home, how do you combine those two necessities? The pastoral and academic role of being a tutor are inextricable, quite inextricable.'

Mary confirms Joyce is 'entirely without jealousy'. Her great secret as a mentor of future generations was that she did not covet their freedom but rather helped them navigate their way through uncharted territory. Joyce considered herself 'part of the 1960s too! One was able to be open-minded.' Within the familial atmosphere of an all-women's college, she provided more than intellectual and emotional support. MM McCabe recalls drinking 'her famous gin and lychees combination at the end of Part I [an exam that was part of tripos] in Joyce's flat'. And there were legendary evening excursions into the Fens. Mary starts giggling. 'I remember in the middle of the tripos she would always take students out to dinner so they got a night off. It was terribly funny, there was a very nice restaurant in Saffron Walden and she would drive – she was an absolutely terrible driver! And we would go in the car.' Mary is now almost snorting with glee. 'And a few years before this, it had been a complete disaster because her car had broken down on the way home. Hahaha! Terribly funny. So, in future she always chose an evening when nobody had an exam the next morning.'

Joyce – timepiece and time traveller – driving her students into the wilds for restorative country air and good conversation and food before they tackled Plato and Euripides. 'It was lovely,' confirms another Classics professor, Charlotte Roueché. 'But it was in the build-up to the exams, and the world had unfortunately just invented contact lenses, and I had them and I dropped one in the dark in the Fens. I don't think I ever found it. It made for rather a complicated evening!'

Mary concedes that nowadays student–tutor relationships are more formalised. The intensity as well as the freewheeling and fun between pupil and teacher is a thing of the past; precautions became an obvious necessity in a few extreme cases, and modern bureaucracy is a thief of time. 'But,' she sighs, 'we've lost something, lost that kind of ... ' Mary doesn't finish her sentence, she doesn't need to. It is unlikely there will ever be another Joyce and that's a great pity.

CHAPTER SIXTEEN

MAKING A HAT FROM KITCHENWARE

EDNA

'I've got something to show you.' Edna presents me with a thoughtfully selected collection of memorabilia. The centenary edition of the Women's Institute magazine, a plastic wallet with one of Edna's first WI membership cards dated 6 November 1947 and a book of sheet music 'especially written for us at the WI'. Every time we meet, without fail, Edna reminds me of the importance of the Women's Institute in her life. 'It empowered me. You must understand, without the WI I wouldn't be able to speak like I am speaking to you now. I was very shy.' Although revolutionary on a personal level, like everything else in Edna's life she had to wait years before she could enjoy the benefits of membership. 'I first went to the WI as a visitor aged twelve cos our cookery mistress was going to show the ladies how to ice a cake for Christmas, but I couldn't fit the meetings in with domestic service. I couldn't do it.'

Formed in 1915 to revitalise rural communities and boost food production during the First World War, the National Federation of Women's Institutes quickly became the largest women's organisation in the post-suffrage era. Denton had a tiny WI in a former purpose-built army hut, but initially Edna didn't attend. 'I was the lowest of the low, you see. Even when I worked for lovely Mrs Fisher at the beginning of the war I couldn't go, cos she was the local chairwoman and I had to stay and give Mr Fisher his supper.' Perhaps it was the extended fifteen-year wait that made membership so sweet. 'I first joined in 1942, when I went to work in the market garden. Oh, it was very simple in Denton, nothing fancy but ... well ...' It meant something. It really meant something.

Edna files through old WI programmes from 1962 (her last year in the Denton branch). Upcoming events at the weekly meetings are listed. *Best addressed envelope by Mrs Otter* – 'now, she was the wife of the Bishop of Grantham, she was important.' The social mixing that men enjoyed on the village green over a game of cricket was finally afforded to women, albeit in a more hierarchical form. Servant Edna shared a homemade bun and cup of tea with Mrs Otter and other ladies (and gentlemen) prepared to impart their wisdom.

Life in Hong Kong by Mr Wilcox.
Care of Hair by Martin Douglas of Mayfair.
Talk on Pop Music by Mr Turner.
Competition: Making a Hat from Kitchenware.

Recreation, social mixing, leisure time, even political activism ('Oh yes, we always had a campaign, you see we carried on where the suffragettes left off; we are fighting for milk and the environment at the moment.') Edna hasn't reneged on her membership since 1942. Although Denton was where it all began, bigger WIs offered greater opportunities. In Sutton on Sea, where Edna looked after the head-master's family, she broke new ground. 'There I had to propose a vote of thanks. Somebody else had to second. Their idea was that if you got up and did that then that was a path to doing more. It gave me the confidence that I needed.' By the time Edna got married to Ern aged forty-seven, she had been a member of the WI for twenty years, it formed the backbone of her meagre social life and rooted her into local communities (Sutton on Sea, Grantham, Denton) in ways otherwise unavailable to domestic servants. The result was a more self-assured Edna in middle age – this was the woman who arrived in Wroughton in 1962 to make her new life as Mrs Cripps.

Husband Ern's wage as a tiler and plasterer enabled her to finally forgo the humility of live-in servitude. Anyway, times were changing and by the 1960s domestic help in a part-time capacity was the norm for most middle-class households. 'The happiest years of my life were working as a batwoman in the RAF houses.'* Daily, Edna pedalled up Brimble Hill to rapturous welcomes. 'It was an officer's privilege, you see, to have a batwoman. But I worked for the wives, twenty-two families in total over twelve years. I had a very good reputation with small children.'

Part-time, Monday to Friday employment proved transformative. 'I've preferred my last fifty years to the first half of my life. The first half was a waste.' Edna is unrepentant. Domestic service stole her youth but how she savoured the delights of creative homemaking when finally in possession of a husband, a home, time and opportunity. History has often maligned the impact of the WI, with derisory 'Jam and Jerusalem' epithets and handbag references. But to mock the movement's post-war focus on consumerism and home decoration risks undermining the lifestyle of rafts of middle-aged and older women in the 1960s and '70s.

Helena and Edna grew up (and will die) rural women. But both have long outlived their respective mothers, whose hard, physical labour in and around the home was continual, exhausting, fatal. In contrast, by the 1960s, time-saving technology meant the home was no longer a space associated exclusively with drudgery, even for Edna. Especially for Edna. Her combined love of gardening and WI crafts inspired a new skill – flower arranging on a grand and competitive scale. Edna has a scrapbook full of local news clippings featuring her artistic exploits with foliage and blooms.

---

* Batwoman and batman are military terms for individuals assigned to Officers' Messes or as personal assistants to high-ranking servicemen and -women and their families.

Oh, I can arrange anything. Daffs, snowdrops, chrysanthemums, hydrangeas; oh yes, you have to grow your own. I loved doing the miniature posies and I always did the church flowers. Ern and I had a lovely garden in Perry's Lane, and an allotment. I remember the two old men in the allotment opposite Ern's staring at me cos women never went down the allotment. They were astounded cos they couldn't understand how I knew what I was doing.

The girl who grew up bobbing her head and scrubbing pots had left the past behind and was forging her own exciting future in Wiltshire. 'I was sitting next to my friend Paddy on the bus after we'd been doing flower-arranging lessons and she said, "Do you think we'll ever get a floral society off the ground?" I said, "Leave it with me, dear."' Half a century later, Edna is not allowed to die. 'It's got nothing to do with my age, it's just that I am the founder and president of Wroughton's Floral Art Society and it celebrates its fiftieth anniversary this summer!'

In 1997 an academic, Maggie Andrews, wrote a book called *The Acceptable Face of Feminism: The Women's Institute as a Social Movement*. There is a chapter heading, 'Can Flower Arranging Be Feminist?', in which she makes the point that 'the utility of flower arranging is virtually nil'. That unlike other manual skills (which Edna also possesses), such as jam-making and patchwork, flower arranging serves no purpose, it is purely decorative. Thus, Andrews argues, floral art is 'an assertion of a woman at one level to spend time in a leisure pursuit with aesthetic rather than utilitarian values'. She concludes that this space women had created for themselves, previously a rarity among the working classes, was an essential precondition for the feminist movement of the 1960s and 70s.[1] As if plucked from the pages of Andrews's book, here was Edna finally taking control of her time in the way she wanted to; she was, after decades of subservience, enjoying her own free will. Edna the feminist giggles. 'And do you know what else I learnt? Lace-making!' Beautifully beaded bobbins and hours of painstaking concentration, all to produce tiny white petalled fancies, whisker-thin doilies and delicate wall hangings that adorn her modest home, magical for their intricate stitches and little else besides. 'Yes, I've loved the last half of my life, well most of it.'

HELENA

Of the six women in this book, Helena is the other (lifelong) member of the WI. 'I was eighteen, living with Mum and Dad as a student teacher at Trallong School, and the head teacher, Miss Walton, said, "It's WI tomorrow night, you must join because there are lots of advantages."' Helena capitalised on every one. 'Well, you met friends and you had the chance to go on courses.' The WI's prestigious Oxfordshire college, Denman, named after the movement's first chairwoman, hosted Helena on several occasions – there she improved her writing and learnt the art of toy-making. (Edna never went to Denman – 'Oh no, I didn't have the money for that.') Already equipped with social confidence and status in her local community, Helena's life wasn't as profoundly impacted by the movement as Edna's, it was one among a rich vista of evening activities. 'The WI drama festival was my thing. It began when I was asked to produce a play at the Trallong WI – ooh, a long time ago now.' Helena chose the drama in the local library and carefully selected her cast.

> There was a girl who played the maid, Rennie she was called, and she had to wear an apron, and we were rehearsing for weeks and we competed and won in the Brecon theatre there. And I remember one night, Rennie's apron fell off and I said, 'Oh, Rennie, you want to tie that tighter than that,' and then it fell off again! I said, 'Oh, Rennie, if those straps are too short make them a bit longer!' Well, you know, the day after the festival Rennie had a baby!

Helena hoots with laughter. 'No, she wasn't married! My God, wasn't I stupid! I never dreamt she'd be pregnant! I'd be a bit wiser today, mind.' Apparently the WI has always been a broad church.

EDNA

'Ern helped me with the WI, and when it came to the Christmas bazaar – can you see up there on the wall – he used to make hedge-hogs out of teasel.' It was a small but important gesture. Men had grumbled about 'losing' their wives to the WI since its inception but Ern, a bachelor for the first fifty-two years of his life, was used to fending for himself. Acutely aware of his long-term single status, Edna made the transition into marriage easy for him. 'I felt that somehow or other he had his life and I'd got to fit in with it. It wasn't a case of him fitting in with me, I felt that because of the way he was, I had to fit in with him.' Tall, devout and quiet, Edna admits that Ern also had 'a very short fuse'. His health impacted on his mood. 'He was always in pain, he had a condition called ankylosing spondylitis.' Plagued by chronic inflammation of the spine, a pronounced stoop restricting his movement, unable to walk arm in arm with his new wife, Ern made do. His job as a plasterer exacerbated the condition but early retirement never occurred to him.

'He was physically handicapped really, you see, but he carried on working.' To sit at home was no life for a man, 'he had to work, being of that generation'. Even on his days off, Ern gently tended his gladioli, painted the church or slowly cycled with Edna. 'We didn't have a car and our bicycles had boxes on the back of them, and he'd come with me if there was anything that had to be carried to a market or competition. He did the flowers, I did the veg. He was very encouraging.' Edna holds these points of common interest dear. 'I remember sitting on the church roof together, watching the sun rise on midsummer's morning. We climbed up through the belfry tower.' Mr and Mrs Cripps, hand in hand, his face lined by the sun, hers soft behind horn-rimmed spectacles. Ern, the clerk of works with Edna, a member of the parochial church council – Wroughton parish fanned before them. It was a blessed, peaceful union. And a short one.

'We were only together thirteen years.' Edna wrinkles her nose. She is 102; their marriage was, in comparison, brutishly minimal. 'He was working, you see, and he got this cough and it wouldn't go away. The doctor took a look and said, "That's it, stop working now!"'

There were lumps too, one on his neck, another 'down below' and ever so many X-rays. 'He was always a smoker, I remember A1 tobacco in a red-and-white tin. I never inhaled, Ern always said a good cigarette was wasted on me!' She smiles. British men smoked, so be it. (A staggering 81 per cent of them, post-war.)* By 1956, the Tory health minister concluded there was probably a link between smoking and lung cancer but he didn't stop smoking himself. Prime Minister Macmillan, worrying about the Treasury's revenues, hoped people would stick with tobacco and the BBC's *Any Questions* provided a reassuring anecdote about Churchill's smoking.[2] Much like the government, Edna wouldn't have dreamt of telling Ern (not her husband until 1962) what to do. Other women were more vocal. Phyllis arrived in Scotland to discover she'd married a heavy smoker. 'Jim was busy lighting one and there was another one lit. You see, you got a hundred cigarettes for half a crown on the ships. I remember the thing about smoking killing in the 1950s and '60s.' Never one to mince her words, Phyllis told her husband straight – '"Jim! Smoking kills!" Oh, and I used to tell him he smelt!' Captain Jim duly stopped, but the damage was done. 'He lost his voice on the ship; it must've been the late sixties and they discovered it was throat cancer.' Phyllis is matter-of-fact: 'They just removed it, they burnt it out, he had a tube in his throat and he was in hospital for a month.' Jim survived and went back to sea. Edna's Ern was less fortunate.

By the time a cautious public health campaign appeared in the mid-'60s, Mr Cripps had been smoking for four decades. Ten years later and he was bedridden in Swindon's Princess Margaret Hospital; the radiotherapy hadn't worked. In 1976, Ern lay clotted with cancer and groggy on morphine, the weather was close, and family flitted in and out. That summer was particularly hot, sunlight teased threatening grey cloud and Edna sat by Ern's bed. Silently, she

---

* In comparison, only 39 per cent of women smoked. None of the six women featured in this book were smokers.

contained a niggling worry. 'You see, he always made mangold wine but that year he hadn't had the chance.' It was no good, she'd have to do something about it. Pecking her husband on the cheek, out she went, away from the squeaky heat of the hospital into Wiltshire's heavy air. 'The weather broke on Friday as he lay dying. It was a terrific thunderstorm but I still had to go and dig these mangolds up.' Beneath open heavens, strong from years of labour, in her welly boots, Mrs Cripps dug her husband's root vegetables. 'They were so dirty but I thought, "I don't care what happens, I am going to make that wine," and I did.'

Ern died two days later, his wife and sister in a vigil by his bed. 'His last words to me were "Rest in the great goodness of the Lord."' Edna took comfort in her husband's faith. Ern had always been a contemplative man, it was important she got her final wifely duty right. She returned to Perry's Lane and shut out the silence with the reassuring weight and words of her husband's Bible. 'It was an old Bible and certain parts of it were marked where he used to go to meetings when he was in his younger days. I came across "*I will trust and not be afraid*." That's it, I thought! That's what I will put on his gravestone.'

The stone has been standing for over forty years. With Edna unable to get there now, niece Carolyn tends to it for her. *I will trust and not be afraid.*

No. I wasn't afraid after he'd gone. I had to pick myself up, because in life there are rough patches and smooth patches. And I suppose I wouldn't have done so many things in Wroughton if Ern had stayed alive. Did I mention, it's the fiftieth anniversary of the Floral Art Society this summer and I'm the president?

⁓

Weeks later, moved by the retelling of this story on the page, I stepped out of the British Library and rang Edna on a mobile from central London. The sun was shining and I wanted to thank her. Out burbled grateful words about Ern, the thunder, mangolds and the summer of '76. Edna was silent. I'd caught her off guard. When she finally spoke, her voice was swollen.

'It wasn't that I don't miss Ern. It's just ... Well, one mustn't moan.'

CHAPTER SEVENTEEN

SWEET DREAMS, FLYING MACHINES

EDNA

August 1915, when baby Edna arrived in Denton village, horse and cart (and shanks's pony) determined the geographical boundaries of her existence. Remote steamships had defined the nineteenth century's international (or rather imperial) scope, but for the ordinary person foreign travel remained a daunting, often irreversible, prospect (there was an uncle Edna never met who'd emigrated to Canada). In its modern context, globalisation – the frantic daily interchange and flow of ideas, goods and people – didn't exist. That required groundbreaking telecommunications backed up by the mass production of diesel engines and gas turbines, an existence where automobiles, aeroplanes and computers were everyday objects. By the late twentieth century, the world had shrunk at turbo-charged speed.

Edna is now bound to her bungalow, and 102 years after her nativity, globalisation doesn't just shimmer on the horizon, it's staked a claim on daily life – a phenomenon that has liberated or left behind a confused humanity in its wake. Edna's watched on with a baleful eye. 'I've never been anywhere but England. I've never felt the inclination.' Day trips to Skegness as a child were supplemented years later when she and Ern occasionally visited her sister (also a domestic servant) in Kent. Edna's never used a computer, she has relied on television and books to fill in the blanks.

> I first travelled through London in 1946 on the train. Later I joined the Dollmakers' Circle in London and with two friends from Wroughton, Pam and Rhonda, we used to go there. As pensioners, we travelled cheaply. We just went to the dollmakers' meetings, no, we didn't go sightseeing. I've never seen the Houses of Parliament. I wasn't very curious, I felt I knew it anyway.

Edna is an English purist. Always a fan of middle England's greatest champion, Prime Minister Stanley Baldwin, she has lived his pre-war vision. Belatedly released from the yoke of service in the 1960s, the freedom to enjoy her green and pleasant land has proved sufficient (there was little money for anything else). 'You can't always want more in life, it doesn't work like that.'

A lifetime's journey from Lincolnshire's Denton to Wiltshire's Wroughton is one version of twentieth-century living and it is Edna's reality. But elsewhere the matrons of one hundred years, too old to cavort in the 1960s and too comfortable to complain in the 1970s, sought to capitalise on the privilege of a smaller, freer world. Travel for travel's sake, once confined to the wealthy, conferred immediate status and freedom.

OLIVE

'Why you not have a car – eh? Ray, he had a new car every three years!' Olive laughs. Ray, her Tory-voting, property developer husband, loved his car. 'Every Saturday afternoon Ray clean his car, all de little silver bits. I say, "You love dat thing more dan me!" He say, "I look after everything that's mine!"' No, she can't remember the model, but the point is he staked his reputation on owning a brand-new set of wheels. There's a picture of young Ray, a carnation in his button hole, leaning on their wedding car. His body language says it all – the baby-blue Ford Zephyr is a thing of great beauty – only the best for his Olive. Before he could afford his own, Ray hired cars. There would be no more hostile stares on public transport; the host country could make way for Mr and Mrs Gordon on the road. He took his 'cutie' to source cassava plants and firm brown rice in Brixton, together they went for a spin to Dirty Dick's, Bishopsgate's famous pub, and soon there were excursions further afield.

By 1956, Olive's teenage children were dropping into their London life – Joye, Gloria and finally Terence. An unfriendly Mother Country *and* a stepfather, the transition wasn't always smooth. Joye was sixteen.

The first thing was, what do I call him? He said, 'Call me Ray,' but I looked at him and I thought, 'I can't call him Ray,' and then one day he was standing like this – with his fingers in his braces – saying, 'I'm de governor of this joint,' and I thought, 'Guv!' That's it, from then on we called him Guv!

Guv took his wife and two teenage stepdaughters on the trip of a lifetime. It was a turning point for family relations, and Olive knows this. 'Let me tell you, when my children came, Ray flew us to Paris with de car! Yes, with de car! He flew us over to Paris for two weeks!' Prior to France, Joye remembers unsatisfactory weekend breaks in Blackpool and Southampton 'in the slinkiest, nastiest, grubbiest places to stay cos the owners were letting themselves down letting you stay ... The suspicion was worse out of London.' Ray decided to raise the stakes. With four earners in the Gordon household, the consumer bubble of the late 1950s afforded the family a slice of luxury that Joye has never forgotten. 'The nicest time I ever had was when we went to Paris with my sister and mother and Ray.' The quartet drove down to Southend-on-Sea and put their car on a biplane, before taking off and touching down in Calais. 'My stepfather was a member of the AA, and he had a big AA badge on his car. We drove to Versailles and we stayed in Hotel Moderne in Paris with Ray's membership.' Poker dens, horse meat, the Eiffel Tower, even a mixed-race couple – Joye couldn't believe her eyes. 'I remember this day walking past and seeing a black man with his arm around a white woman and she kissed him. I looked absolutely shocked and she looked at me and said, "He French!" In other words he is French so it doesn't matter.' British Joye was struck. 'I thought, "Hmmm, so if you're black and French it's all right!"'

In 1971, twelve years after the Gordons' French trip, only 4 million British tourists went abroad on holiday; within a decade that number would treble to 13 million. Mr and Mrs Gordon were ahead of the curve and France was just the beginning. Sixty-five years after docking in 'dismal Britain', Olive loves to regale visitors with the extraordinary list of countries she and Ray later ticked off in the name of leisure.

Precariously balanced in black patent heels, her diminutive frame leaning heavily on a wheeled Zimmer, she can't resist a commentary on the pictures that adorn her walls. 'Der is me on a camel in Egypt, hahaha!' Sure enough, an attractive, mature woman dressed in cherry red straddles a camel against the sandy brick of the world's most famous ancient wonder. 'Ha, you see! I tellin' you Ray took me everywhere.' In another she walks with assurance, tote in hand, pearls bright against a crisp navy shirt, a smart foreground focus for the Swiss Alpine chalets and viridescent trees. 'Not just Switzerland! I been to Scotland, you know, I been to Princes Street, Edinburgh, Ray took me.' Olive gleefully barks out countries, the list is long – Gibraltar, Cyprus, Spain, Greece, Holland, America ... 'But, no, I didn't go so much to de West Indies.' Olive's daughter Joye married a Jamaican but Olive wasn't tempted to holiday near home turf.

'Guyana is de country of my birth, and in Georgetown were relatives of mine. I felt happy to go back der. I went in de '60s. They all came and visited me and brought gifts and so on.' Initially by ship and latterly in the air, Olive made the occasional return trip to Guyana, where she nodded approval at the progress: 'a woman used to sell at de gate of de market little packets of coffee and chocolate when I was a child, and den she opened a big place like Safeways. So yeah, people moved on.' But she was too pragmatic to feel homesick. 'My object of interest no longer der.' Her children, her mother and most importantly Ray were all in England. Returning to Guyana was a pleasing duty but it was recreational travel she hankered most. Framed on the wall, Ray is standing beneath a lemon tree, his stomach plump with success under a cool blue shirt. The couple are on holiday in Havana. 'Cuba was de most expensive holiday, £1,800 for me alone! Yes, it was about fifteen years ago. Oh my Lord, it was amazing, de food and de hotel.' In retirement, Ray's gift to Olive was to place the world in the palm of her hand; she received the compliment with abundant gratitude and goodwill and still generously shares her anecdotes.

Olive loves to be social; at 102 there are exercise classes where local MP Jeremy Corbyn has popped in, St George's Church for God and a good sing-song, and frequent community activities and afternoon teas with other elderly people. It is at one of the latter, over cake with her (near) contemporaries, I first learnt of Olive's travels. Some have heard the stories before, and all are very aware of her special 102-year-old status. Old East End women in their nineties, minus Olive's vim and stylish wardrobe, mutter loudly between themselves. Piqued that they will always be her juniors, they refuse to believe the holiday stories. 'Her husband was just working on a ship, he didn't take her to all these places.' Tut tut. Olive doesn't hear their waspy comments (or chooses not to). Long ago she blocked out the cynicism and judgement of that generation; instead she shouts her status loudly over the hum. Yes, of course she went all over the world, she was Olive Gordon, illustrious wife of businessman Ray Gordon. And she has the photographs to prove it!

Helena

'You were one of the dolly birds of the air, weren't you?' There's a hint of pride in Helena's voice. Like her mother, daughter Meryl trained to become a teacher but a 1970s classroom couldn't compete with the glamour of open skies. A pretty girl with hazel eyes and hair, Meryl's teaching colleagues encouraged her. 'Look at this advert, you don't want to be moulding away here, you should apply, Meryl.' For both mother and daughter, it was a seminal moment.

> 'Back then, to be an air hostess, they wanted people with an education!'
>
> 'You know, I forget the number of people applying, but it was thousands and thousands.'
>
> 'I remember you saying you had to have matching leather shoes and a handbag, and how you had to put your handbag down to show they matched.'
>
> 'You had to look the part for British Caledonian, these girls were the trolley dollies, you see.'

Pencil skirts and vertiginous high heels, wheeling champagne flutes through turbulence with a fixed smile – the Boeing 747 jumbo jet era was specific in its demands. Equal Pay and Sex Discrimination Acts defined the 1970s as the decade when change for working women was formalised, but they still played by a different set of rules and nowhere more so than in the air. Meryl was summoned to a 'really nice hotel in Kensington' for an interview. 'It was in quite a big room and I remember them saying, "Would you get up and walk down there and come back."' Full frontal, pert behind, all eyes were upon Miss Jones. 'You couldn't do that these days, could you?' Meryl isn't really asking a question, but regardless Helena shakes her contemporary (100-year-old) head. 'No, you wouldn't be allowed to interview people like that now!'

In the 1970s, it had all felt very exciting when Meryl landed her flash air hostess job in London. There were considerable perks for her mother too.

> Oh, I went all over the world with Meryl. I'd never flown before but I could go to America for about twenty-five pounds. Canada was my first country. We were coming down and it was all snow and ice and I thought, 'Oh my God, we've come here to die!'

Perhaps the biggest success story was a trip to Ireland. 'Father had finished the harvest, do you remember, Ma? So I got these tickets to Ireland purely on a whim as my father had never flown, and we hired a car and he loved it.' Helena nods. Ireland, especially the north, had been centre stage since 1968 – news bulletins ricocheted with protest and bombs, the shadows of fear and uniformed men – a grim idea that lay in stark contrast to the verdant reality the Joneses discovered on the other side of the Irish Sea. Sheep, Celtic charm, local dialect and comfort food, 'I loved Ireland, it was a bit like Wales.'

Home from home underscored the broad appeal of both Canada and Ireland. For indefatigable Helena, post-teaching ('I kept on going till I was sixty-three, they wouldn't let me retire, haha!') it was also the inspiration behind her second career. 'We built our own bungalow and I ran a bed and breakfast. It was the best job I ever had, I went on a tourism course in Brecon.' People dropped into her Welsh home from all over the world. Among her papers, there's a 1981 copy of *Nursery World* magazine. Under the heading 'Farmhouse fun in Wales', the gushing writer assures her readers that

> our hostess, lively, friendly Mrs Jones ... is a keen musician and a member of the Women's Institute. She obviously enjoys having visitors and nothing seems too much trouble. Her husband is still actively farming and during our stay he was out early feeding calves and tending his sheep. To his delight, our twelve-year-old son was allowed to feed the ponies.

By the 1980s, recreational travel was emerging as a cultural and economic powerhouse that nations eagerly sought to control and expand; effortlessly, Helena adapted her Welsh home to accommodate this mobile world. 'I met so many interesting people, and I did it for twenty-three years.' In her ninth decade, Helena was still frying Breconshire bacon and smiling at her breakfast guests, daffodils dancing beyond the window. 'Well, I suppose I was an ambassador for Wales ... in a way. People would come back year after year.'

Phyllis

Phyllis hasn't had a paid job since that Edinburgh munitions factory during the war but, like many of her female contemporaries, she never stopped. Her husband, Captain Jim Ramsay, was, for most of their married life, absent at sea. When she could, she joined him. Unafraid of the macho onboard culture, Phyllis embraced the opportunity to scuttle back down (Nasser's) Suez Canal and revisit her one-time 'homeland' – independent India. ('Well, in Bombay the imperial quarter was gone; we'd had nice clean streets and gardens, and when I returned it was washing hung across the streets.') But despite her wanderlust, two sons born ten years apart kept Phyllis bound to the British mainland for the majority of the 1950s and '60s. Like so many post-war wives and mothers, she had to adapt to the requirements of her family. When second son Geoff got into a good school in Edinburgh, she left their east coast home and moved back to the Scottish capital. There, a proliferation of causes and voluntary organisations gave shape and meaning to her life.

It started with the Townswomen's Guild, which I joined in 1967, and one thing just led to another. There was Lamb's House, the National Trust, Save the Children shops, I worked for the blood transfusion service and the Red Cross, and in the Western General Hospital, and I volunteered in Edinburgh Zoo for years.

Phyllis inflected her adventuresome personality to fit the demands of her husband's leave and sons' school holidays. She was the mistress of flexibility. As proved the case for many women, this left Phyllis much better equipped to deal with the challenges of old age and 'retirement' than her husband, Jim. For Captain Ramsay, that masculine belief in a 'job for life' proved a painful chimera in 1973 when he was summoned to BP's headquarters and released early after decades at sea. 'It was very cruel the way they got rid of Jim. They just said, "We're cutting the fleet, you finish at the end of the month."' It wasn't the money (his pension was generous), but rather the burden of empty time. Phyllis watched her proud, upright husband bend under the weight of enforced retirement. His problems had always been her problems and now his weakness needed her strength. She had to find a solution, a means to somehow reboot her husband and encourage him to look to the future as an opportunity. 'He wasn't used to being at home, and I realised I had to get him away. So I bought a ten-foot caravan, invited my sister and her husband over from Australia, and the four of us toured all around Europe, even England!' The early 1970s was boom time for caravanning, the beginning of the decade saw British manufacturers make 70,000 mobile homes.

> Our first one was very simple but it was a proper little caravan – it had a cooker, relied on Calor Gas, and if you went to the toilet you had to leave the door open because there wasn't room for your knees. Me and my sister would throw the two men out!

Phyllis laughs. The caravan offered an escape; four mature adults playing at keeping home out on the open road, led by the family's Triumph car. Hope was restored, and after several months the Ramsays returned with a new, unifying hobby. 'That's right, we became members of the Caravan Club.'

JOYCE

Charlotte Roueché, Professor Emeritus at King's College London and another of Joyce's high-achieving former students and colleagues, is wiry, with a brainy face and grey, bobbed hair.

We are sitting across a table from one another in a noisy common room, Charlotte is deep in thought about Joyce's legacy (academics rarely shoot from the hip when discussing their erstwhile tutors). Eventually she decides, 'Joyce took the opportunities that the 1950s, 60s and 70s offered, actually going out and dealing with material on the ground, that had been rare before. She engaged with all this stuff and put it in a truly historical context.' What comes next is an epic description of redoubtable Joyce (with young Charlotte in tow) en route to the ancient site of Aphrodisias in Turkey's western Anatolia. 'It was the '70s, by then flying was the quick, easy way. We flew to Istanbul and got a bus down to İzmir. You couldn't have predicted some of the places were going to turn into great tourist monstrosities, then it was just camels and donkeys.' Ringed by snow-capped Aydın Mountains echoing the beautiful call of a local imam, the two women arrived amidst the hot white marble of ancient Aphrodisais. The site was run by a 'completely dictatorial Ottoman Turk, a fascinating, terrifying character called Kenan Erim'. Elegant, unpredictable and anti-women, according to Charlotte few people survived under this pasha's rule. Joyce, in her capacity as an epigraphist, proved an exception. 'She just kept her head down and was one of the last women standing.' Employed to interpret 'an unbelievably important set of inscriptions on a wall dubbed the archive wall', Joyce published her most outstanding piece of work – *Aphrodisias and Rome* ('an extraordinary glimpse of the working relations between an eastern town and those in charge of the empire'[1]) and outlasted Kenan, who died in 1990.

The Joyce Charlotte recalls was intrepid.

> We stayed in the dig house, the showers were just water that you leave outside and by the evening it has been warmed up by the sun. Joyce was hardy, very, very hardy – sometimes she would bash bits of herself on rocks etc., but she'd just carry on. Occasionally, Kenan suggested she wore trousers when clambering over rocks . . .

Unlike so many of the on-site Americans (fussy about the food, keen for a knees-up in the local village, blaring their opinions at any opportunity), Joyce quietly got on with the job. 'We were dealing with an Ottoman; his family language was French, but Turkish was what he spoke to the servants. Joyce handled him with great care. I suppose she's always had to be careful.' Charlotte was impressed by her tutor's dexterous management of the country, the site and their challenging leader. By the 1970s, Joyce had form. She places her relationship with Kenan Erim in context. 'I had a longish wartime experience in the civil service, where if you wanted something done you had to jog your seniors along – persuade them that it was interesting and the best thing for this to be done or that. You sometimes had to think rather carefully about how you put things.' Joyce knew how to get her way, and ultimately grew to like Kenan. 'He cared about Aphrodisias – really cared.' As for travel, she'd been 'moving about' in earnest since the 1950s.

Introduced to inscription work in Tripolitania after the war, Joyce was soon spending her Cambridge vacations further along the coast, on-site at Cyrenaica in eastern Libya. 'I got my fare paid if I catered and cared for the student members of the dig. I had to buy the food, make sure it was properly cooked, allocate beds. The buck stopped with me.' Operating unaided in a Muslim world, it was in Libya Joyce met an academic from West Germany called Elizabeth, who shared her enthusiasm for the classical world (and would later introduce her to Kenan Erim). Together, they planned an archaeological road trip.

'I think it was in the late 1950s, I got a ferry across the Mediterranean from Naples to Libya and worked for several weeks at Cyrenaica, then we set off.' Two women, one additional female student and a sturdy jeep, together the trio negotiated North Africa. 'I didn't think I was being terribly intrepid. European women had been working in Egypt during the war.' They crossed the Red Sea and headed through the sands into the Middle East. 'Mostly it was fine, but in parts it wasn't very easy to be alone as a woman but we were ... yes, that's right ... kindred spirits. We went to Palmyra. I remember walking down ancient streets, there was nobody else there. No one else.' Three friends picking their way through the monumental ruins of a great city, an oasis of distant history in the Syrian desert. Joyce shudders. 'Now, bitterly, I think ... ' She doesn't finish her sentence. Four times besieged in the current Syrian civil war, reverberating with gunfire, Palmyra is no longer silent. After several millennia, its very existence is under threat. So too Aleppo.

On that occasion, we spent three nights in Aleppo and a local family felt impelled to entertain us to a delicious home-cooked lunch. It is terrible what's happening now. I should doubt there will be anything left. The centre of Aleppo was very beautiful, a major antique square with a lot of early buildings and several early mosques. I think they've gone ...

The women finished the road trip in modern-day Turkey. Joyce concedes that their trio was greeted with surprise in more distant places. Occasionally, she felt alarm.

We crossed the Turkish frontier at a very high point, and very remote. We turned up, three girls in a car, and the customs chap came out and saw us, and he asked us some questions, and said, 'Get out of your car!' So we got out of our car, thinking he was going to do goodness knows what to us.

Joyce holds up her hand to resist an interjection, a smile pulling at the corners of her mouth. 'He said, "Come into the office" quite fiercely and when we got in, all he wanted to do was offer us some coffee!'

Now in her ninety-ninth year, Joyce is confined to a very English setting – her own Edwardian home in residential Cambridge, scented roses bobbing heavy heads in the back garden, familiar rain spitting at the window, Bernard next door, chopping oranges for marmalade. But anytime Joyce likes, she can mentally travel through decades of adventure and academic quest. Every summer involved carefully planned trips to Libya and Turkey. Small wonder she waves away concerns about the absence of a husband or a professorship. In her long life, Joyce has found numerous alternative destinations.

'Yes,' agrees Charlotte, 'Joyce was a trailblazer.' After our rendezvous at London's King's College, she emails four pictures of her former tutor. I anticipated a middle-aged Joyce in retro spectacles and the obligatory skirt, perhaps examining a marble document alongside Kenan Erim. But the photographs are almost contemporary. In 'Reynolds blue', equipped with a money belt and notebook, nonagenarian Joyce is standing next to a Libyan man examining ancient graffiti; in another, she's walking down a street adorned with patterned rugs and platters and salesmen, stick in hand, sturdy ankles visible, eyes forward. Yes. Of course. Joyce would still be out there now, were it not for a second broken hip in her nineties. 'It's maddening. I miss travelling and on-site work very much.'

CHAPTER EIGHTEEN

IRON LADIES

My voice is wheedling, 'You must have an anecdote on Thatcher? A story? An impression? She was a Somerville girl like you!' 'No, not really, I don't' is Joyce's stout reply. Margaret Thatcher, eight years her junior, did not overlap with her at Oxford, and anyway she wasn't Joyce's sort, or rather, 'Thatcher was competent but in a way that I didn't approve of.'

'It's like a dream,' declared Margaret Thatcher on becoming the first female leader of the Conservative Party in 1975, having trounced her four – male – rivals. Within as many years, she'd added to that victory by winning the 1979 general election; Britain had its first female prime minister. But it wasn't just Thatcher's gender that took a while to get used to. In the late 1970s, the post-war political consensus collapsed. The nadir for a minority Labour government stymied by inflation and industrial action was the Winter of Discontent, 1978–9, when swathes of public sector workers went on strike; fetid rubbish clogged Britain's streets and hospitals admitted emergency patients only. Opposition leader Thatcher, with her sharp blue suits and home economics enunciations, had won on the promise of change. However, the rigorous application of her free-market remedies for sickly Britain proved unpopular and painful. Teeth were pulled from the unions, Britain's heavy industries were hit hard and deflationary policies cut family finances to the bone. In the early years, Joyce wasn't alone in disapproving of Thatcher – her poll ratings were dismal. Despite falling inflation, things didn't improve for the Conservative leader until she brandished big guns at the Falkland crisis and found her footing, courtesy of the elixir of a military victory in 1982.

It's hard to imagine this post-imperial gamble impressing Joyce – Somervillians Mrs Thatcher and Miss Reynolds could not have been more different. But when we next speak, Joyce has generously discovered a Thatcher anecdote. 'There was a garden party, some sort of celebration at Somerville, with lots of alumnae there. I was in the college gardens when Thatcher arrived. By that time she was prime minister but she did come.' Joyce was impressed that Thatcher turned up. After all, Oxford women's college Somerville was renowned throughout the twentieth century for left-wing credentials among both students and staff. 'I had the strong impression that the Fellows would rather have had their Lib Dem girl Shirley Williams as the first female prime minister.' Regardless, Thatcher toughed it out among the delphiniums, and everyone was far too polite to actually say anything.

In the 1980s, while Britain's Iron Lady found her controversial stride on the world stage with new friend Ronald Reagan and crushed the miners beneath a well-positioned heel, Joyce was 'officially' retiring from her post in Newnham College. There's a picture of her looking remarkably young: dark hair in a trademark bun, her considerable bosom pronounced by a hand on the hip, the other holding notes. 'Oh, I expect I said something nice about the college.' Joyce had no intention of stopping work, but freedom had just been injected into her schedule and the photograph captures arch good form. Officialdom, full-time commitments, even the impact of Thatcherism were not Joyce's concerns. Soon appointed an honorary fellow, she could teach, travel, publish her extensive research and still enjoy free meals in college. The possibilities were endless ('I haven't thought of it as a twilight period, it's just life!'). To talk too much about Thatcher would be a misrepresentation of her focus. Nor is Joyce prepared to cut Britain's first female prime minister any slack for being a woman ('like I say, I didn't think of it as a glass ceiling'), but contemporary doom in her daily edition of *The Times* does force a grudging long view. 'Look, Thatcher was properly educated, she was clever, a lot cleverer than Theresa May.' (This opinion offered when Britain's second female prime minister rode high in the polls, three months before she crashed in the dismal 2017 'Brexit' election.) Her former pupils are right, undimmed at nearly one hundred, Joyce often knows best.

With a cold manner and hectoring tone, even those not in her line of fire found Thatcher hard to love; perhaps harder still if one is older and wiser than the brazen Tory leader. Redoubtable Ann stiffens on the telephone. 'No, I've no memory of Thatcher other than tolerating something one disapproved of.' What about her being a first for women? 'Oh no, that was old hat by then. No, that didn't mean anything.' Ann is unequivocal, although later she will mutter something about Thatcher being talented to get that far without the weight of Establishment support. The grammar school girl didn't elicit much sympathy. Being a woman simply wasn't enough to excuse her politics.

At best, Thatcherism provokes an ambivalent response. Helena sighs. 'People didn't like her, did they? She wasn't very popular, was she?' In comparison with the clearly staked out Liberal versus Labour Wales of her youth, Thatcher represented a seedier, greedier modern era. 'Politics is a dirty game. They promise and then they don't do these things. It was different when I was young.' She's right, idealism had given way to consumerism and the deferential prism through which politics was interpreted vanished. The more recent 24/7 assault on television, in print and now online has bled into Helena's living room for decades, leaving its recipient feeling uncertain. She doesn't really care about Thatcher. Nor does Phyllis. Although a staunch Conservative and ready to admit that she voted for and admired the woman, Phyllis would rather talk about her husband's collection of Churchill books. Scotland still bears the scars of Thatcher; Phyllis's restrained appreciation reflects the difficulties Conservatives north of the border have felt ever since.

The only woman prepared to offer a strong view is Edna.

'Ooh, don't get me started.'
'But I thought you were a Conservative?'

Edna is defiant. 'I am, but Thatcher was a selfish so-and-so.' One flagship policy in particular stands out. 'The worst thing Thatcher ever did was to sell off the council houses.' Widowed Edna never had the money to buy her home, and anyway decades earlier Granny Parks cautioned against ever owning one. 'It was the cost of the maintenance, you see, for people like me.' She looks up, there's a flash of anger in her face. 'And nowadays, because Thatcher sold so many there is a chronic shortage.' In the 1960s, Edna's life had been transformed when, finally, as a married woman she moved into the Cripps's 'lovely council house' in Wroughton. But that privilege has not been available to one of her few living relatives, a great-nephew who's been stuck on the housing list for years. Edna pins the blame back to Thatcher, under whom the peachiest council properties sold like hot cakes, with little concern for future population growth. So yes, she has a specific reason to rail against Britain's first female prime minister. But the uncharacteristic edge in Edna's voice suggests an additional, more personal antipathy.

> That woman was far too full of her own importance. They couldn't even put up a memorial to her in Grantham cos she is not liked. She was born at Grantham and I was born four miles away. Her father was the mayor in Grantham and he wasn't any good. You know, I would have gone to the same high school as her but I was dyslexic and Mother couldn't have afforded the uniform anyway.

To be squashed at the bottom of England's hierarchy as a domestic servant was one thing, but to watch a local pipsqueak – the grocer's daughter – leapfrog across that impenetrable divide was quite another. Grantham girl Thatcher, ten years Edna's junior, posturing at the dispatch box and on television, distributing council houses like candy to those who could pay, proved an uncomfortable reminder of opportunities that were always just out of Edna's reach. 'No, I didn't like her. Mind you, I still voted Conservative.'

So Prime Minister Thatcher failed to impress the women in this book, but as the indisputable figurehead of the 1980s, her timing didn't help. Whether any generation ever owns a particular era is a moot point, but just as the Century Girls weren't swinging in the '60s, nor were they striking with the miners or banking fat bonuses in the '80s. By the time Margaret Thatcher was in power, women born in or before 1918 were in their sixties and seventies. Ann, who's still independent at 103, considers the once common phrase 'declining years' both quaint and faintly ridiculous, yet even she concedes the onset of old age comes with its own particular challenges. For Ann, as well as for Helena and Phyllis, Thatcher's decade was particularly tough, irrespective of the politics.

ANN

Bernhard Baer very rarely mentioned the Holocaust to his wife. Ann believes 'this is indicative of a silent burden'. Only recently has she discovered that another German Jewish refugee advised her husband after the war, 'We have to realise that we will never see our parents again.' So Bernhard guessed his parents had died; he survived off memories and there were meagre letters written by his mother. 'They were very small Red Cross letters written in German, only twenty words were permitted. They were sent from a concentration camp. I think the letters just hope that her children were all right. Horrible.' Ann shudders. It is a pain hard to imagine.

Her husband, Bernhard, highly educated with a distinct German accent and pebble spectacles, 'was an extraordinary, marvellous man'. Working together through their combined dependence on Ganymed Printing and a high understanding of art, Ann and Bernhard's sudden marriage in 1953 was the beginning of something special. Both at work and in their elegant Richmond home, the couple enjoyed a profound compatibility and a deep, grown-up love. They even turned high culture into everyday conversation. 'He was immensely well informed on English literature. We used to sometimes amuse ourselves by talking in Shakespeare quotations.' His death in 1983 came as a terrible shock, but Ann, a reserved, private person, doesn't mention her husband's heart attack. It is Bernhard's daughter Susan who explains: 'Father died in his sleep. It must've been horrible for Ann.' It is a loss she does not detail, Ann's own silent burden.

A youthful sixty-nine and in good health, overnight in the summer of '83 Ann had to face down the future alone. Here she had form. The first thirty years of her adult life were spent single and now, twenty years later, she was alone again. But this time there was a painful, irreplaceable absence. With its billowing corners and empty hours, widowhood is hard, solitary work, usually minus a day job to distract. (Ganymed had shut its doors in 1980, technology rendering their high-end printing obsolete. The archive is in the V & A Museum.) Ann reluctantly admits being without Bernhard wasn't easy to handle. 'I mean, it still has its repercussions but there are diversions, of which that is one.' She nods to a book at her feet. *Medieval Woman: Village Life in the Middle Ages* by Ann Baer. It was three years after Bernhard's death before she felt sufficiently recovered to begin this intimate portrait. As an unpublished older woman, when it was finished in 1996 commercial options were limited but talent is hard to suppress. The historical novel was so beautifully researched, years later it caught the eye of Philippa Gregory (Britain's most famous historical novelist), who proclaimed in *The Times*, 'this is an account of a medieval woman's life completely persuasive and ringing with truth'.[1]

The book had a long gestation period, with seeds sown decades earlier.

When I was helping my stepson, James, with his homework I saw a chapter in his school book called 'A Day in the Life of a Medieval

Peasant'. The portrait of a man was done on a Sunday in June and I thought how stupidly false the whole thing was. I decided a story should be done from a female point of view, as men had easier lives. I started to invent a village in Kent, I invented a woman, I picked the names from the Shakespeare song 'When Icicles Hang by the Wall'. The woman, Marion, was going to have lost several babies because probably everybody did, and she recently lost a twelve-year-old daughter because people did . . .

Ann's book is a staggering feat of empathy, historical knowledge and meticulous research. On the page, Marion is very real. Ann, during those acute early years of widowhood, escaped into a darker, harder world than her own, and made art.

To Marion, people were a natural part of the earth. As the deer that lived in the forest, the hares that ran in the fields, the thrush that sang in the ash tree, the spiders that hid in the cottage thatch, so to her thinking, people were a product of earth, sustained by it while they lived, returned to it when they died.[2]

PHYLLIS

May 1984: Life was very lonely then, after being married for forty-three years and such happy ones even though his [Jim's] life at sea kept us apart so often and long.[3]

There is a sting in the tail of (successful) marriage; death is the ultimate victor. After her husband's sudden early retirement in 1973, Phyllis could finally enjoy having Jim at home full time. He found a modest local job 'for his self-respect' and their touring holidays with (or without) the caravan became more frequent – Ireland, Norway and Australia several times, where Phyllis had family. She satiated her thirst for travel and Jim kept her company.

'He died in Australia. I found his diary right up to the day he died. We were touring south-east Australia and he mentioned pain, we didn't know about this pain. Jim never ever complained, but when he wasn't well he'd go quiet.' Belonging to a generation of men who came of age in the crucible of war, Jim was brave; he had little time for ill health and hospitals. But eventually he relented. 'He kept saying, "I think I have a lump in my throat, I have a sore throat." I said, "Tell the doctor." He said, "No, no, I'm coming home!" Jim left hospital and returned to his sister-in-law's house in Perth. It was Australia's autumn; mulberry trees shed their leaves in the garden and evening light danced across the eiderdown. Jim lay in bed.

I went to see him and he jokingly said, 'Come on, come into bed with me!' He was laughing. I said, 'I'll come back and see you when we're finished playing cards.' But he was asleep, then about 1.30am I heard the door creak. He just walked across the room. 'Jim?' He never said anything, he just fell on the bed ... He didn't go straight away ...

The memory, its emotion and colour, the finality and the love is etched for ever in Phyllis's mind. Just like that, she can return to 18 April 1984. 'In your fifties and sixties you start slowing down [sexually]. Well our generation did anyway. It's the companionship I miss. I began writing memories and diaries because I missed having Jim to tell my stories to.'

It's these memories, written in her considered hand, that have made Phyllis's contribution in this book so vivid. Talking to the page helped her recover a sense of self, it provided a path back to the resilient girl who crossed continents and forged new beginnings all by herself. 'After Jim died, that's when I started working in Edinburgh's Western Hospital three days a week. And I had a huge garden, one third of an acre. I returned to Australia for three months a year to see my sisters until I was ninety-two, but then the insurance said no!' There's a picture of Phyllis in the Rocky Mountains – alone, she crossed Canada in a bus and responded to China's attempts to attract tourists, flying with a friend to Shanghai. I first heard of her, aged ninety-nine, looking for a tea towel in my friend's craft shop on the remote Scottish island of Iona. 'I was touring the west coast with my niece, we visited Fingal's Cave and my picture made the papers!' Still physically fit, that inner tomboy, forged so long ago, propelled her into an energetic old age. Phyllis didn't stop and she still hasn't. 'That's the secret – forward plan, meet people, do things, don't just sit at home.'

HELENA

'Old age is not for the faint-hearted.'

'Well, no.' Helena laughs. 'But life is what you make it and God's been good.' Helena lives alone, she has done ever since Percy died in 1989. 'Too soon, too soon. He was eighty when he died. I was seventy-three, with another quarter of a century in front of me.' Helena charted the decline of her husband. The catalyst was when he jumped off a gambo and missed his footing: 'He fell on a stake and it didn't cut him, but it damaged him.' Percy lived on for two or three years but without his usual zest. 'I noticed him try to do things and he couldn't, you see, he was breathless.' She pauses. 'Well there we are, he died.' She parcels up the story into a neat sentence and tucks the emotion away as convention dictates she should. In her contemplative moments, Helena admits the two great losses in her life were the death of her beloved sister Vanu and Percy leaving her behind. Her mainstay and great companion had departed, and he took with him the last vestiges of a way of life. Helena missed her husband and she also missed the farm and her active engagement with the livestock and abundant landscape that still surrounded her. She turned her sorrow into words.

> But watch – with pain – the black-faced lambs at play
> Their frisky chasing hurts – they are not mine!
> This flock belongs to younger hands today!
> With moist blurred eyes, I make a sad retreat
> The sun and birdsong fail to cheer my heart

Soft daisies crush beneath my heavy feet!
'Twas my farm once but now I share no part.

Widowed, with so much life left, like Edna, Ann and Phyllis, Helena
sought solace through activity, occupation and writing. Still physically able in early 'old' age, they had the time and energy to recover
and re-chart their lives. 'Well, sometimes I do feel lonely now, yes.
I'd never lived on my own before but you have to keep going. And I
was lucky because Meryl's son, my grandson, Steffan, was just two
and I helped look after him. Yes, that helped a lot.' The son she never
had arrived instead as a perfect grandson. The handsome blond
boy remains the apple of her eye; today he sits in his graduate garb
smiling down at us from the mantelpiece. 'He's a handsome lad, isn't
he? But I do worry he'll be lonely. He's twenty-seven, you know, but
he still hasn't settled down with anyone!' The young replaced the
old; all his life, perhaps without even realising it, Steffan has helped
Helena adjust to a world without Percy. Gradually the ache shifted.
Once acute, it's now a distant throb.

> After he died, people came to me straight away. I said, 'I don't do
> bed and breakfast any more.' I wasn't going to, I couldn't face it,
> you know. I said to this couple. 'I don't do bed and breakfast,' and
> they said, 'But you must! We always come here!' So I let them, I
> remembered them, and once I had done it once, I knew I could
> do it again, and it was company you see, something to live for ...

Continuing bed and breakfast was a baby step in what would
become a full and vital old age. If Thatcher talked of the end of
society, Helena – and her Wales – weren't listening. A tidal wave
of London-led free market deregulation and moneymaking had
scorched Britain's Celtic nations. Blighted by miners' strikes and
poll tax riots, Wales and Scotland asked more angrily than ever
what was in it for them? The Scottish National Party, fuelled by
the discovery of oil in the 1970s, was resurgent; in Wales, Plaid
Cymru's political push was more modest but other results thrilled

Helena. 'I think Wales is probably too small to manage on its own, but I've always believed two windows in the world is better than one.' Over the next decade, in local schools, on television and at adult learning centres, the Welsh language proliferated; in 1993, an Act of Parliament put Welsh on an equal footing with English in the public sector. Eighty years earlier, the imperative to get on in an Anglocentric world had seen her father sideline his mother tongue, and Helena had always carried a quiet regret she couldn't speak the language of her predecessors. Now finally she'd lived long enough to see that trend reversed. 'You know in my nineties I took my first ever GCSE – in Welsh!'

A keen eisteddfod performer, Helena had recited Welsh language poetry and prose at a competitive level since childhood, but after her nonagenarian studies she could write her own. 'In 2013, I entered to speak in the Welsh learner category on family history. I had to speak in Welsh for about twenty minutes.' It's a serious matter competing at the annual National Eisteddfod. One of the largest poetry and music festivals in Europe, they attract thronging crowds – 150,000-plus people under canvas, a druidic celebration revelling in the Welsh language and the performance it inspires. In 2013, the competition was in Denbigh, a market town in North Wales. A lifelong competitor and winner at numerous regional eisteddfods, Helena had never won on the national stage. 'There are always prelims, and you have to succeed there to get through to the final.' Helena was one of three finalists. Her authored family story was about Vanu's premature death, the burden of breaking the news to her younger siblings and Helena's magical explanation that Vanu had joined the angels on a sunbeam.

The adjudicators took their job seriously, posing with pen and paper, solemn-faced. Helena, a seasoned performer of ninety-six, was nervous; adrenalin pumped through her body, the hand holding her notes shook slightly, and so in Welsh she began – wide-eyed, eloquent, expressive – all the things her father had taught her a lifetime ago. Vanu was reimagined in the language of her forefathers, and the farm, the sunset, the emotion. 'After I finished, no one made

a sound, nothing. I thought, "Oh gosh, I've made a mess of that."
Then I looked across at the judges and I saw that one of them was
crying.'

When it came, the applause was thunderous. 'Oh my goodness!
Yes. Yes, winning an eisteddfod at ninety-six, that was quite something! I was very thrilled.'

CHAPTER NINETEEN

Do Not Go Gentle into That Good Night

Over the last twenty years, the rise of nationalism, exacerbated by Scottish and Welsh devolution on the one hand and increased European integration on the other, now threatens the previously unimaginable – the break-up of Great Britain. Scotland, and Wales to a lesser extent, pillory Westminster's power, and England attacks Brussels.[1] The perceived failure of the neoliberal, laissez-faire economic model introduced by Thatcher in the 1980s has heightened tensions. No one seemed to have an answer to the 2008 economic crash. 'It's just been more of the same,' says Ann gloomily, grateful she is cushioned by her extreme age and a pension. But if the Century Girls are now bystanders not active participants in Britain's economic life, the recent uncertainty has demanded an unprecedented flurry of political engagement – two national referendums* and two general elections since 2014.

This glut of electioneering has taken them by surprise. The timing almost feels personal – a test of their democratic mettle neatly arriving at the end of women's first politically enfranchised century, a postscript to check they are still awake. 'Of course I voted, I always

---

* Only voters in Scotland could participate in the Scottish independence referendum of 2014.

vote!' is their stock reply, although Edna does concede postal voting is now her preferred (even essential) option. It's hard to imagine that within their living memory, female voters were handled with caution, their numbers restricted in 1918 to ensure they didn't outvote men. The political landscape today has changed beyond recognition; where once gender was the dividing line, now age is the perceived culprit of discord.

In the wake of the 2017 general election, pollsters loudly concluded the seventy-plus generation were much more likely to vote Conservative than any other, with YouGov claiming 'for every ten years older a voter is, their chance of voting Tory increases by around nine points'.[2] Similar judgements were made a year earlier, after Britain's 2016 'Brexit' referendum, when apparently the older the voter, the more likely they were to opt out of the European Union. 'Absolute nonsense!' mutters Joyce and she may well have a point. For society's very oldest, these are untested generalisations. Opinion polls divide voters into ten-year age categories,* that is until they reach sixty-five (occasionally seventy) and then they are all lumped together under the vague headings 'sixty-five-plus' or 'seventy-plus'. But today, eight million citizens in Britain are over seventy – it is an age group which spans more than two generations.[3] Dominated by vast numbers of septuagenarians and octogenarians, no one really knows how the small minority of men and women over ninety vote (of whom there are about half a million), nor those over one hundred (centenarians number approximately 14,000). Widespread extended living is a relatively recent phenomenon, and politics has not caught up.

This clay-footed approach mirrors modern society's attitude towards the elderly in general. No longer revered, old people are shoved into one homogenous category, an amorphous group who look and apparently behave and think in a uniform fashion. This is an error of judgement in a modern world where each decade has seen momentous change. It assumes that those who witnessed Europe

---

* With the exception of those aged between 18–24, who tend to be given their own six-year bracket.

rip itself asunder and fought in the Second World War feel the same about national identity and international politics as those who grew up in the shadow of that legendary war. It forgets that a computer means something completely different to a seventy-year-old, who will have operated one at work, than to a 100-year-old, for whom such technology is often alien. (Of the six women in this book, only Joyce has an email address – but then she's never stopped working.) Meanwhile, those born in Britain between the wars can remember a country with few effective medicines and no National Health Service. As Edna wisely observed, 'More people in them days often died when they weren't old.' Women aged one hundred have lived very different lives from the seventy-year-old generation they brought up. Both deserve better than to be crushed into one age bracket.

Ann assures me that, on a personal level, things changed somewhat once she hit a hundred – 'Then I got a degree of interest and special attention!' Invisible old age comes full circle for centenarians – in 2017, both Channel 4 and BBC1's *Panorama* made documentaries about daily life for those over one hundred. When Edna hit a century, she was featured in the local *Swindon Advertiser*, Clive James referred to Ann in his *Guardian* column and recent poetry anthology,*4 and Olive is continually being asked to appear on television and talk about her great age. But that interest can't be taken for granted. Recent surveys suggest that one third of girls born in 2011 will live to celebrate their hundredth birthday. The last century has proved that the extraordinary can quickly become ordinary. No one knows that better than the six women featured in this book.

JOYCE

It is July 2016. The EU referendum has been and gone; in an unpredicted result, Britain voted to leave the European Union. Brexit has shaken the nation, people are in shock and none more so than

---

* See page [269] for details of what happened when, unsolicited, Ann wrote to Clive James.

Joyce. 'I found myself saying at once, "Thank heavens I have no children!"' Lying before her is a copy of *The Times* and an edition of the *Cambridge Evening News*, featuring Mary Beard's analysis of Brexit. 'I thought for a local paper she spent too much time on the intellectual side and the difficulties that will arise for academia.' (The tutor is as uncompromising as ever.) 'One of the startling things is, I can't remember joining Europe. There was a vote, but I can't remember it at all. I think it was voting for something looser, it has evolved.' Joyce puckers her brow, briefly disturbed by a lack of recall.

Twice vetoed by French president de Gaulle, Britain eventually became a member of the European Economic Community in 1973 and held a referendum on whether to remain in the group two years later. Joyce is right, the union was looser then and the decisive result in 1975 less memorable. Alongside Labour prime minister Harold Wilson, leader of the opposition Margaret Thatcher, in a tight sweater, featuring all nine Common Market members' flags, demanded a big vote for 'yes'. Sixty-seven per cent of the population did what they were told. Post-imperial trading habits were abandoned and thirty years after the end of the Second World War, little Britain turned to embrace its inner European. Joyce sighs. 'The whole Brexit thing is a disaster. It was run so badly. It shouldn't have been run, but if you decide to run it then you do it properly.' Born at the end of the First World War, daughter of liberal internationalist parents, this astute scholar, who's spent the vast majority of her adult life pushing academic boundaries, is unimpressed by a campaign fuelled with fake facts and anti-immigrant rhetoric. Five months later, and the advent of Donald Trump's American presidency on the uncompromising mantra 'America First!' confirms her worst suspicions. In her ninety-eighth year, Joyce did what she could – she voted. Of course she voted, on every level Joyce remains engaged. Still receiving prestigious Classics awards, proofing Mary's latest book, translating inscriptions for Charlotte's digital collections, voting is an important footnote in a busy existence.* She operates

---

* For more on the latest award Joyce received, see Acknowledgements, p. 303.

more slowly now and is occasionally caught napping in the faculty library, but remains a perfectionist. 'Check your references!' that would be my advice to young girls today.'

We're summoned to lunch by her nephew Bernard. He shakes his head vigorously. 'No, it's not the food, she's still alive because her students love her.' A reminder of their affection was the 'JoyceFest' held at Newnham in September 2013. This esteemed gathering was described by Mary Beard in the *Times Literary Supplement* as an event 'celebrating Joyce ... celebrating her ongoing achievements'. Four classical lectures, a generous buffet lunch, 'softies and prosecco' in the Museum of Classical Archaeology and 'dinner in King's, where Joyce got a presentation to mark her greatness ... and made a robust speech'. The day was long and full and impressive – an appropriate metaphor for Joyce's own life.[5] One can only wonder about her hundredth birthday in December 2018.

Bernard pulls out a chair and Joyce clumps into the dining room behind a Zimmer frame; Sylvana, her weekly Italian helper (a fixture for the last twenty-five years), brings in plates of fried fish and stewed fruit. An adoring helper, she admits, 'Joyce has always been a mama to me.' Joyce smiles. 'I'll tell you what, if the country doesn't want any more immigrants, we're going to have to get much better at doing our own housework.' A ringing telephone interrupts the laughter; it's one of Joyce's former pupils confirming their walk that afternoon.

'Ah yes, Cambridge is a very good place to get old.'

Olive

'Here! I'll go if you come get me.' Olive will vote in the referendum if I take her to the polling booth and stay a while. 'I'm not sure what to vote. What you think I should vote?' She might be teasing, it's hard to tell. Olive doesn't really want to talk about politics, as usual Ray is her focus. 'Don't tell me about your husband, you make me jealous!' She's still angry with Ray, five years her junior, for dying first. 'Ray got ill when I went to America. I was at my cousin's hundredth birthday and when I come back at de airport it's my daughter, not

Ray.' Instinctively, Olive knew something was wrong. Ray was in hospital; he'd had a stroke. 'He was sick, never again good.' She shakes her head. The white pulley Olive used to haul her dying man into an upright position is still in her living room, she sits in the reclining chair that was once his. There's a detailed story of how she nursed him, it involves orange juice and resuscitation, tablets and funny noises. A second time he went by ambulance to the hospital. 'When I get there, he is lying stretched out and his eyes open. I went to him and put my hand on his tummy and he closed his eyes. He was waitin' for me.' Olive returned to an empty home and the tears came. 'I was cryin' all de time. Why he leave me?' She was ninety-four when her husband died – too old to fully readjust to life without her man in a country she'd never tackled alone. Olive's still grieving, eight years on. Solitude is easier to manage if you've had decades of practice. Edna, Joyce and Ann will testify to that.

Now a staggering 102 years of age, Olive's America-based son Terence has also died, but it's Ray's passing that consumes her. She's seen his ghost, she talks to him in the dark and, swaddled in her own loneliness, she bemoans the absence of her daughters. They are dutiful, but Olive wants more. She tended her own mother into the grave the Guyanese way and expects the same. 'Someone to comb my hair and clip my nails. I am stuck in dis chair now.' But Joye and Gloria, two accomplished British women, widows and grandmothers in their own right, take a different view. They visit their mother, they call her, there is money for carers and parties. Olive's 101st birthday celebration was enormous – family tipped out of the church into the street, the birthday girl sang and shimmered in sequins and white feathers – but the next day she felt lonely again.

An extrovert who was always surrounded by family and bundles of friends, it's tough being alone over a hundred. Children don't guarantee a companionable old age.* Olive and I chat for an hour before the taxi comes to take us to the polling station. The driver discusses the referendum with his extraordinary passenger. 'Over

---

* See Appendix 2.

one hundred! Wow! Yeah, I'll be voting later. I liked Britain how it used to be.' Quick as a flash, Olive shoots back, 'What? When dey had up de signs – no blacks, no dogs. Ha?' The driver is contrite and Olive delighted. And, proving politics is always personal, she's finally made up her mind. 'I don't like de talk of immigrants. I'm votin' to stay in! I tell you, I've had a won-derful life!'

EDNA

'No, I don't have a birthday card from the Queen. I didn't want one, so I haven't got one.' It was the Pensions Office that rang Edna. 'I just told 'em not to bother sending it.' She giggles, thrilled with the idea that she rebuffed a tradition established by the king who ruled over her childhood.

> We all liked George V and I think the Queen is lovely. Really, I do! But she doesn't know me from Adam. Think about the people she's got around her and then on a card there is a stamp and that's it. I know how these big houses are run. It's very impersonal and you don't want a card from someone you don't know.

Edna's decision to reject the birthday card was a small but hugely symbolic act against the British Establishment that has ruled so much of her life. Aged one hundred, she was at last free to do as she pleased. The same year she broke with another tradition. 'I've always voted Conservative but in 2015 I voted UKIP.' Beneath a crest of hair, her soft eyes glimmer. Within the confines of her modest brick home, Edna had made an important decision and has thoroughly enjoyed watching the politics play out ever since – perfect armchair sport for an ancient Eurosceptic. A second referendum was the culmination of a forty-one-year wait.

> I've been ready since the 1970s to see that change. It's nothing to do with immigration. You will find I am right on Germany. Hitler wanted to control the whole of England and Europe, and you will

see they are still in control. We have freedom now. I know because
I have been alive a lot longer than you.

She has leaned forward in her chair to make this point, her concave
frame craning with the need to make herself understood. Now she
slumps back, satisfied. Edna wasn't treated well during the first
fifty years of her life, but a 1930s conservatism is still embedded
deep within her. She's held dear to the idea of an old England; an
enduring continuity, a deep Anglo-Saxon instinct, a way of life
that was unforgettably threatened by Germany in two world wars.
This unequivocal loyalty to a nativist construct makes her epically
contemporary. She is the 102-year-old populist, the woman who
outlived Baldwinism, Powellism and Thatcherism, but took with her
the kernel of their message: For ever England!

'Look, take down the file! Yes, that's the one with my bank
statements. See, that's all the money that I have a month. Ooh,
I'm showing you everything, aren't I? Well, you see, with all I get
now I am richer than I've ever been. My life's been much easier
than my mother's.' Dependent on a state pension, topped up with
a care and fuel allowance in line with her great age, Edna no
longer considers herself poor. 'I've a cleaner once a week. She's
called Heather – she's lovely. She massages my legs and, yes, we do
spend a lot of time chatting.' For three hours a week, the former
servant is the recipient of her own domestic helper. Edna smiles. 'I
can't complain. And my friends come and do my garden and take
me to Floral Art. Most mornings, her opposite neighbour brings
in the milk bottle and checks on her welfare. Friendship, flowers
and a sense of belonging – Edna is surrounded by the trappings
of a loving community she's contributed to for decades. Her last
years have been spent enjoying a rural idyll – one secured by both
government supplements and the yolk of kindness. In 2016, she
voted for change in order to keep things the way they are. 'Yes, I
like Mrs May, our new prime minister. She is a vicar's daughter.
I shall be putting a Conservative poster in my window.' With
Britain's departure from the EU under way, Edna reverted to the

Conservative Party in the June 2017 election. 'I have a good life now. People don't realise how lucky they are, they don't know what it means to be really poor.'

HELENA

'Well, now you come to ask, yes, I have voted already, I filled in a postal form. I voted for the Liberal candidate that we knew from our days farming in Rhayader.' A week later, Wales lost its last Liberal Democrat seat in the general election of 2017. Over Helena's lifetime, this small Celtic nation has grown out of an old voting allegiance that once defined her father's farming family. She shrugs, keen to avoid political discussion. The referendum bemused her, but recalling the fragility of the British Isles in the Second World War, she opted to stay within Europe. Edna voted differently from Helena, yet both women want things to more or less remain the same. 'I suppose what's important for me is being Welsh.'

In August 2016, Helena celebrated her one hundredth birthday. There were two parties, 216 birthday cards and a special Welsh rendition of 'Happy Birthday' at the National Eisteddfod in Abergavenny, where Helena was recognised as the festival's oldest-ever competitor. 'Well, that was nice, wasn't it? And I felt so happy when they all sang, but the television cameras photographed me crying!' BBC Wales captured the birthday girl momentarily overcome beneath her round spectacles and beamed the footage across the country. Turning one hundred is generally accompanied with a certain local caché, but Helena has garnered headlines well beyond Brecon. In August 2017, the National Eisteddfod will be held in Anglesey, North Wales. There, Helena will join a long and esteemed list of Welsh greats at the Gorsedd of the Bards. 'I've been invited to be a druid! I know, can you believe it!' A centuries-old tradition inspired to emphasise the Welsh claim on Celtic culture, the Gorsedd of the Bards recognises individuals who've made exceptional contributions to Welsh life. Sportsmen, television personalities, musicians, scientists and Helena. Her family have booked a holiday cottage in

Anglesey; their ancient mother, trussed up in startling blue robes, will become an honorary druid at the Gorsedd and they want to be there. Meryl is overcome. 'All her life, my mother has sought to work and now she's been given accolades for that. I am very glad.'

Welsh Helena, the teacher, the mother, the writer, the producer, the actress, the performer. Enquire after Helena Jones in Breconshire today and people will nod fondly. Often, they give you an affirming anecdote or tell you how much she means to the community. They will certainly mention her age or her plays. But it's unlikely anyone will be surprised that she's achieved so much and is a woman. Like the vote, today her gender is taken for granted. Even Helena needs reminding. 'Well, now you come to mention it, my mother never did any of the things I did, no, she didn't. She had a much harder life than me.'

It's easy to forget how far women have travelled in one hundred years.

PHYLLIS

A century ago, Scots, Irish, Welsh and English melted into one under tropical sun. An identity hammered out on the dusty planes of the subcontinent, Phyllis was born into a gigantic, ambitious version of Britishness on the other side of the world. She tuts. 'Now it all seems so unsettled. I don't want Scotland to survive on its own. I am a British citizen, I've still got seven British passports!' Phyllis isn't particularly interested in the EU referendum, her recent frame of reference is Scotland's 2014 independence referendum and the prospect of a second one. It turns out the British brand misses the glue of empire that once held it together at home; Great Britain is shrinking into itself, behind small borders. Resurgent nationalism has seen Edna's 1930s England re-chime with the times; Helena's Welshness has never been more feted; but for Phyllis the Scottish National Party's independence quest threatens her keen sense of self. A Conservative, a unionist, a traditionalist – according to Phyllis, all this talk of independence is not progress. Things have not got better.

'Nowadays, I feel sorry for you all. I feel sorry for what's ahead of you all. We've had the best years after the war in the 1950s and 60s and 70s.' At least, that's how it feels to the colonial wife of a captain who manned the sea's shipping lanes with his supertanker. Phyllis has always understood the world for its scope and size; rising nationalism and old age challenge both. But of other threats she is impervious. 'Well, no, terror doesn't bother me. I grew up with riots and things in India. Life was cheap there, it didn't shock you.' The old-school colonial is stamped deep within. Phyllis is still tough (she lives alone, medicates with cod liver oil and has only just started using a stick). But her first home – British India – has vanished and at her core there is a gap. After seventy-six years of learning to call it home, Phyllis doesn't want British Scotland to disappear as well.

It's June 2017. 'Yes, of course I'll vote,* but I resent having to vote tactically just to get the nationalists out. I preferred it when politics was simpler.'† She makes the point that Glasgow is different from Edinburgh, 'more manual workers, less well paid'. More national-ist. Phyllis is an Edinburgh lady, she feels at home in this regal city, resplendent with its elegant New Town, Princes Street and cut-glass accent. She's served the Scottish capital with numerous voluntary hats as befitted her social standing as a captain's wife, including Edinburgh Zoo. It's among their exotic animals that she will cel-ebrate her one hundredth birthday in July 2017 with a traditional sit-down lunch. Her son Jim, a successful accountant, has flown in from Australia to be there. Her other son, Geoff, an aerospace engineer, is co-ordinating the event. An abundance of friends and family are congregating from far and wide. 'U-huh, I consider myself a citizen of the world, I suppose.' And she laughs. Her world is not a modern one, but it's a better one, she thinks.

---

* In the June 2017 general election.
† In 1950, Churchill talked of saving Scotland (predominantly Conservative) from English socialism. The significant rise of the SNP in the 1970s and the dis-appearance of Conservative Scotland in the 1980s were just two of the seismic changes in the political landscape of post-war Scotland.

ANN

'You haven't got an end for your book because I haven't died yet!'
Ann is gleeful and, at 103, rightly so. I protest that I never intended
to end on a funeral, but admit to imagining there would be one.
Although non-religious ('There are four things I have no interest
in – religion, pets, sport and music'), I first heard of Ann from
Richmond's former vicar, Reverend Reindorp. 'There's a woman
called Ann Baer, one of my congregation knows her; she will talk to
you but says, "Don't wait too long!"' I nearly didn't bother calling – a
woman born before the First World War, it sounded too precarious.
But there was a certain gumption in the vicar's description. 'Don't
wait too long!' An impatience even, as if Ann had anticipated my
enquiry. 'Do write to her!' urged his email, so I did.

A watchful woman, Ann has been observing life for over a century; she understands about as well as anyone can that living isn't
good or bad,

> it's patchy. I can't tell you if it's better to be born today or in 1914 –
> they're not comparable. Then, things were slower, we were more
> ignorant but it felt more secure. Perhaps there are more people
> born into more pleasant circumstances today but there are other
> issues, different inequalities.

Two eras separated by more than one hundred years are worlds
apart – Ann's life bridges that divide, but she too has changed. The
young girl is now very old, wisdom has replaced naïvety, realism
overtaken optimism and where once the future lay, now she sees
mainly the past. 'One doesn't know when one is going to topple over.
That's the thing. I still look forward to things – I looked forward to
seeing you today, for instance – but one simply doesn't know whether
one will be here next week.'

With such an uncertain future, Ann is making the most of the
present. 'I can't tell you why I've lived so long – it's sheer fluke!' An
avid correspondent, her beautiful handwritten missives penned in

the extremity of life have impressed numerous recipients. Out of the blue, broadcaster and writer Clive James received a poem ('I had no idea he was a television personality, I came across his work in the *Times Literary Supplement*'). They now correspond regularly; Ann headlined at his book launch in 2015 and Clive wrote a poem, 'Verse Letter', 'In reply to Ann Baer, aged 101, of Richmond upon Thames' that appeared in his latest anthology. His words marvel at her handwriting, her love for language, her great age.

> No wonder that you write a hand so fair.
> I swear that you'll be here when I am gone.[6]

Ann's junior by some three years, writer Diana Athill was graced with a seven-page letter regarding their lifelong associations in the publishing world. The nonagenarian scribe replied she was greatly relieved that, for once, pages of unsolicited ink from an unknown sender made luminous good sense. I, meanwhile, have been thoroughly scolded for my illegible scrawl. 'Your handwriting is indeed difficult to read and only by my familiarity with written English can I decipher some of it.' I tried to explain that rusty writing is due to over-dependence on computers and laptops. Ann isn't interested. 'I don't do technology. I once thought iPod was the past tense of the verb iPad.'

Ann is the only woman in this book minus a television. Edna enjoys watching *Bake Off* and Brexit's incremental progress; Joyce checks in when Mary Beard has a classical offering on the BBC ('I think she holds the viewer very well'); and Olive has the television on all the time, it easies the silent pinch that surrounds her. Not Ann, however. 'I am currently halfway through George Eliot's longest book, *Middlemarch*. I've read it many times. And Jane Austen can be perpetually reread. I know some almost off by heart.' Literature's classics provide Ann with that which modern society can't – a high seriousness no longer in fashion, and a reminder of what once was. Some classics were her contemporaries. 'My father knew A. A. Milne. *Winnie the Pooh* was written when I was a child.'

Meanwhile, today's world silts up her doormat. 'I suppose I do read the political leaflets, mind you they all tend to say the same thing.' It's 8 June 2017. Ann has a bad leg, but because it's polling day she must walk around the corner and do her duty. 'Yes, it is a duty, I regard voting absolutely as an obligation.' Ann has fulfilled that obligation since 1935, this will be her twenty-first election

> and surely my last! It's impossible to compare today with 1935. Then, I was very aware of fascism on the Continent and that the national government weren't doing anything about it. And today I suppose is uncertain, but in a very different way.

Ann lives in a swing seat, vigorously contested by the Conservatives and the Liberal Democrats (forty-five votes will determine Richmond's outcome in June 2017), but she will not disclose whom she's voting for. 'Absolutely not. What's the point in all the secrecy, the little booth and pencil and so on, if one tells everybody?' This discreet woman solemnly makes her way to the polling caravan wearing a blue trouser suit and faded gym shoes (yes, she's still stylish). A young mother with a buggy almost derails her on the pavement, it's a near miss. No one would guess just how old Ann is and that she has a very sore leg, or that she's worried at any moment she may topple over. She's walking on her own, with a stick and white hair, her extraordinary history folded up inside her.

'What advice would I give to young girls today?' She looks at me as if the question is a trick. But when her answer comes, it's almost a shout.

'Get on with it!'

Ann is.

ACKNOWLEDGEMENTS

Spending time and developing firm friendships with the six women in this book has been one of the great privileges of my life. Not only have they welcomed me into their homes and shared so many extraordinary memories, they've also introduced me to many of their friends and family members. It was therefore with tremendous sadness that I dedicated this book to Joyce's late nephew, Bernard Reynolds. He had lived with Joyce and been her devoted carer for over twenty years. I looked forward to him opening the door of their Cambridge home, thrusting his hands in his pockets and declaring, 'If you don't stay for lunch, you'll queer us something rotten!' The onset of an aggressive cancer and his sudden death in September 2017 was a shock for everyone, particularly Joyce. As she sagely pointed out during my last visit, 'You were lucky to have met him.' Indeed I was.

When I came up with the idea for this project, I anticipated it would be emotionally challenging. Great age comes with illness, adversity and loss. What I didn't expect was that the women would provide me with the most extraordinary support when I faced adversity. I lost a longed-for pregnancy midterm last year and they looked after me as if I was their own family. Joyce wrote one of her wonderful soothing letters (and four months later reminded me to start the book!), Helena let me cry on her knee (twice), Edna listened for hours and hours (and hours). Phyllis reminded me to be tough and Olive rang up and exclaimed down the phone. She relived her own pain from 1953 and, in doing so, eased mine. Ann assured me that, when it came to grief, 'rationality doesn't apply', and explained how she got over her own emotional hurdles. It is impossible to put my gratitude into words. If ever there was an example of the sisterhood in action it was Joyce, Helena, Phyllis, Ann, Olive and Edna over the last eighteen months. Thank you and thank you all some more.

I finished the first draft of this book in July 2016, but I could have carried on writing. Tomboy Phyllis wore a stunning blue dress at her hundredth birthday party later that same month – Edinburgh Zoo didn't know what had hit them! The last time I chatted to her, she had just attended the opening ceremony of Edinburgh's new bridge over the Firth of Forth, proof if any were needed that she remains the matriarch of Scotland's capital. Edna appeared in the *Swindon Advertiser* wearing a smart blazer and a winsome smile – she'd had a cracking evening at the fiftieth anniversary of her very own Floral Art Association, aged 102.

Helena's lifetime of endeavour and achievement in Wales was recognised in August 2017 when she was made an Honorary Druid by the Gorsedd of the Bards at the National Eisteddfod in Anglesey. Everyone was there, her whole family, the Welsh press, even the sunshine. It was a deeply moving ceremony and my first eisteddfod!

Joyce was worried about a description of her in the book as 'Britain's leading epigraphist'. 'There were older and eminent others,' she noted on the relevant page, scoring a line through the claim. However, after a late and prestigious evening at the British Academy, where Joyce was awarded the Kenyon Medal 'for her lifetime contribution to the research and study of Roman epigraphy' in September 2017, she relented and the description survived!

Both Ann and Olive generously appeared in a 'taster' film to convince the BBC that *The Century Girls* really ought to be on television (even though Ann still doesn't have one). Olive wore her finery and Ann wrote a letter to chivvy things along, pointing out the 2017 election was her twenty-first and that it was doubtful she'd be here for another. However, I harbour a sneaking suspicion that at 103 she will survive longer than our current prime minister, Theresa May.

I'm not sure it's possible to get to one hundred with the panache of the Century Girls without legions of friends and loyal family members providing help and support. But meeting, talking to, even feeding a writer is surely beyond the job description of most companions and relations ...

Thank you, Meryl Davies, for helping shed light on the latter half of your mother Helena's life, for sending her poetry and generally egging me on. Thank you, Joye Manyan, for chatting so openly about your mother, Olive, and for explaining more about the history of Guyana and your transition into British life. Thank you, Sue Wragg, for a delicious lunch and candid conversation about your stepmother, Ann, in the sixties, not to mention the lift to and from the train station.

I agree with Edna, Carolyn Venn really is the best niece one could wish for – Carolyn, thank you for remembering your grandparents so brilliantly and for sharing your own memories about 'stylish Aunt Edna'. Irene Ramsay is another extraordinary niece, thank you for the lunches, chats with (and about) Phyllis, not to mention the endless emailing of photographs. Ditto Geoff Ramsay, a son and a half, who made me feel so welcome at Phyllis's hundredth birthday.

Joyce, the list of professors I have spoken to about you is long and impressive, courtesy of your legacy as a teacher and academic. Thank you, Prof Pat Easterling, for generous incites (and a free Newnham lunch); thank you, Prof Charlotte Roueché, for lengthy chats and email exchanges; thank you, Prof Mary Beard, for giving 'Joyce the tutor' a fulsome and funny report; thank you, Prof MM McCabe, for a comprehensive 'Joyce analysis' over the telephone. Thank you, Prof Bryan Ward-Perkins (who happens to be my former tutor), for childhood memories of Joyce and thanks also to your sister, Catherine, for sharing family photographs of Joyce in 1950s Italy. And thank you, Prof Sir Fergus Millar, for confirming that Joyce the academic is indeed a 'dedicated searcher after truth.'

All books in the early 'ideas' stage need inspiration. I would like to thank Peter and Jean Connah, Rosey Hickson and Eve Reynolds, Sheila Harris-Taylor and Rosalie Naydorf, Pauline Owen and Vera Keenan and Nina Thomas, as well as dear friends Pamela Rose and

Pat Murray, plus numerous others, all of whom either knew of, or were living proof that, women of one hundred always have a story worth telling.

The broad sweep of history across one hundred years under my clumsy navigation needed careful stewardship. I don't know what I would have done without Prof Bruce Collins. Thank you so much for granting me a year's leave from my PhD studies to write this book, and for recommending certain texts that proved invaluable for a better understanding of the last century, as were your own observations. Thank you also for reading and fact-checking the final manuscript (any errors are entirely mine!).

Thank you, agent Robert Kirby, for believing in the project and coming up with a great title and many thanks to editor Iain MacGregor for grasping the appeal of *The Century Girls* and for giving me the space to get on with it. I am indebted to copy-editor Jo Whitford for kindly agreeing to revisit the text with a mission 'to cut' – the book is a tighter, brighter read after your pruning. Thank you to all the other team members at Simon & Schuster whom I have yet to meet but who I know are part of the vital engine room that takes pages of copy and turns them into a finished (hopefully readable) product!

Anne Thomson and Dr Gillian Sutherland, I really enjoyed the afternoon we spent together in Newnham archive. Tips, photographs and valuable background information on Joyce – thank you! Ditto Dr Howard Bailes for the lowdown on life at St Paul's Girls School during the 1930s. Of course, there would have been no Joyce in the book had it not been for access to Somerville's alumnae, so thank you Elizabeth Cooke and Brett de Gaynesford.

It was the remarkable Dana Winogron who provided the vital human link between Olive on a TV documentary to the real Olive Gordon, and old school friend Micky Gordon who spotted Phyllis's talents in his craft shop on the Scottish Isle of Iona. Everyone needs a reverend in their life, and mine – Rev. Julian Reindorp – never fails to deliver. Thank you for Ann. She is epic.

There are many personal thank yous. I have leant heavily on the six women in this book as well as on many long-suffering friends. Katie Gordon, Hilary Murray, Danny Fagerson, Charlotte Robertson, Emma Marinos, Fran Voss, Liz Wallace, Lucy Wainwright and Jo Varney, to name but a few. It's very different being a woman today but I'm not sure that necessarily means it's altogether easier. As the Century Girls have helped me understand, our capacity for resilience and compassion remains as important as ever.

My nine-year-old daughter, Mara, has met four of the women in this book. To watch the exchange between old and young has been a delight. Struck by her singing, it was Mara's idea that Olive should visit her London primary school where she was a big hit! Visits to Wales have seen Mara's love of drama nurtured by Helena and journeys down the M4 were broken up with lace-making and daisy chains, courtesy of Edna. Back at home, Mara has introduced me to the research benefits of Google Maps and listened to extracts of the book as they took shape, shaking her head (and returning to 'Minecraft') when I overwrote and leaning in when it got interesting. Thank you, Mara, and thank you, Dan, for letting me read aloud around the house, for understanding the importance of the project and for never objecting when I cooked for my 100-year-olds and you cooked for me.

Appendix 1

Olive speaks with a distinct, old-fashioned Guyanese accent. When she appeared on BBC Radio London in October 2016 for Black History Month, several Londoners with Guyanese or West Indian heritage commented on how her voice made them nostalgic for a generation that's almost disappeared. Olive knows her words are written phonetically in this book – 'as it should be', her response. Other accents featured are much less pronounced but where colloquialisms etc. have occurred, I've left them in.

APPENDIX 2

It appears that women who live beyond a century generally buck their own generation's trend for big families. Three women in this book never had children. During my research I came across, spoke to, met or discussed with their friends and family, nearly fifty women who were in reasonable physical and mental health and born in 1918 or before. Almost half of them didn't have any children and very few had three or more in an era when nine out of ten women had children and often more than two. Given the paucity of women alive over one hundred (under 10,000), this anecdotal research suggests not bearing children may be one factor in extreme longevity in women. A 1998 survey reported in the *Independent* newspaper corroborates this finding. http://www.independent.co.uk/news/longer-life-for-childless-women-1194163.html

NOTES

1. A Richer Dust Concealed

1 A. Sidgwick, 'Biblio-vignettes 5', *The Book Collector* vol.61, no.1 (Spring 2012), pp.95–6
2 A. J. P. Taylor, *English History 1914–1945* (Harmondsworth, Penguin, 1981), p.1
3 http://www.telegraph.co.uk/finance/property/pictures/11072925/Britains-top-20-places-to-raise-a-family.html?frame=3025891; https://www.theguardian.com/money/2011/sep/16/move-to-great-missenden-prestwood-bucks
4 http://www.bsiarchivalhistory.org/BSI_Archival_History/Sidgwick_obit.html
5 A. Baer, 'Unpublished Wartime Memoir' (2004), p.1
6 Taylor, *English History*, p.174
7 S. Baldwin, *On England and Other Addresses* (London, Phillip Allan, 1926), p.64

2. Education for All

1 H. Jones, *My First School, by a Libanus Lass*, copy printed by the Brecon and Radnor Printers, no date
2 Ibid., pp.5–6
3 Ibid., pp.11–12
4 http://www.wsfg.waltham.sch.uk/page/?title=Our+School+History&pid=16
5 A. Holdsworth, *Out of the Doll's House: The Story of Women in the Twentieth Century* (London, BBC Books, 1988), p.50
6 Ibid.
7 A. J. P. Taylor, *English History 1914–1945* (Harmondsworth, Penguin, 1981)

8 M. Stopes, *Married Love* 4th edn (London, A. C. Fifield, 1918); M. Stopes, *Wise Parenthood* (London, A. C. Fifield, 1918)

9 Taylor, *English History*, p.302

10 H. Bailes, *Once a Paulina ... A History of St Paul's Girls' School* (London, James & James, 2000), pp.9–28

11 J. Reynolds, handwritten memoirs, St Paul's Girls' School archive

12 M. Pugh, 'The Impact of Women's Enfranchisement in Britain', in C. Daley and M. Nolan (eds.), *Suffrage and Beyond: International Feminist Perspectives* (New York, New York University Press, 1994), p.321

13 A. Baer, cited in R. Goyder, *Hayseed to Harvest. Memories of Katherine Cox and Hayes Court School* (Colchester, Fletcher & Fletcher, 1985), p.7

14 S. Markham, 'Guardian of the Ganymeds, Ann Baer at 100', *The Book Collector* vol.63, no.3 (Autumn 2014), p.417

3. Empire Girls

1 A. H. Halsey cited in J. M. MacKenzie, *Propaganda and Empire: The Manipulation of British Public Opinion, 1880–1960* (Manchester, Manchester University Press, 1984), ch. 7, 'Imperialism and the school textbook', p.193

2 G. Orwell, cited in J. M. MacKenzie, '"In touch with the infinite": the BBC and the Empire, 1923–53', in J. M. MacKenzie (ed.), *Imperialism and Popular Culture* (Manchester, Manchester University Press, 1986), p.184

3 N. Ferguson, *Empire: How Britain Made the Modern World* eBook edn (London, Penguin, 2012), p.113

4 This Kipling poem is cited and the broader point made by E. Buettner, *Empire Families: Britons and Late Imperial India* (Oxford, OUP, 2004), pp.1–2

5 P. Ramsay, 'My Life as I remember it' (unpublished memoir, 2001), p.27

6 G. Orwell, cited in Buettner, *Empire Families*, p.19

4. A Green and Pleasant Land

1 S. Baldwin, 'England' in *On England and Other Addresses* (London, Phillip Allen, 1926), p.1

2 Ibid., p.7

3 R. Kipling, cited in M. J. Wiener, *English Culture and the Decline of the Industrial Spirit* (Cambridge, CUP, 1981), p.56

4 H. V. Morton, *In Search of England* 15th edn (London, Methuen, 1931)

5 Ibid., pp.22, 77, 109

6 M. Cunningham, 'Ethos and Politics in the Youth Hostels Association (YHA) in the 1930s', *Contemporary British History* vol.30, no.2 (2016), p.177

7 N. Crane, *The Making of the British Landscape: From the Ice Age to the Present* (London, Weidenfeld & Nicolson, 2016), pp.466–9

8 H. Jones, *My First School, by a Libanus Lass*, copy printed by the Brecon and Radnor Printers, no date, p.20

9 A. J. P. Taylor, *English History 1914–1945* (Harmondsworth, Penguin, 1981), p.303; https://www.gov.uk/government/statistics/reported-road-casu-alties-great-britain-provisional-estimates-january-to-march-2016

10 J. B. Priestley, *English Journey Jubilee Edition,* (London, Heinemann, 1984), p.297

11 Morton, *In Search of England*, p.190

12 H. E. Bates, cited in P. Rich, 'Imperial Decline and the Resurgence of English National Identity, 1918–1979', in T. Kushner and K. Lunn (eds.), *Traditions of Intolerance: Historical Perspectives on Fascism and Race Discourse in Britain* (Manchester, Manchester University Press, 1989), pp.37–8

13 H. G. Wells, *Kipps*, cited in L. Lethbridge, *Servants: A Downstairs View of Twentieth-century Britain* eBook edn (London, Bloomsbury, 2013), loc 65

14 G. Orwell, *The Road to Wigan Pier*, in P. Davidson (ed.) *The Complete Works of George Orwell* 5th edn (London, Secker & Warburg, 1986), pp.81–2

5. Growing Pains

1 J. Davies, *A History of Wales*, (London, Allen Lane, 1993), pp.566, 590

2 I. Zweiniger-Bargielowska, *Managing the Body: Beauty, Health, and Fitness in Britain, 1880–1939* (Oxford, OUP, 2010), p.242

3 C. Moran, *How to Be a Woman* eBook edn (London, Ebury Press, 2011), p.15

4 http://www.mum.org/kotexadwords.htm, although the first disposable san-itary towels were produced in America by Johnson & Johnson in the 1890s

5 *Vogue* cited in A. Holdsworth, *Out of the Doll's House: The Story of Women in the Twentieth Century* (London, BBC Books, 1988), p.168

6 Ibid.

6. Winberries and Lipstick

1 J. Davies, *A History of Wales* (London, Allen Lane, 1993), p.579. A total of 190,722 people born in Wales had settled in south-east England by 1951

2 http://www.artbiogs.co.uk/2/schools/chelsea-school-art

3 A. Baer, 'Painting for John Hayward', *The Book Collector*, vol.59, no.1 (Spring 2010), p.70

4 I. Zweiniger-Bargielowska, *Managing the Body: Beauty, Health, and Fitness in Britain, 1880–1939* (Oxford, OUP, 2010), p.239

5 Baer, 'Painting for John Hayward', p.70

7. But Today the Struggle

1 J. V. Gottlieb and R. Toye, *The Aftermath of Suffrage: Women, Gender and Politics in Britain, 1918–45* (Basingstoke, Palgrave Macmillan, 2013), p.11
2 Ibid.
3 A. Baer, 'Unpublished Wartime Memoir' (2004), p.1
4 P. Adams, *Somerville for Women: An Oxford College 1879–1993* (Oxford, OUP, 1996), pp.232–3
5 A. Baer, 'The Meidner Portrait', in I. Sinclair (ed.), *London: City of Disappearances* (London, Penguin, 2012), pp.283–5
6 A. J. P. Taylor, *English History 1914–1945* (Harmondsworth, Penguin, 1981), p.419
7 Ibid., pp.298–9
8 Ibid., p.317
9 C. Jayawardena, 'Culture and Ethnicity in Guyana and Fiji,' *MAN*, New Series, vol.15, no.3, (September 1980), pp.430–50
10 G. Chamberlain, 'British Maternal Mortality in the 19th and Early 20th centuries', *Journal of the Royal Society of Medicine*, vol.99, no.6 (2006), pp.559–63
11 A. L. Stoler, cited in E. Buettner, *Empire Families: Britons and Late Imperial India* (Oxford, OUP, 2004), p.6
12 Buettner, *Empire Families*, p.6
13 P. Ramsay, 'My Life as I remember it' (unpublished memoir, 2001), p.27
14 P. Ramsay, 'Thoughts of when I started Nursing' (unpublished memoir, no date) p.1

8. Storm Clouds

1 S. Baldwin cited in J. Gardiner, *The Thirties: An Intimate History* eBook edn (London, Harper Press, 2010), p.378
2 P. Adams, *Somerville for Women: An Oxford College 1879–1993* (Oxford, OUP, 1996), pp.232–3
3 J. Reynolds, handwritten memories, St Paul's Girls' School archive, no date
4 Adams, *Somerville for Women*, p.233
5 *The Times*, 13 April 1939
6 P. Corner, *The Fascist Party and Popular Opinion in Mussolini's Italy* (Oxford, OUP, 2012), p.230
7 T. Dunlop, *The Bletchley Girls* (London, Hodder & Stoughton, 2015), p.43

9. This Country is at War with Germany

1 Cited in L. Noakes, *Women in the British Army: War and the Gentle Sex, 1907–1948* (London, Routledge, 2006), p.105

2 P. Adams, *Somerville for Women: An Oxford College 1879–1993* (Oxford, OUP, 1996), p.239
3 Ibid., p.244
4 D. Lloyd George, cited in A. J. P. Taylor, *English History 1914–1945* (Harmondsworth, Penguin, 1981), p.445; N. Chamberlain, cited ibid., p.446
5 A. Baer, 'Unpublished Wartime Memoir' (2004), p.2
6 Noakes, *Women in the British Army*, pp.105–7
7 A. Baer, 'Unpublished Wartime Memoir' (2004), p.3
8 Ibid., p.5
9 J. B. Priestley, *English Journey, Jubilee edition* (London, Heinemann, 1984)

10. Love Bombs and War Boys

1 N. Ferguson, *Empire: How Britain Made the Modern World* eBook edn (London, Penguin, 2012), p.347, fn. 11
2 L. Feigel, *The Love-Charm of Bombs: Restless Lives in the Second World War* (London, Bloomsbury, 2013)
3 V. Nicholson, *Singled Out: How Two Million Women Survived Without Men After the First World War* eBook edn (London, Penguin, 2008), p.xiii
4 A. Baer, 'Unpublished Wartime Memoir' (2004), p.5
5 Ibid., p.7
6 P. Ramsay, 'My Life as I remember it' (unpublished memoir, 2001), p.35

11. It's a Lovely Day Tomorrow

1 A. Baer, 'Unpublished Wartime Memoir' (2004), p.8
2 A. Baer, unpublished notes on Henry Moore
3 V. Nicholson, *Millions Like Us: Women's Lives in the Second World War* eBook edn (London, Penguin, 2012), p.337
4 *Manchester Guardian*, 5 July 1945
5 A. Holdsworth, *Out of the Doll's House: The Story of Women in the Twentieth Century* (London, BBC Books, 1988), p.26
6 A. Mayer, *Access to History: Women in Britain, 1900–2000* (London, Hodder & Stoughton, 2002), pp.99–100

12. Places, Loved Ones

1 The Beveridge Report 1942, cited in V. Nicholson, *Perfect Wives in Ideal Homes: The Story of Women in the 1950s* eBook edn (London, Viking, 2015), loc 800
2 *Daily Mail*, cited in V. Nicholson, *Millions Like Us: Women's Lives in the Second World War* eBook edn (London, Penguin, 2012), p.355. They were wrong, a labour shortage defined the post-war period

3 J. Bowlby, *Maternal Care and Mental Health* (New York, Schocken Books, 1966; 1st edn, 1950). His work was soon converted into a new mother's bible, *Childcare and the Growth of Love*

4 Nicholson, *Perfect Wives in Ideal homes*, loc 1344

13. A Brave New World

1 V. Markham, cited in W. Webster, *Englishness and Empire 1939–65* (Oxford, OUP, 2005), p.92

2 J. M. Keynes, cited in N. Ferguson, *Empire: How Britain Made the Modern World,* eBook edn (London, Penguin, 2012), p.353

3 R. Winder, *Bloody Foreigners: The Story of Immigration to Britain* (London, Little, Brown, 2004), p.255 Citation was David Maxwell Fyfe, a member of Parliament for the Conservative opposition, addressing the House of Commons.

4 J. M. Reynolds and J. B. Ward-Perkins (eds.), *The Inscriptions of Roman Tripolitania* (Rome, London, British School at Rome, 1952)

5 V. Nicholson, *Perfect Wives in Ideal Homes: The Story of Women in the 1950s* eBook edn (London, Viking, 2015), loc 266

6 Dr E. Chesser, *The Sexual, Marital and Family Relationships of the English Woman* (London, New York, Toronto, Hutchinson's Medical Publications, 1956)

7 Mike Phillips, 'Pitt, David Thomas, Baron Pitt of Hampstead (1913–1994)', *Oxford Dictionary of National Biography*, Oxford University Press, 2004 [http://www.oxforddnb.com.ezproxy2.londonlibrary.co.uk/view/article/55254, accessed 24 Sept 2017]

14. Elizabethan Britain

1 For a good analysis of the impact of Elizabeth II's coronation see V. Nicholson, *Perfect Wives in Ideal Homes: The Story of Women in the 1950s* eBook edn (London, Viking, 2015), ch.1, loc 206–789

2 D. Kynaston, *Family Britain, 1951–57* (London, New York, Bloomsbury, 2009), p.293

3 https://www.royalcollection.org.uk/collection/themes//fashioning-a-reign-90-years-of-style-from-the-queens-wardrobe/buckingham-palace/coronation-dress

4 Nicholson, *Perfect Wives in Ideal Homes,* loc 322

5 C. Davidson, cited ibid., loc 1041

6 http://news.bbc.co.uk/onthisday/hi/dates/stories/july/20/newsid_3728000/3728225.stm

7 Kynaston, *Family Britain*, pp.97–8

8 Ibid., p.98

9 R. Winder, *Bloody Foreigners*, The Story of Immigration to Britain, (London, Little Brown, 2004), p.339
10 Ibid., p.365
11 M. Donnelly, *Sixties Britain, Culture, Society and Politics* (Harlow, Pearson Longman, 2005), p.112

15. The Times They Are a-Changin'

1 A. Phillips (ed.), *A Newnham Anthology* (Cambridge, CUP, 1979)
2 https://www.theguardian.com/books/2007/nov/10/featuresreviews. guardianreview19
3 M. Donnelly, *Sixties Britain: Culture, Society and Politics* (Harlow, Pearson Longman, 2005), p.77
4 Ibid.
5 A. de Villiers, H. Fox and P. Adams (eds.), *Somerville College, Oxford, 1879–1979: A Century in Pictures* (Oxford, Somerville College, 1978), p.25

16. Making a Hat from Kitchenware

1 M. Andrews, *The Acceptable Face of Feminism: The Women's Institute as a Social Movement* (Chadwell Heath, Lawrence & Wishart, 1997), pp.146–65
2 D. Kynaston, *Family Britain 1951–57* (London, Bloomsbury, 2009), p.630

17. Sweet Dreams and Flying Machines

1 J. M. Reynolds, *Aphrodisias and Rome: Documents from the Excavation of the Theatre at Aphrodisias Conducted by Kenan T. Erim: Together with Some Related Texts* (London, Society for the Promotion of Roman Studies, 1982); Mary Beard, *Times Literary Supplement* 29 September 2013

18. Iron Ladies

1 *The Times*, cutting from Ann's personal archive, no date
2 A. Baer, *Medieval Woman: Village Life in the Middle Ages* eBook edn (London, Michael O'Mara Books, 1996), loc 866
3 P. Ramsay, 'My Life as I remember it' (unpublished memoir, 2001), p.48

19. Do Not Go Gentle into That Good Night

1 Northern Ireland is a complicated case. For a brief introduction to the subtleties of Northern Irish nationalism in a recent context read http://www.nybooks.com/articles/2017/09/28/brexits-irish-question/

2 https://yougov.co.uk/news/2017/06/13/how-britain-voted-2017-general-election/

3 The figure was 7,844,972 in 2014 (Office for National Statistics)

4 'My friend is 101 and I'm hoping to catch some of her secret' *Guardian*, 5 December 2015; 'Verse Letters' in C. James, *Injury Time* (London, Picador, 2017), p.55

5 Mary Beard, *Times Literary Supplement* 29 September 2013

6 C. James, *Injury Time*, (London, Picador, 2017), p.55. The poem which first inspired Ann to contact Clive was 'Japanese Maple' in C. James, *Sentenced to Life* (London, Picador, 2015), p.53

BIBLIOGRAPHY

Unless cited all references concerning the six Century Girls and their friends and family featured in this book were taken from face-to-face interviews and subsequent telephone conversations, letters, email exchanges and visits between 2015–17.

It would be nearly impossible to specify every book and text that fed into the historical narrative supporting the Century Girls' stories. Not to mention historical dramas! Without Netflix's *The Crown*, I would've clean forgotten to ask Ann and Olive about London's Great Smog in 1952. Like most, my general knowledge of twentieth century history has come from a pick-n-mix of sources and experiences beginning with a (ploddish) school syllabus in the 1980s and 90s, and enriched through three bouts of post-graduate historical study in adulthood. Researching and writing *The Bletchley Girls* in 2014–15 provided a solid base for understanding the pressures on women growing up in the 1930s and conscripted in the 1940s. In comparison, *The Century Girls* has proved a far broader, more exciting challenge, which required great swathes of historical context. While the bibliographical list below cites the books and journals I referred to specifically for this project, certain historians whose work transformed my understanding of particular decades and subjects over the last hundred years deserve a special mention.

Yes, he's a bit dated but the late, great A. J. P. Taylor cannot be beaten for his thorough and enjoyable portrayal of *English History*

1914–1945. For life across the border in Wales, my comprehensive bible was *A History of Wales* by J. Davies.

To access imperial Britain in the twentieth century, N. Ferguson's bold *Empire* was great for a flamboyant overview, while the meticulous research and intimate portraits in E. Buettner's *Empire Families* proved invaluable. R. Winder's *Bloody Foreigners* offered both context and rich anecdote for the arrival of West Indian migrants in the Mother Country post-war.

Virginia Nicholson's trio of feminist histories – *Singled Out*, focusing on the 1920s, *Millions Like Us*, dealing with the war years, and *Perfect Wives* for the 1950s – provided an elegant voice on British women mid-century. I also found K. Holden's *In the Shadow of Marriage* particularly insightful on single life amidst decades of marriage and children.

My 1950s go-to historian was (of course) D. Kynaston, particularly *Family Britain, 1951–1957*, and M. Donnelly held my hand through the next decade with *Sixties Britain*. More than any other book, it was Christopher Lee's *This Sceptred Isle: Twentieth Century* that yielded numerous illuminating facts and statistics thrown up by the last hundred years.

Without the above shoulders to sit upon, the researching and writing of this book would have been a far lonelier, more arduous task.

~

General Reading List

Books

Adams, P. *Somerville for Women: An Oxford College 1879–1993* (Oxford, OUP, 1996)

Andrews, M. *The Acceptable Face of Feminism: The Women's Institute as a Social Movement* (Chadwell Heath, Lawrence & Wishart, 1997)

Baer, A. *Medieval Woman: Village Life in the Middle Ages* eBook edn (London, Michael O'Mara Books, 1996)

Bailes, H. *Once a Paulina ... A History of St Paul's Girls' School* (London, James & James, 2000)

Baldwin, S. *On England and Other Addresses* (London, Phillip Allan, 1926)

Bates, D. *A Diary of a Wartime Affair: The True Story of a Surprisingly Modern Romance* (London, Viking, 2016)

Bowlby, J. *Childcare and the Growth of Love* (London, Pelican Books, 1955)

——*Maternal Care and Mental Health* (New York, Schocken Books, 1966)

Buettner, E. *Empire Families: Britons and Late Imperial India* (Oxford, OUP, 2004)

Chesser, Dr E. *The Sexual, Marital and Family Relationships of the English Woman* (London, New York, Toronto, Hutchinson's Medical Publications, 1956)

Corner, P. *The Fascist Party and Popular Opinion in Mussolini's Italy* (Oxford, OUP, 2012)

Crane, N. *The Making of the British Landscape: From the Ice Age to the Present* (London, Weidenfeld & Nicolson, 2016)

Daley C. and M. Nolan (eds.). *Suffrage and Beyond: International Feminist Perspectives* (New York, New York University Press, 1994)

Daly, V. T. *A Short History of the Guyanese People* (London, Macmillan, 1975)

Davidson, P. (ed.). *The Complete Works of George Orwell* 5th edn (London, Secker & Warburg, 1986)

Davies, J. *A History of Wales*, (London, Allen Lane, 1993)

Donnelly, M. *Sixties Britain, Culture, Society and Politics* (Harlow, Pearson Longman, 2005)

Dudgeon P. (ed.). *Village Voices: A Portrait of Change in England's Green and Pleasant Land 1915–1990* (Pilot Productions Ltd, 1989)

Feigel, L. *The Love-Charm of Bombs: Restless Lives in the Second World War* (London, Bloomsbury, 2013)

Ferguson, N. *Empire: How Britain Made the Modern World* eBook edn (London, Penguin, 2012)

Gardiner, J. *The Thirties: An Intimate History*, (London, HarperPress, 2010)

Gilbert, M. *The Second World War* (London, Weidenfeld & Nicolson, 1989)

Gottlieb, J. V. and R. Toye. *The Aftermath of Suffrage: Women, Gender and Politics in Britain, 1918–45* (Basingstoke, Palgrave Macmillan, 2013)

Goyder, R. *Hayseed to Harvest: Memories of Katherine Cox and Hayes Court School* (Colchester, Fletcher & Fletcher, 1985)

Harris, C. *Women at War 1939–45: The Home Front* (Stroud, The History Press, 2010)

Holdsworth, A. *Out of the Doll's House: The Story of Women in the Twentieth Century* (London, BBC Books, 1988)

James, C. *Sentenced to Life* (London, Picador, 2015)

——*Injury Time* (London, Picador, 2017)

Jenkins, S. *Thatcher & Sons: A Revolution in Three Acts* (London, Allen Lane, 2006)

Jones, H. *My First School, by a Libanus Lass*, copy printed by the Brecon and Radnor Printers

Kipling, R. *Plain Tales from the Hills* eBook edn (South Australia, Adelaide University Library, 2014)

Kushner, T. and K. Lunn (eds.). *Traditions of Intolerance: Historical Perspectives on Fascism and Race Discourse in Britain* (Manchester, Manchester University Press, 1989)

Kynaston, D. *Family Britain, 1951–57* (London, New York, Bloomsbury, 2009)

Lee, C. *This Sceptred Isle: Twentieth Century: From the Death of Queen Victoria to the Dawn of a New Millennium* (London, Penguin Books, BBC Books, 1999)

Lethbridge, L. *Servants: A Downstairs View of Twentieth-century Britain* eBook edn (London, Bloomsbury, 2013)

Light, A. *Forever England: Femininity, Literature and Conservatism between the Wars* (London, Routledge, 1991)

MacKenzie, J. M. *Propaganda and Empire: The Manipulation of British Public Opinion, 1880–1960* (Manchester, Manchester University Press, 1984)

Mann, J. *The Fifties Mystique* eBook edn (London, Quartet Books, 2012)

Mayer, A. *Access to History: Women in Britain, 1900–2000,* (London, Hodder & Stoughton, 2002)

Moran, C. *How to Be a Woman* eBook edn (London, Ebury Press, 2011)

Morton, H. V. *In Search of England* 15th edn (London, Methuen, 1931)

Nicholson, V. *Singled Out: How Two Million Women Survived Without Men After the First World War* eBook edn (London, Penguin, 2008)

——*Millions Like Us: Women's Lives in the Second World War* eBook edn (London, Penguin, 2012)

——*Perfect Wives in Ideal Homes: The Story of Women in the 1950s* eBook edn (London, Viking, 2015)

Noakes, L. *Women in the British Army: War and the Gentle Sex 1907–1948* (London, Routledge, 2008)

Orwell, G. *Burmese Days* (London, Secker & Warburg, 1985)

Phillips A. (ed.). *A Newnham Anthology* (Cambridge, CUP, 1979)

Priestley, J. B. *English Journey (Jubilee Edition)* (London, Heinemann, 1984)

Pym, B. *Excellent Women* eBook edn (London, Virago Modern Classics, 2011)

——*Jane and Prudence* eBook edn (London, Virago Modern Classics, 2011)

Reynolds, J. M. *Aphrodisias and Rome: Documents from the Excavation of the Theatre at Aphrodisias Conducted by Kenan T. Erim: Together with Some Related Texts* (London, Society for the Promotion of Roman Studies, 1982)

Reynolds, J. M. and J. B. Ward-Perkins (eds.). *The Inscriptions of*

Roman Tripolitania (Rome, London, British School at Rome, 1952)

Ross, S. *At Home in World War Two: Rationing* (London, Evan Brothers Ltd, 2002)

Sayers, D. L. *Gaudy Night: A Lord Peter Wimsey Mystery* (London, Hodder & Stoughton, 2016)

Sinclair, I. (ed.). *London: City of Disappearances* (London, Penguin, 2012)

Smith, H. *War and Social Change: British Society in the Second World War* (Manchester, Manchester University Press, 1986)

Stevenson, D. *1914–1918: The History of the First World War* (London, Penguin, 2004)

Summerfield, P. *Reconstructing Women's Wartime Lives: Discourse and Subjectivity in Oral Histories of the Second World War* (Manchester, Manchester University Press, 1998)

Summers, J. *Jambusters: The Story of the Women's Institute in the Second World War* (London, Simon & Schuster, 2013)

Sutherland, G. *Faith, Duty and the Power of the Mind, The Cloughs and their Circle, 1820–1960* (Cambridge, CUP, 2006)

Taylor, A. J. P. *English History 1914–1945* (Harmondsworth, Penguin, 1981)

de Villiers, A., H. Fox and P. Adams (eds.). *Somerville College, Oxford, 1879–1979: A Century in Pictures* (Oxford, Somerville College, 1978)

Webster, W. *Englishness and Empire 1939–65* (Oxford, OUP, 2005)

Wiener, M. J. *English Culture and the Decline of the Industrial Spirit* (Cambridge, CUP, 1981)

Winder, R. *Bloody Foreigners: The Story of Immigration to Britain* (London, Little, Brown, 2004)

Woolf, V. *A Room of One's Own* eBook edn (London, HarperPerennial Classic, 2014)

Zweiniger-Bargielowska, I. *Managing the Body: Beauty, Health, and Fitness in Britain, 1880–1939* (Oxford, OUP, 2010)

Articles in Journals

Baer, A. 'Painting for John Hayward', *The Book Collector*, vol.59, no.1 (Spring 2010)

Baer, A. 'Biblio-Vignette 5', *The Book Collector*, vol.61, no.1 (Spring 2012)

Chamberlain, G. 'British Maternal Mortality in the 19th and Early 20th Centuries', *Journal of the Royal Society of Medicine*, vol.99, no.6

Cunningham, M. 'Ethos and Politics in the Youth Hostels Association (YHA) in the 1930s', *Contemporary British History*, vol.30, no.2 (2016)

Jayawardena, C. 'Culture and Ethnicity in Guyana and Fiji', *MAN*, New Series, vol.15, no.3 (September 1980)

Markham, S. 'Guardian of Ganymeds, Ann Baer at 100', *The Book Collector*, vol.63, no.3 (Autumn 2014)

Phillips, M. 'Pitt, David Thomas, Baron Pitt of Hampstead (1913–1994)', *Oxford Dictionary of National Biography* (Oxford, OUP, 2004)

Thomas-Hope, E. 'Hopes and Reality in the West Indian Migration to Britain', *Oral History*, vol.8, no.1 (Spring 1980)

Todd, S. 'Domestic Service and Class Relations in Britain, 1900–1950', *Past and Present* (May 2009)

Newspapers

Daily Mail
The Guardian
The Independent
Telegraph
The Times
Times Literary Supplement

Websites

www.artbiogs.co.uk
www.bbc.co.uk

www.ons.gov.uk
www.mum.org
www.royalcollection.org.uk
www.yougov.co.uk
www.wikipedia.org
www.wsfg.waltham.sch.uk

INDEX